Timothy Goo[...]
1955, when h[...]
to read a bo[...] ...... Keynoe which
detailed sightings by highly qualified observers such
as military and civilian pilots. Now regarded as a top
authority, he has travelled worldwide interviewing
key witnesses and amassing a wealth of evidence,
including several thousand declassified intelligence
documents.

Timothy Good has lectured on his subject since 1967,
at universities, schools, and to many organizations,
including the Institute of Medical Laboratory
Sciences, the House of Lords All-Party UFO Study
Group, and the Oxford and Cambridge Union
Societies. He has been interviewed on numerous
television and radio programmes throughout the
world, and in 1989 became the first Ufologist from the
West to be interviewed on Soviet television.

Alien Update is the sequel to the bestselling *Alien
Liaison* (Arrow 1992).

ALIEN UPDATE

EDITED BY
Timothy Good

ARROW

First published 1993

7 9 10 8 6

© Timothy Good

Timothy Good has asserted his
right under the Copyright, Designs and Patents Act, 1988
to be identified as the author of this work

First published in the United Kingdom in 1993 by Arrow
Random House, 20 Vauxhall Bridge Road, London SW1V 2SA

Random House Australia (Pty) Limited
20 Alfred Street, Milsons Point, Sydney
New South Wales 2061, Australia

Random House New Zealand Limited
18 Poland Road, Glenfield
Auckland 10, New Zealand

Random House South Africa (Pty) Limited
PO Box 337, Bergvlei, South Africa

Random House UK Limited Reg. No. 954009

A CIP catalogue record for this book
is available from the British Library

ISBN 0 09 925761 0

Photoset by Deltatype Ltd, Ellesmere Port, Cheshire
Printed in Great Britain by
Cox & Wyman Ltd, Reading, Berkshire

CONTENTS

Contents

ACKNOWLEDGEMENTS

I am indebted to the team of dedicated contributors who have made this book possible, and to the numerous journalists, investigators, magazines and newspapers whose reports are included herein. My apologies for any omissions of credit.

FOREWORD

'The heady days of flying saucers and close encounters with unearthly beings appear to be numbered,' wrote Jonathan Margolis in *Time* magazine in August 1992. 'In Western Europe at least, even evidence in the form of UFO sightings is fast disappearing. It may be a function of earthly worry caused by the recession, or a fading of fear now that the cold war is over, but 1992 has not been a vintage year for strange flying objects, be they flying saucers or cigars. Hard data are hard to come by, and the picture is confused by competing reports from rival UFO-spotting organizations, but a common downward trend, even a collapse, in the sightings market is evident.'[1]

A glance at my world round-up of sightings, covering a fourteen-month period from July 1991 to August 1992, shows that the reverse is the case. The national media in general remain not only uninformed about what is going on, but reluctant to carry out any investigations into the numerous sightings reported worldwide, many of which have been made by sensible down-to-earth witnesses. Fortunately, local newspapers continue to carry such reports, and often publish the results of follow-up investigations.

There are encouraging signs, too, that national television journalists are now beginning to realize that something of extraordinary significance is happening on our planet. On 20 April 1992, for example, NBC *Nightly News* showed a short extract from a video film taken at night by an NBC TV crew in the vicinity of the Nevada Test Site, where many unusual sightings have been reported and where, according to physicist Bob Lazar and others, actual extraterrestrial vehicles are being examined and even test-flown, as reported in *Alien*

1

Liaison. The NBC film (of which I have a copy) shows what was described as 'something that seems to defy the laws of physics', and reporter Fred Francis added that 'hundreds of witnesses have seen the bright light hovering motionless over the mountains, then move quickly across the night sky at high speed – like a flying saucer.' Japanese TV crews have also filmed anomalous objects in this vicinity. In March 1992, the chief news cameraman for a CBS affiliate station filmed a cigar-shaped UFO in Bellevue, Wisconsin (see p. 255). Additional video films have been taken by various TV crews, including Fuji-TV of Japan, in Gulf Breeze, Florida. Furthermore, *Dateline NBC* has been investigating the claims of a computer hacker (whose identity is being protected) who maintains that he has gained access to top secret files on UFO materials – including references to alien autopsy reports – stored at Wright-Patterson Air Force Base, Dayton, Ohio[2].

Several programmes on the subject were televised nationwide in the United States in 1991–2, such as *Intruders* (a CBS fictionalized mini-series on the abduction phenomenon) NBC's *Unsolved Mysteries*, and the *Now It Can Be Told* series (one of which included an extract from the tape-recorded conversation between former National Security Agency director Admiral Bobby Ray Inman and Bob Oechsler, during which it was implied that the United States Government has access to alien vehicles, as described in Chapter 13). In Japan, documentaries on the subject are commonplace, but in Britain we lag far behind – so far. I am pleased to report that a British company currently is filming a major documentary, to be shown in late 1994.

On 12 October 1992, NASA initiated a new SETI (Search for Extraterrestrial Intelligence) programme, designed to explore a far wider range of frequencies than hitherto for signs of intelligent radio signals. One half of this $100 million, ten-year programme consists of the so-called 'Targeted Search', which is focusing on the nearest sun-like stars, eighty light-years from Earth, scanning two billion channels over the 1,000 to 3,000 megahertz frequencies. This will use the giant radio telescope at Arecibo, Puerto Rico, and the Green Bank National Telescope in West Virginia, and computers will search 15 million channels every second for signs of an intelligent signal.

One of the problems involved in this search is that it could take many years before we receive a response. Nonetheless, Dr Frank Drake, the astronomer who in 1960 conducted the first radio search for extraterrestrials, has stated that he fully expects a positive response before the year 2000[3]. Jesuit priests who run the Vatican Observatory are also involved in the programme, and the Vatican has helped build a new reflector telescope (a joint venture with the University of Arizona) in Tucson, Arizona. Father George Coyne, Director of the Vatican Observatory, who will run the Tucson Observatory with other clerics, commented (apparently seriously) that, in the event aliens are discovered, 'the Church would be obliged to address the question of whether extraterrestrials might be brought within the fold and baptised . . .'[4]

It is my conviction that NASA and the US intelligence community have proof (at a restricted level) that aliens have already landed on Earth and that contact has been established. The evidence suggests that large amounts of money are spent on top secret extraterrestrial research programmes (funded by so-called 'black' budgets) in the United States, and information about these 'Special Access Programs' is so restricted that few have knowledge of them. If this is the case, the SETI programme would seem to be something of an anachronism. However, as noted in my previous book, even if contact has taken place with one or more alien species, there will always remain a need to search for signs of communications from the extraterrestrial intelligence community which, in my view, is widespread throughout the universe. Furthermore, the money spent on SETI is very small in comparison to the black budget: the Fiscal 1993

3

Department of Defense requests included a total of almost $16 billion for black programmes alone!

If intelligent signals or communications are received via SETI, red tape will delay any public announcement. At a conference of the International Academy of Astronautics held in August 1991, a set of guidelines was drawn up by scientists – *The Declaration of Principles Concerning Activities Following the Detection of Extraterrestrial Intelligence* – which states that news of the discovery of extraterrestrial signals must first be relayed to other scientists worldwide to verify them, followed by notification to the International Astronomical Union, which in turn will send out an official notification through the Central Bureau for Astronomical Telegrams. Finally, the Secretary-General of the United Nations, the Institute for Space Law, as well as the International Telecommunications Union, will be told. In theory, the public will then be informed of the discovery. In practice, as Dr John Mason of the British Astronomical Association points out, there will be a great deal of argument among scientists, 'during which time an investigative journalist will be almost bound to get wind of it'.[5] Quite so. And in any event, since these matters will have repercussions affecting national security, we can be certain that the intelligence community will monitor and control the release of any such extraterrestrial communications (see Chapter 10).

Investigative journalists would do well to take the current UFO situation seriously and forget about SETI for the time being. I find it ironical that the latest SETI programme was initiated at the Arecibo radio telescope (which in 1974 was one of the first used to transmit a coded message to the stars) in Puerto Rico, a country where numerous encounters with UFOs and aliens continue to be reported. Even a local director of the State Agency of Civil Defence stated in 1992 that he had observed a flying disc being chased by a US Navy jet, as well as UFOs entering and leaving the Laguna Cartagena, leading to his conviction that an actual alien base is located in that area (see Chapter 1).

During an Oprah Winfrey show in 1991 which featured some of the Apollo astronauts, the subject of UFOs cropped up. Dr Edgar Mitchell, following the rather negative comments of his former colleagues, rejoined: 'I do believe that there is a lot more known about extraterrestrial investigation than is available to the public right now [and] has been for a long time . . . It's a long, long story. It goes back to World War II when all of that happened, and [it] is highly classified stuff.'

I wrote to Dr Mitchell, asking if he would elaborate on that statement. 'I really have little that I can add to what I have already said, for frankly I know very little,' he replied. 'My own assessment after years of sceptical observation is that the evidence has become so consistent and overwhelming that it can hardly be ignored. This being the case it will sooner or later break open and we will all be pleased to know the results. . . .'[6]

That the results of top secret extraterrestrial investigations will break open eventually is a certainty. But will we all be pleased to know the results?

Timothy Good

Notes

1. Margolis, Jonathan: 'Are We Alone?', *Time*, 31 August 1992.
2. *Dateline NBC* featured a story about the computer hacker on 27 October 1992.
3. Begley, Sharon: 'ET, Phone Us', *Newsweek*, 12 October 1992.
4. Johnston, Bruce: 'Vatican sets evangelical sights on outer space', *Daily Telegraph*, 28 October 1992.
5. Highfield, Roger: 'Red tape will delay news of Little Green Men', *Daily Telegraph*, 10 August 1991.
6. Letter from Edgar D. Mitchell Sc.D, 21 April 1992.

1
IS THERE AN ALIEN BASE IN PUERTO RICO?

Jorge Martín

Leading Puerto Rican investigator Jorge Martín is the editor of *Enigma!*, a monthly magazine featuring articles on UFOs and the paranormal. He has investigated hundreds of UFO incidents in the island of Puerto Rico since 1975, and has written many articles and reports for Puerto Rican as well as foreign newspapers and magazines.

Jorge has written two previous articles for the *UFO Report* series, dealing with numerous incidents involving sightings in Puerto Rico of UFOs alongside military aircraft, the apparent 'abduction' of US Navy jets, as well as an encounter with alien beings in the Cabo Rojo area. Several of these accounts are also published in *Alien Liaison*. I have twice visited Puerto Rico in order to meet some of the principal witnesses, and came away with the conviction that these extraordinary incidents had in fact taken place as described.

Since 1987, the island of Puerto Rico, a US territorial possession in the Caribbean West Indies, has experienced its most important UFO wave. For the purpose of this report, I have focused on some of the many UFO-related incidents in the south-west region of the island, mostly in the towns of Cabo Rojo and Lajas, and more specifically in the Laguna Cartagena area (a lagoon several kilometres long and wide, located at the borders of these towns) and the Sierra Bermeja (a small mountain ridge next to the Laguna Cartagena). The incidents there seem to imply that there may be a joint US/alien undersea/underground base in that area.

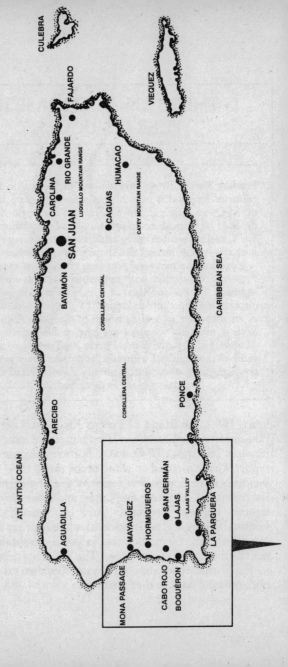

PUERTO RICO

CULEBRA

VIEQUEZ

FAJARDO

RIO GRANDE

LUQUILLO MOUNTAIN RANGE

CAROLINA

HUMACAO

SAN JUAN

CAGUAS

BAYAMÓN

CAYEY MOUNTAIN RANGE

CORDILLERA CENTRAL

ARECIBO

CORDILLERA CENTRAL

PONCE

CARIBBEAN SEA

ATLANTIC OCEAN

AGUADILLA

MAYAGÜEZ

HORMIGUEROS

SAN GERMÁN

LAJAS

LAJAS VALLEY

MONA PASSAGE

CABO ROJO

BOQUÉRON

LA PARGUERA

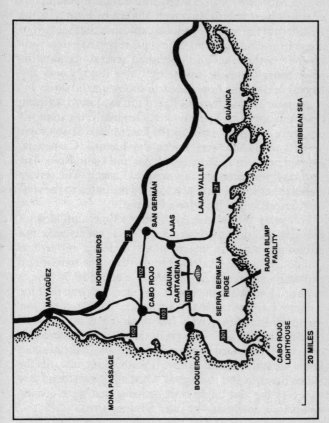

Fig. 1.1 Map of Puerto Rico showing (inset) locations of sightings and encounters. *(Tania Long)*

ANOMALOUS INCIDENTS

On 31 May 1987, at 1.55 p.m., thousands of inhabitants of south-west Puerto Rico were shaken by both a strong tremor and the sound of a loud explosion that seemed to come from underground. The press reported extensively on the 'earthquake' and published several accounts by neighbours from the towns of Cabo Rojo, Lajas and Mayagüez, stating how the earth shook up and down for some moments as they all heard the explosion, causing cracks to appear in some homes. Originally, the tremor's epicentre was pinpointed by the Puerto Rico Seismologic Service at 81,000 feet under the Laguna Cartagena, located between the towns of Lajas and Cabo Rojo. The next day, however, the report was changed. The service stated that the epicentre was located out at sea to the west of Puerto Rico, in the Mona Passage.

Following the 'earthquake', other events unfolded on that day and on subsequent days. These events were not published, but our investigations added a mysterious component to the incident. The day after the tremor and explosion, on Sunday, 1 June 1987, at about 10.00 p.m., a huge unidentified flying object was seen hovering over the Laguna Cartagena. Many witnesses, among them our friend Wilson Sosa, who has observed many unusual incidents in the Laguna Cartagena area[1], saw the incredible object as it remained hanging in the sky above their homes in the community of Betances. 'I was looking towards the Sierra Bermeja and the laguna when all of a sudden I saw two very big and bright stars or lights that were coming down very slowly side by side,' Sosa reported.

'I called my wife and got my binoculars. The lights were at the end of something very big that looked like a huge metallic-looking silvery pipe. It was cylindrical with two big spheres of greenish-white light at each end. On the object's underside there was something like a revolving reddish light.'

Mrs Rosa Acosta, also resident in that community, gave us her testimony as follows:

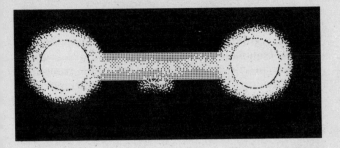

Fig. 1.2

It was really large. I observed it from several kilometres away and it still measured about 6 inches long [at arm's length] . . . It was incredible! That thing came down and hovered in the air, motionless over the Laguna Cartagena. Then, about fifteen minutes later, it flew up and disappeared to the south behind the Sierra Bermeja.

This isn't new here. These mysterious lights and artifacts have been seen here for years, especially in that particular area. There have been occasions when I've been lying down in my hammock here on the terrace and all of a sudden a bright light shines on me from above. When I look up, one of these things – something saucer-shaped – is over me and shining a bright white light on me. This has happened a couple of times. Why they do it, I don't know . . . and why me?

Mrs Haydeé Alvarez, another neighbour we interviewed about the incident, reported that 'they were like two very big stars the size of a half dollar coin, joined by a long, big pipe with lights underneath'.

Carlitos Muñoz, a young lad present during the interviews, explained that his whole family has been seeing this type of object for some time. 'One night about a year ago,' he began, 'all of us at home saw a very big "platform" – something that came down from the sky and remained there motionless over the Laguna Cartagena. It had very bright yellow and green lights, and from the platform, many smaller luminous objects were coming out from the underside and flying away in different directions. They kept going in and out of that thing. After some minutes, the smaller objects entered the big one and it flew away and disappeared in the sky. It happens regularly . . . and always over the Sierra Bermeja and the Laguna.'

Many people called the regional radio stations to report the huge UFO over the lagoon. Amazingly, these objects returned for two more consecutive nights, remaining motionless for a few minutes over the Laguna at about 500 feet altitude before leaving.

STRANGE CIRCLES AND WEIRD 'X-RAYS'

Intrigued by the reports of witnesses indicating that the objects always flew away over and behind the Sierra Bermeja next to the Laguna Cartagena, we went to the Olivares area in the municipality of Lajas, next to the 'La Parguera' resort. During our investigations we made an unexpected discovery: several clearly defined perfect circles, as if cut into the terrain, could be seen in a field next to the Sierra Bermeja.

When measured, most of the circles were 35 feet in diameter and defined by a rim almost totally devoid of grass, in which the soil seemed baked and harder than in the remaining soil from the rim or inside the rim. The small quantity of grass still in the rim's area was totally dried up and dead. The rim was 3 feet wide.

When asked, all the neighbours said they were surprised by the circles, never having seen them before. It seemed as if they had been formed overnight. The neighbours go to bed early, so they were unable to explain how they were formed, but they all stated that for several nights, beginning with the night after the so-called 'earthquake', they had seen 'strange lights and a very big object with many coloured lights hovering in the sky and flying over the Sierra Bermeja in the direction of Cabo Rojo and the Laguna, to the other side of the Sierra'. The descriptions of the objects seen by them were similar to those given by the witnesses on the other side of the Sierra.

Roosevelt Acosta, together with his brother Heriberto and relatives, attested to this, also stating that on some occasions neighbours had seen strange small beings that seemed to have a faint glow to their bodies and which disappeared very quickly whenever approached by the witnesses.

On one occasion, Mrs Dolín Acosta, also a resident in the Olivares sector, was on her balcony when a bright beam of light suddenly engulfed her from above:

It was a very bright white light, and it came from above the balcony ceiling. There was a hole in the ceiling and I looked up. There was something like a big ball of light, and a ray of light came out of it and shone on me. When I looked at myself, I couldn't believe it – I could see my bones! It was like looking at an X-ray plate. I could see the bones in my fingers, in my arms, my body . . . even my toes! That object was up there and I could hear a soft sound that was coming from it, something like air being ejected at intervals, like psss . . . psss . . . psss. It then left, but for some minutes I could still see myself like that. My sister Eunice came out of her room to see what was causing the bright light and we *both* could see our bones. When I looked at her, she had no eyes: I could clearly see her empty eye sockets, and she saw the same thing on me. After about five minutes, we were back to normal.

No after-effects were ever felt by either Dolín or her sister.

To return to the circles, Fidel Avilés, owner of the land where they appeared, stated: 'I've lived here for fifty years and never saw anything like this. Those circles appeared there overnight after the explosion and the tremor which we felt here.'

Avilés has a small food store in Olivares, and three other circles had appeared behind the store that early morning. His son, Fillo, who works in the store, reported that the same morning, a young man had come to the store and nervously explained to him that he was camping with a group of friends further down the road and went out for a ride on his motorcycle at about 3.00 a.m. when, as he passed in front of the store, he saw three strange luminous objects that were hovering next to the ground behind the store. According to the young man, the luminous things were round, soundless, and looked like upside-down dishes, with bright yellowish light emanating from them. He became frightened and left immediately.

At first, there were eight circles, but two days later there were twelve. Intrigued, we talked about it with our friends Captain Luis Irizarry, a pilot of many years experience, and Julio César Rivera, a flying student, who agreed to fly us over the area. We were surprised by what we saw: there were thirty-eight of those circles in the terrain! They were totally symmetrical and tended to be in pairs. Some days later, we took soil samples from the circles and sent them to the Agricultural Extension Programme in Mayagüez, a big town near Cabo Rojo, in order to check if a type of mushroom that we found at the place could have been responsible for the circles. The programme's cytologist certified that the type of fungus involved could not have formed the circles. Also, the samples showed that the pH (hydrogen ion concentration) in the soil had changed, but only in the rim area. The other samples taken from the inside and the outside of the circles were totally normal.

There were many other strange incidents relating to the so-called 'earthquake', as we shall learn.

BLUE SMOKE AND MYSTERIOUS PERSONNEL IN LAGUNA CARTAGENA

Several neighbours in the Maguayo region, next to the Laguna Cartagena, reported that on the night prior to the explosion and tremor of 31 May 1987, they saw a strange 'red ball of fire' moving over the lagoon and descending in a controlled and steady fashion, making a buzzing sound. Then it slowly disappeared into the waters of the lagoon. At 2.00 a.m., many residents were awakened by a strong white light coming through all the windows and openings in their houses. Curious about it, the neighbours looked out and were amazed by the sight of a huge flying saucer-type craft hovering low over the lagoon as if searching for something. According to everyone, the craft was covered by bright white light and it was circling the area very slowly. After about two minutes it left, swiftly disappearing in the sky.

The next day, at 1.55 p.m., the tremor and explosion occurred. We must remember that the epicentre was initially pinpointed by the authorities to be 81,000 feet under the Laguna Cartagena. But what really happened? We know that an unidentified object was seen entering the lagoon, another UFO was seen late at night as if looking for something there, and the next day, an explosion that rocked the whole region was felt.

After the tremor, several fissures appeared in different areas of Lajas and Cabo Rojo, and many witnesses stated that a bright, cobalt blue-coloured smoke issued with some force from these crevices. Pedro Asencio Vargas, resident in sector La22 of Llanos Tuna, Cabo Rojo, and a teacher, reported as follows:

I saw clearly that some cracks had appeared in the ground in my yard – and this blue smoke frightened me. Some people from the Mayagüez Agricultural and Mechanical Arts College [part of the University of Puerto Rico complex, specializing in engineering and agricultural techniques] came to check on what happened, but strangely, they refused to take samples of residue from the blue smoke and powder that remained on some of the plants. That was strange, because they were supposedly investigating what had happened. Why then did they refuse to take the samples and analyze them? I still don't understand.

This bright cobalt blue smoke also issued from the Laguna Cartagena, according to several witnesses. Carlos ('Carlencho') Medina, together with other residents in the Maguayo community, stated that after the explosion, blue smoke issued from the laguna (such smoke has nothing to do with vulcanism or seismological activity), and the area of the lagoon was cordoned off by unidentified personnel. Some of these personnel consisted of men dressed in camouflaged fatigue-type military uniforms, while others were dressed in plain clothes, and still others were dressed in white, head-to-toes anti-contamination-type coveralls. The latter wore thick, dark grey gloves and boots and were putting samples of the lagoon's water, mud, soil, and plants into large translucent canisters. According to the witnesses, they had some type of radios they were using to check something in the water; their descriptions of the 'radios' reminded us of Geiger counters.

The military men prevented anyone from getting inside the area, stating that special personnel were there to investigate what had happened. Medina and others said that the following day, a dark green military helicopter with no markings flew over the area, and a big metallic ball with what looked like electronic equipment was lowered into the water, attached to a very long metallic line, as if looking for something. The witnesses also noted the presence of a number of beige-coloured vans and bronco-type vehicles with small revolving parabolic-type antennae on top of them.

Mrs Zulma Ramírez de Pérez, whose family at that time owned part of the land where the Laguna Cartagena is located, went to the area with her sister to see what had happened, since they had seen bright blue smoke issuing from the lagoon. Several American men dressed in dark suits with a red badge approached and ordered them to leave the place at once. The women explained that the land was theirs, but the agents replied that they would have to leave anyway, since they were trying to find out what had happened. If the official explanation was true – that the explosion and tremor were caused by an earthquake – why did these personnel say they were trying to find out what had happened? The men were tall, Caucasian, blond, and dressed in fine-looking suits, but wearing what seemed to be black rubber boots. They also had metallic, silvery-looking briefcases with them, according to the two sisters.

At this point, Mrs Ramírez told us something very significant. Her entire family, she said, had seen flying saucer-type craft coming out of or entering the waters of the Laguna Cartagena since 1956:

At first, they were very bright and luminous, and as they came out, you could define their shape more clearly. They were disc-shaped, silvery and metallic, with translucent domes on top and they had many beautiful coloured lights all around them. They made a 'whooshing' sound. You could see people or figures inside the domes, because on some occasions, when they came out, we yelled at them and they would stop in the air in front of us. We tried to report these things we were seeing to the media, but no one would listen to us then, so we just let it be.

In fact, my brother Quintin, now dead, one night back in 1964 yelled at them that he wanted to know who they were, to see if they were really from outer space, as people said. And that same night he had an encounter with them. He went to bed and suddenly felt an urge to go to the lagoon. He got dressed, got in his jeep and drove toward the Las Guanábanas dirt lane, to the back of the lagoon. Getting out of the jeep, he saw two figures approaching him from the lagoon. They were tall white men, about 6 to 7 feet tall – with blond long hair and dressed in one-piece, tight-fitting silvery suits. 'They were very beautiful and delicate, almost female looking,' he said. He was too nervous, and asked them not to come any closer as he couldn't take it, so they smiled sweetly at him and walked back into the lagoon.

He fled the place and in the morning explained everything to us. He was very upset because we wouldn't believe him. After that, he never said anything else to us. I know he had other encounters with these beings, because some nights he disappeared into the lagoon area, and he wouldn't talk about what he was doing there all night. But we knew he was with his 'friends', as he used to call them. I'm sorry he's dead now, because I know he'd be happy hearing all the things people are saying about the lagoon and aliens being there, because it would back up all he used to say.'

The day after the explosion and tremor, a green military unmarked helicopter landed on top of the hills of the Sierra Bermeja, just behind the residence of Milton Vélez. Vélez, his wife and children all saw several men dressed in green military fatigues and boots, with black berets, get off the helicopter and begin scanning the soil on the hill with instruments that looked to Milton like metal detectors. 'They looked like special forces people to me,' Vélez said. 'They were looking for something there. After an hour or so, they left in the helicopter without any explanation.'

More recently Vélez, his family and neighbours have all seen luminous flying saucers that come down from the sky in the night and remain motionless next to a radar aerostat (blimp) installed there by the government. After some minutes, the UFOs leave very quickly. This has become a common event in that vicinity.

TWO POLICEMEN, A BLACK HELICOPTER AND 'FEDERAL AGENTS'

We also interviewed a policeman who was at the lagoon with a fellow policeman friend a couple of days before the explosion when something weird happened there that they will never forget.

According to the policeman, they had gone to the lagoon to do some fishing when suddenly his friend saw strange movements on a slope in one of the hills of the Sierra Bermeja, as well as smoke coming from the ground. He went up the hill to have a look and saw several men dressed in silvery-looking coveralls, gloves and boots, who appeared to be checking something in the area with what looked like Geiger counters. His friend called him to follow, and as he climbed up the hill, they both noticed some other men, dressed likewise, hauling three large rolls of thick black rubber-covered electrical or communications cables, several inches wide, from big black trucks. The men then put one of the cables into the lagoon, specifically in the area free from the grass that grows on most of its water surface (the area where most of the sightings have occurred and where the Ramírez family saw the UFOs emerge). The other trucks entered a lane in one of the cattle ranches to the right and disappeared.

At that moment, a helicopter appeared as if from nowhere and someone ordered them through a loudspeaker to stop where they were and get down the hill at once. The policeman, whose name we cannot divulge for obvious security reasons, described what happened as follows:

It was a big black helicopter with no markings. They ordered us to stop and said they knew we were armed. How did they know that we had our guns with us? I still can't understand that. Maybe they had some type of equipment in the helicopter that enabled them to know about it. We came down from the hill and they landed next to us, very quickly. Two armed men dressed in black jumpsuits jumped down from the helicopter and asked my friend to come closer. They were white, with dark hair and moustaches — latin-looking. He joined them and came back with a very worried look. 'Now we're in trouble,' he said. 'These are federal agents.'

I told him not to worry, and we both approached the helicopter. They asked what we were doing and we explained that we were off-duty policemen fishing in the area. They answered in perfect Spanish with a Puerto Rican accent: 'You can't go up there. This is a restricted place under the federal government and we are doing an experiment here.' What type of experiment, they never said. They took us away to an area between two hills in the sierra, where there was a camping tent. A tall white man dressed in a military suit came out of the tent. He seemed to be an American officer. This man talked to the other men, and we perceived he was asking why they had taken us there. He seemed very annoyed by our presence.

After talking with the military man, one of the men approached the policemen, and the next thing they were aware of was that they were lying face down in the dirt road that goes from the Laguna Cartagena to Route 101. Our policeman was the first one to recover consciousness. When he did so, he heard a man say in perfect Spanish: 'Hey, they're waking up. Let's go.' Then some men got into a car and left very quickly. The other policeman woke up, but both remained dazed for a while as they sat there in the dirt road. They left the place and never returned. Our policeman's friend remained somewhat disturbed after the experience, moving later to New York, and does not intend returning to Puerto Rico.

'I don't know what happened,' our witness told us. 'Those men did something to us, because we can't remember what happened after the man with the military officer approached us at the tent, only that we woke up in the dirt road and in a dazed state. It was as if we had been drugged and taken there – I'm sure they drugged us somehow. But why? We didn't see anything important – I think – only these men in silvery suits with the cables going into the water. Who knows, maybe that is what they didn't want us to see? And then, some days later, there was the explosion and earthquake. This is all very weird . . .'

The statement by the helicopter personnel that the area was 'a restricted place under the federal government' is a fallacy, because the Laguna Cartagena was not 'leased' to the US Federal Government (by an 'agreement' between the Puerto Rican local government and the US Wildlife and Fishing Service) until August 1989.

THE US FEDERAL GOVERNMENT 'LEASES' THE AREA

After the tremor, the number of sightings and incidents continued to grow, and then an extraordinary event occurred one night when two US Navy jet fighters were abducted in mid-air by a huge triangular-shaped UFO which disappeared in front of more than 100 witnesses. This happened on the night of 28 December 1988. To date, Puerto Rican and US authorities still refuse to acknowledge that the incident happened. And prior to this, a similar incident occurred on 16 November 1988 in the town of San Germán, next to Lajas and Cabo Rojo, as described in *Alien Liaison*[2].

Following these incidents, many jet fighters, helicopters and big AWACS-type radar planes were seen, constantly flying low and circling over the lagoon as if searching for something, and the fishermen and neighbours observed UFOs entering and coming out of the sea near the coast, as well as hovering over the Sierra Bermeja. In one of these sightings, in November 1988, almost 300 people participating in a political rally saw a cigar-shaped luminous UFO hovering above the Betances community, and then over the Sierra Bermeja and the lagoon, while releasing many smaller luminous objects from its interior. The sighting lasted for half an hour.

On 8 August 1989, following rumours to the effect, the Laguna Cartagena was 'leased' by an 'agreement' to the US Wildlife and Fishing Service, in order to 'preserve animal species in danger of extinction'. By this agreement, the area is now under US control for fifty years – and possibly for another fifty years after that.

Later on, the federal authorities took control of another UFO hot spot in the Sierra Bermeja, a field next to the Pitahaya-Olivares sector on the coast, by the mangrove channels between La Parguera and the Cabo Rojo lighthouse, where many UFOs are seen regularly entering the water or flying out of it; an area that has been closely monitored by US Navy vessels and planes, and which was recently restricted and placed under the control of numerous US military troops for two months, without any explanation. The 'official' reason for controlling the field in the Pitahaya-Olivares area was that the authorities wanted to install a radar blimp (aerostat), in order to detect and prevent drug smuggling by air and sea. Eventually, the aerostat was anchored and deployed there.

On numerous occasions since then, many local witnesses have seen UFOs hover next to the blimp, emitting strange flashes of light in a pattern similar to the one given out by the blimp. To some, this seems as if both airborne objects communicate via the light flashes. Sometimes, the UFOs are chased away by US military aircraft, but the fact of the matter is that, whenever the UFOs appear next to the radar blimp, it malfunctions and has to be repaired. According to certain sources, all the computer systems in the installation go blank, and have to be re-programmed. To many, however, the reason for this installation is linked with the UFO situation in the area. Most believe the facilities were placed there to monitor UFO activity and try to detect the UFOs' trajectories and pinpoint the areas they enter or exit from.

CREATURES IN THE MANGROVES

As described in *The UFO Report 1992* and *Alien Liaison*[3], five small, apparently alien creatures were observed by many witnesses in the Cabo Rojo area in the early hours of 31 August 1990. One of these witnesses, Miguel Figueroa, approached the beings, and he reported that they were grey, very thin, with large heads, pointed ears, a slit-like mouth, small nose, and large white almond-shaped eyes. As he drew closer in his car, Figueroa said that a blinding bright light emitted from the beings' eyes, forcing him to stop. They turned and continued walking down a road, then jumped over a small bridge and headed along a river bed towards the Laguna Cartagena, leaving three-toed footprints.

Later that day, an anonymous telephone caller warned Figueroa not to discuss what he had seen or in what direction the beings were headed, threatening that if he did so, something bad could happen to him. This frightened Figueroa, particularly since his telephone number was listed in another person's name. By a strange coincidence, both Timothy Good and I, together with other investigators, were in that very area during the afternoon of 31 August, but the report did not come to my attention until days later. The encounter is by no means unique: further sightings of alien creatures in this vicinity have been, and are continuing to be, reported.

One afternoon in July 1989, Arístides Medina, a resident of La Parguera, Lajas, decided to go fishing out to sea in his boat. At about 3.00 p.m., as he took the exit through the mangrove channels in La Pitahaya sector, he came across what at first he thought was a group of children:

. . . They were about 3 to 3½ feet tall, like five- to six-year-old children. I got closer so as to have a better look at them. What would children be doing in such a desolate place? They were all alike, and that's when I realized they weren't children at all. They were all skinny, about the same size, and dressed in tight-fitting greyish-silvery suits, similar to leotards used by dancers. Strangely, the suits seemed to be slightly fluorescent – they had a mild luminosity to them.

Two of them were standing there looking straight at me, and the others were half-hidden in the mangroves. Their heads were larger than ours, but not much, and rather egg-shaped, elongated to the back – with no hair at all. They were very pale, with a greyish tinge to their skin. They had big elongated black eyes and a small nose, with a barely noticeable mouth.

They seemed to be very curious about me, but also very cautious. When I tried to approach them, they fled very quickly and disappeared in a slope between the Sierra Bermeja mountains. Since then, I've seen them a couple of times . . .

Medina was initially reluctant to tell us about his experiences. 'I've told you this because what's happening is important,' he said. 'People have to understand that these people [the aliens] do exist, and that they are here with us already. Many are afraid of them, but they are not coming to harm or conquer us. They come to help us, and whoever says that they want to invade is fantasizing or lying, because that's just not true.'

Medina believes the aliens have some type of under-ground base in the area. 'For some reason, the authorities are trying to force them to remain down there . . . for what reason, I don't know. To me, there seems to be a sort of disagreement between the government and them. The last time I saw them [in the Sierra Bermeja sector], three hours later the place was full of federal agents, and the area was sealed off by so-called representatives of the Puerto Rico Natural Resources Department. Now the area is off-limits to everyone, and the government has given away that area to the federal government. They know what's there – there's no doubt about it.'

A VISIT BY TWO STRANGE CREATURES

On the night of 13 August 1991, Mrs Marisol Camacho, a young woman who lives at the back of the Maguayo community next to the Laguna Cartagena, received an unexpected visit at her home by two strange creatures:

I was asleep, when at about 2.00 a.m. I heard strange noises outside, next to my balcony. I got up and went to the balcony window. Someone was there mumbling in a strange gibberish. I opened the venetian blinds very slowly and – Oh, God – there were two of the weirdest creatures you can imagine, standing there on the balcony.

They were examining one of my plants, one we call 'Queso Suizo' ['Swiss cheese', the scientific name of which is *Monsterosa deliciosa*, an ornamental tropical plant whose leaves have many holes]. They were taking leaves from the plant and mumbling. They looked really interested in it. I was surprised and – I don't know why – but I couldn't move. I was frozen to the spot, looking at them. They were almost 4 feet tall and had large egg-shaped heads, big at the top with a narrow chin. They were skinny and seemed to be grey, and were naked. They had big black elongated eyes that tapered to the sides of their heads, with no pupils and no whites in them. Their faces were flat, with a narrow slit for a mouth, no lips, and two small holes for a nose. I never felt any fear – I was fascinated by what I was seeing. They seemed like children to me . . .

They had arms longer than ours, and long skinny hands with four long fingers. They didn't seem to notice me at the window. They took leaves from the plant and left, talking among themselves in that fast mumbling gibberish. They walked slowly towards the Laguna Cartagena, entered the brush there at the end of the street, and disappeared.

I just couldn't believe it. What people were saying around here was true – there are aliens here! I saw them, and I'm sure of what I saw. After they left I was able to move again. I went to bed and later told my husband what I had seen.

Two weeks later, the aliens returned to Marisol's house. 'It was again late at night,' she told us. 'I heard the same sounds, got up and went to the same window, which was partially closed, and there they were again! They were either the same ones or identical to the others,

24

examining the plant again and talking in that mumbled gibberish. But this time I was able to move and I tried to tell them something. I began opening the blinds, but when they heard this, they looked at me quickly then ran away at high speed down the street towards the Laguna again, and disappeared.

'I don't know what they want, but they don't seem to be dangerous. They didn't harm me, and they didn't harm my dogs, who slept all the time they were here. One thing is for sure: they are already here, living among us. We should prepare to face that fact. And I'm convinced they are there in the Laguna Cartagena. That's their territory . . .'

A week after this second visit, many of Marisol's neighbours were witness to a brilliantly coloured disc that hovered for about three minutes some 50 feet above her house at 9.30 p.m.

AN ALIEN IN THE IRRIGATION CANAL

Ulises Pérez was riding his motorcycle on a dirt road in a desolate cattle ranch in the Cuesta Blanca sector, located between La Parguera and the Laguna Cartagena. The time was 11.30 a.m., sometime at the end of August 1991:

. . . As I was riding along, the bike fell into a water-filled hole and the engine sputtered then cut out. I began to check it, and after fixing what I believed to be the problem and trying to start it again, I looked into the irrigation canal – and I saw that thing there.

I saw something seated or crouched over a log beside a tree [Fig. 1.3]. The creature's skin looked as if raw – you know when you cut off a slice of skin and the cut looks whitish with pinkish-red spots in it? That's how it looked. It was a pale, whitish skin, like those pale salamander lizards.

We looked at each other for a moment, without moving. I'm not ashamed to admit that I was scared by that thing, and I tried to start the bike and get away. As I moved, the thing jumped and disappeared under the water in the canal: I saw its feet as they disappeared under the water lilies. I started the bike and fled.

Fig. 1.3 (*Jorge Martín*)

On reaching home, I nervously explained what I had seen. My friends and relatives wouldn't believe me, but agreed to come with me to the site. Seeing the crushed lilies there, they believed me, and were scared . . .

According to Ulises, the creature was identical to the ones previously described. 'What impressed me most was its big head and those huge black eyes,' he stated. And as with the other encounters, there is a direct link with the Laguna Cartagena, since the irrigation canal leads there eventually.

All these cases seem to suggest that beings of this type possibly have established their habitat under the Laguna Cartagena and other bodies of water in that region. Several investigators believe that these beings may be amphibian in nature, due to the webbing between their fingers, frequently described by witnesses.

MISCELLANEOUS ENCOUNTERS

Another encounter near the Laguna Cartagena was reported by Eleuterio Acosta, a very serious eighty-year-old man who lives in the Olivares sector, just in front of the radar blimp facility. He says that he was once surrounded by five of these small grey creatures as he entered his home. He managed to confront them with a stick and yelled at them, at which point a sixth, taller creature of the same type communicated with the other five, and they all jumped out through a window and fled quickly, heading towards the Sierra Bermeja.

Eunice Acosta, another resident of the Olivares sector, who has also witnessed many UFOs near the radar blimp and is the sister of Dolín Acosta (whose case is described earlier), claims to have fought off and prevented an apparent attempt at abduction by these creatures, in May 1991.

There is also a claim by some of the policemen who stand guard at the radar facility, who say they encountered several of the creatures when the facility was being built in 1989. But there are even more significant encounters, which may provide us with some answers.

'THEY TOOK ME TO THEIR BASE . . .'

Carlos Mañuel Mercado, one of many witnesses to the apparent abduction of US Navy fighters in December 1988, and whom we have come to know very well and to respect as a sensible and honest man [this was also the impression I formed when I met him briefly in August 1990 – Ed.], revealed during an interview with us that something shocking had happened to him one night in June 1988, six months before the UFO/jets incident:

I was trying to get some sleep that night, but it was so hot that I simply couldn't. My family was asleep. I got up and lay down on the sofa in the living room, trying to get some sleep there, but to no avail.

Suddenly, I saw a flash of light outside and heard a buzzing sound. A few moments later, someone knocked three times on the venetian blinds. I got up and opened the window, and there they were – three small men looking at me, but they weren't human. I was shocked, but a voice told me in my mind: *Do not be scared, everything is fine. Nothing is going to happen to you. Do not be scared. We want to show you something.*

I was shocked at first, but when I heard the voice I felt very calm. They asked me to come out, but not with their mouths – they never opened their mouths – this was in my mind. So I opened the door. I felt I had to do it – somehow I knew they wouldn't harm me . . .

According to Mañuel, the little men were almost 4 feet tall, with big pear-shaped heads, pale grey skin and big black slanted eyes with no pupils. They had no ears, a small slit for a mouth and just two holes for a nose. Additionally, Mañuel noticed that the beings had small bumps in the skin of their faces; 'perhaps something like acne,' he suggested. They were humanoid in shape but their arms were a little longer than those of humans. All three were dressed in tight-fitting, sandy-coloured one-piece suits, like those of mechanics, and only their hands and heads were outside the suits.

. . . Two of them took me by my hands to the front of my home [opposite the Sierra Bermeja] and down the road. I couldn't believe it – there was a flying saucer there! It was standing on three metallic legs. It was round, with a dome on top with windows, and many coloured lights around the rim . . . There was an opening on its underside, a hatch, from which a long stairway came down to the ground. They asked me to climb up the stair and board the craft.

There were more of those little men inside, and the place was full of machines with many coloured lights and panels: this was in the area with windows – like a flight deck in a dome. The little men introduced me to a taller being who was about my size [5 feet 9 inches]. I felt more comfortable with this one because, even though he was like the others, he was taller and looked a little more human-like. He was dressed in a white robe, and they said he was their 'captain-medic'.

This taller being explained that they did not mean to harm me; that they only wanted to show and tell me something so I could later relate it to other people. He said something to the others at the panels and I felt the [landing] legs coming up, and a clamping sound. The hatch closed and the craft began moving. I was impressed, but not afraid – they kept me calm somehow. The craft shot up, and I believed we would go far away, but instead, it seemed to veer to the left and descended toward the Sierra Bermeja. I was afraid we would crash, but a hole appeared in a depression to the side of El Cayúl mountain and the craft went all the way down it through a tunnel and came out in a big place that seemed to be like a long, large cavern.

There were many barracks-like structures or buildings inside the place, and hundreds of the little aliens working as if on production lines, assembling electronic, mechanical parts or machinery. There were many crafts down there, but not like airplanes or helicopters; they were saucer-shaped, or triangular- and hexagonal-shaped.

Then the tall being said: *As you can see, we have a base here for the maintenance of our crafts' systems. We have been here for a long time and don't intend to leave. We want the Earth people to know that we mean no harm, that we don't mean to conquer you either. We want to reach out to you and establish a direct relationship which will be beneficial to both parties. Earth people can rest assured that we don't mean harm in any way.*

I said, 'Why me? I'm a simple man, and no one will believe me.' He replied: *It doesn't matter. People will hear you as well as many others we are contacting and bringing here to show them the same. When people with knowledge hear what you simple people – as you call yourself – are saying, they will know that you are telling the truth.*

After that they brought me home, and before leaving told me that they would come back someday. At first I was afraid to talk about this. But when this thing with the jets happened, I worried. Maybe this has something to do with the beings down there, and I know – I felt – that they are good, and harmless. Knowing this, I decided to talk to you and let you know what happened.

We know of another man residing in the area who was supposedly abducted and taken to the same underground base by the same type of aliens. This man is a high-ranking military officer in the west of Puerto Rico. We are unable to disclose his name now. But everything he says corroborates the details given by Mañuel Mercado, especially the place where the mountain slope opens down to the purported base in El Cayúl mountain.

A SUSPICIOUS SUICIDE

A man we consider to be completely reliable told us how, together with a fisherman friend (called Rodríguez) from La Parguera, he accidentally gained access to this supposed base via a concealed ventilation shaft located near the radar blimp. Our witness, whose name we cannot for the time being reveal for security reasons, insisted that there really are aliens in this base, and that they had also seen US military soldiers down there. Frightened, they fled, worried that they may have seen something they should not have. Some days later, Rodríguez was found dead, hanging from a small tree in La Parguera. According to the authorities, he hung himself with his shoe laces. However, the circumstances of the hanging tend to rule out such a conclusion.

We spoke to 'Lindo' Rodríguez, the dead man's brother, who has himself witnessed several UFO sightings in the vicinity. He said that no one in the family could understand the alleged suicide. 'My brother didn't drink alcohol nor use drugs,' Lindo told us. 'He wasn't depressed and didn't have any emotional or romantic problems, and he was in good health. So, why did it happen? I don't know, but something isn't right about this.'

Our investigations into this case are continuing.

OFFICIAL CONCERN AND DISINFORMATION

During the last months of 1991, a disinformation programme was set in motion by Aníbal Roman, director of the Mayagüez area Civil Defence Agency office, and Lieutenant Rodríguez of the Lajas police headquarters, together with officers from the US Wildlife and Fishing Service, using the Puerto Rican TV, radio and press media in order to discredit all the reports about UFOs and aliens. This was revealed to us in the course of a recent interview by Freddie Cruz, director of the Civil Defence Agency of Lajas. While this was going on, Roman's supervisor, Colonel José A. M. Nolla, director of the Puerto Rico State Agency of Civil Defence, sent an internal directive to all regional offices in the country, laying down guidelines for a secret investigation of UFO sightings, part of which [translated by Margaret Barling – Ed.] states as follows:

. . . we judged it fitting and necessary that the Civil Defence of Puerto Rico should investigate and study the cases of sightings of unidentified objects with the purpose of guaranteeing that the same do not represent a threat to the safety of the Puerto Rican people.

The study . . . will be the responsibility of a special committee comprising the State Director, Assistant State Director, Head of Geographical Intelligence, Head of Government Operations, the Representative of the Observatory of Arecibo, the Representative of the Department of Natural Resources and the Representative of the National Guard of Puerto Rico. Other Government representatives . . . will take part in the study should the need arise . . . [4]

A copy of this directive, written in Spanish (see Fig. 1.4) was given to us by a source within the State Agency of Civil Defence, who explained that even though it was stated that the study was the responsibility of the agency, the results were really for analysis by the US Department of Defense. In this way, the American agency would not be seen as officially involved in the UFO investigations.

We also learned recently that Colonel Nolla, who used to be the liaison officer of the Puerto Rican/US Army and National Guard with the US Defense Intelligence Agency (DIA), stated under oath in a hearing at the Senate of Puerto Rico that he, the military and the Agency of Civil Defence, had been investigating the many UFO sightings and animal mutilations that had taken place over the years in Puerto Rico.

During our interview, Freddie Cruz described an important incident when he and others witnessed a jet

AGENCIA ESTATAL DE DEFENSA CIVIL
Estado Libre Asociado de Puerto Rico

7 de octubre de 1991

DIRECTRIZ INVESTIGATIVA NO. 1-91

A : Inspector General
Director de Operaciones Gubernamentales
Director de Inteligencia Geográfica
Coordinador de Areas Operacionales
Coordinador de Areas Especiales

DE : *José O. M. Nolla*
José A.M. Nolla
Director

ASUNTO : OBJETOS NO-IDENTIFICADOS

En el pasado y más recientemente han ocurrido avistamientos de objetos voladores no-identificados (OVNIS) y objetos marítimos no-identificados (OMNIS) en el territorio del Estado Libre Asociado de Puerto Rico. A tenor con el Artículo 6, inciso F de la Ley Núm. 22 del 23. de junio de 1976 hemos estimado conveniente y necesario que la Defensa Civil de Puerto Rico investigue y estudie los casos de avistamiento de objetos no-identificados con el fin de garantizar que los mismos no representan una amenaza a la seguridad del pueblo puertorriqueño.

El estudio de los casos de avistamiento será responsabilidad de un comité especial compuesto por el Director Estatal, Sub-director Estatal, Director de Inteligencia Geográfica, Director de Operaciones Gubernamentales, Representante del Observatorio de Arecibo, Representante del Departamento de Recursos Naturales y Representante de la Guardia Nacional de Puerto Rico. Otras instrumentalidades del Gobierno de Puerto Rico participarán en el estudio cuando surja la necesidad.

Será responsabilidad de los Coordinadores de Areas Operacionales (Zonas) y Especiales efectuar las entrevistas iniciales de testigos de avistamientos, utilizando la Forma DC-DIG 001. Una vez se efectúe la entrevista inicial la Forma DC-DIG 001

Apartado 5127, Pta. de Tierra Station San Juan, Puerto Rico 00906
Tel. 724-0124   FAX 725-4244

Fig. 1.4 Puerto Rico State Agency of Civil Defence internal directive on UFOs, proving serious official concern.

fighter chasing a UFO in Lajas, on the afternoon of 28 April 1992:

It happened at 5.00 p.m. I was repairing my truck when one of my kids and I heard a jet flying low. We looked up and saw a thing like a flying saucer being chased by a military jet [an F-14 Tomcat, according to the witnesses]. The saucer was metallic, silvery, very polished, and it seemed to be playing with the jet. It was a little bigger than the plane. It would continually stop in the air suddenly, then as the jet was just about to catch up, it would move ahead quickly and stop further away.

The saucer was just that – a flying saucer, like two flattened dishes joined by the rims, and it had a dome on top. Finally, as the jet was about to close in again, the saucer split in half! The upper part came away from the lower part, and then each part flew away, one to the south-west and the other to the east. The jet remained there circling the area, as if not knowing what to do, then departed to the east.

'This convinced me that I should say what I knew about the situation,' Cruz continued. 'It's unfair for Roman and others to continue the disinformation. Currently, there's a secret investigation being made by the Civil Defence Agency of Puerto Rico. And I know everything is true, because I've seen UFOs myself. And last November [1991], the police received a tip-off about the expected arrival in boats of a number of illegal immigrants from the Dominican Republic, in the El Papayo beach area, between La Parguera and Guánica. While there, at 9.00 p.m., we saw a large bright star in the sky. Suddenly, the "star" began to descend – and it was a huge thing, a flying saucer the size of a stadium! It was very bright, with coloured lights all around it.

'It remained motionless about 25 feet above the sea for about half an hour, then it flew upwards and disappeared in the sky. That really shook us up. I'll be honest: when that thing came down I crawled under my truck and stayed there until it left. Also, we have made vigils at the Laguna Cartagena, and have seen brightly coloured ovoid and round objects as they fly over the area doing right-angled turns, and sometimes they enter the laguna and disappear underwater.

'The UFOs are there – they really are. So that's why I can't remain silent while Roman and the others ridicule those who have seen things here. It's not fair. The people say what they've seen because they know that whatever is going on here is important. I know most of these people and they are serious and decent people, and they deserve some respect.

'There are UFOs in the Laguna Cartagena, and something weird is going on at the aerostat radar facility. If not, why do NASA white trucks have to enter the premises at about 2.00 a.m., escorted by military jeeps? Why do this in such a furtive way? What does NASA have to do with the anti-drug war? [the official explanation]. Nothing, that we know of. To me, there's an alien base around here and the authorities know about it, but don't want anyone else to . . .'

A high-ranking police officer told us in confidence that when policemen were selected to stand guard at the entrance of the road leading to the radar facility, they were debriefed by American federal agents [supposedly from the FBI]. Our source said that they were all surprised by the many UFO- and alien-related questions asked by the agents, who would begin by asking about the policemen's experience and background, but would then change the line of questioning to ask the interviewees if they had seen any UFOs; if they had been contacted by aliens; if anyone in their family had had a UFO experience, and so on. From time to time a lie detector would be used during the debriefings.

It is evident that enough circumstantial evidence now exists to suggest that something strange and very important is going on in south-west Puerto Rico, particularly in the Lajas-Cabo Rojo area. The more such incidents happen, the more people believe that there really is a UFO base there. The reports I have included here are but a fraction of those we have investigated, but I hope nevertheless that they give the reader a general idea of the significance of what has happened – and is continuing to happen – in my country.

Notes

1. Martín, Jorge: 'US Jets Abducted by UFOs in Puerto Rico', *The UFO Report 1991*, ed. Timothy Good, Sidgwick & Jackson, London, 1990; Good, Timothy: *Alien Liaison: The Ultimate Secret*, Century/Arrow, London, 1991/2, published in an updated edition as *Alien Contact: Top-Secret UFO Files Revealed*, William Morrow, New York, 1993.
2. Ibid.
3. Martín, Jorge: 'Puerto Rico's Astounding UFO Situation', *The UFO Report 1992*, ed. Timothy Good, Sidgwick & Jackson, London, 1991; Good, Timothy, op. cit.
4. Investigative Directive No. 1–19, from José A. Nolla, Director, State Agency of Civil Defence, US Commonwealth State of Puerto Rico, to the Inspector General, the Head of Government Operations, the Head of Geographical Intelligence, the Co-ordinator of Operational Areas, the Co-ordinator of Special Areas, 7 October 1991.

2
SPEAK PLAINLY, AND GO POLITICAL

Hal McKenzie

Hal McKenzie worked as an editorial writer, reporter and editor at the *News World* newspaper in New York City from 1976, and first became interested in UFOs in 1981, when he was made editor of a weekly supplement called 'UFOs and Cosmic Phenomena'. In 1983, after the paper changed its name to the *New York City Tribune*, he edited the Commentary and Science sections until it ceased publication in 1991. He is now Current Issues editor at the *World & I* magazine, a publication of the Washington Times Corporation, in Washington, DC.

'Do you believe in UFOs?' This annoying question, asked of me more times than I would like to count, is, in my opinion, the most oppressive sentence in the English language. In particular, the words 'believe' and 'UFOs' form a semantic straitjacket which makes up a large part of that frustrating wall of confusion and denial that confronts almost everyone involved in serious UFO research. I believe there is a way, however, to break out of that straitjacket and bring down that wall.

The answer lies in *semantics* and *politics*: semantics, because the terms popularly used to frame the UFO controversy tend to euphemize and confuse the issue; and politics, because it was political leaders making political decisions whose cowardice threw the entire issue of extraterrestrial contact into its present intellectual limbo. To clear up the fog and solve the UFO mystery itself, we must first explain plainly what we mean, and second, throw the entire issue into the political arena.

Consider the word 'believe'. The whole point of Unidentified Flying Objects is that they are seen, which puts them in the category of facts, not belief. It is in one's *reaction* to the facts that belief plays a role. One can either deal with the facts rationally, drawing the most direct and logical conclusions from them without fear or favour; or one can allow personal conceits, myths and/or social conventions to intervene.

Here emerges a gross abuse of language and a semantic fraud of major proportions: UFO researchers, as well as ordinary people whose lives have been turned upside down by close encounters of whatever kind, are labelled UFO 'believers' when, in fact, they are only drawing the most logical conclusions from the data, or reacting with normal human emotions to bizarre or terrifying sense-experiences.

The real believers, in fact, are those who keep insisting that what is happening *can't* be happening; who deny, ignore or cover up the facts because the facts would upset their cherished belief systems.

THE DENIAL SYNDROME

Psychologists have a word for this kind of stubborn, irrational belief that flies in the face of facts: *denial*. The denial syndrome is all too common in human life and history, where we can find innumerable examples, and not just in the area of UFOs.

Consider, for example, the tragic and all-too-common case of a little girl who reports to her mother that her father often comes into her room at night and sexually abuses her. The mother angrily rebukes the child and tells her to stop telling 'lies'. The truth is so painful to the mother that her mind rebels against it or blocks it out: she is in a state of denial.

The child, facing this wall of rejection and with no one to turn to, goes into a denial of her own to survive; she blocks out the painful experiences, suppressing the memories of them deeply in her subconscious. Yet the memories cannot be suppressed forever, and when the child reaches adulthood they force themselves to the surface, causing psychoses.

Today, an understanding therapist would help such a patient come to terms with the fact of her victimhood as a step towards healing. There was a time, however, when incest victims faced a wall of denial, even from so-called psychoanalysts. The late great Sigmund Freud often dealt with women who revealed under analysis that they were raped by their fathers. The good Dr Freud just couldn't believe it – the societal taboo against even discussing incest was too strong. So he denied the truth of his patient's testimony and concocted a nifty theory to explain it: the famous Oedipus complex. Freud theorized that these women as little girls, driven by their infantile libidos, *fantasized* that they had sex with their fathers!

Nowadays, incest is no longer kept 'in the closet' but is openly discussed on television programmes. No longer do victims of incest have to suffer as in the past. The age of denial has ended and truth and understanding have dawned; at least as far as incest victims are concerned. The same is not yet true of those claiming abduction by aliens, whose stories are recounted, for example, in Budd Hopkins's books, *Missing Time* and *Intruders*[1], and in Whitley Strieber's best-selling *Communion*[2] and the movie based on it. Most big-media reviews of the above-mentioned works express the fervent belief that Strieber and hundreds of others all independently fantasized the same thing. So learned men keep coming up with half-baked theories to explain this mass 'fantasy', while its victims continue to suffer from their terrifying experiences under a cloud of official rejection.

In other words, our society, in particular the intelligentsia, is locked in a state of denial when it comes to evidence of 'off-world' contact. It is not that there aren't enough facts to prove the case, it is that the facts themselves are being ignored, suppressed and ridiculed because they point to a conclusion too threatening for many to contemplate.

TERMINOLOGY

Getting back to semantics, ask yourself the question: How do you end the state of denial of, say, an alcoholic? The answer is, you get the person to say 'I am an alcoholic' – not a tippler, not a social drinker, but an *alcoholic*. Once the person accepts that key word, he or she is on the road to recovery.

Ending the fog of denial regarding extraterrestrial issues may also involve nothing more than a change in terminology. 'UFO' is an acronym originally coined by that boundless fount of obfuscatory language, the US Government, for the very purpose of euphemizing the evidence of alien spaceships in our atmosphere. The word 'UFO' can mean different things to different people. To some it means off-world craft, but to others it might mean 'misidentified natural phenomena' or even 'hallucinations of crackpots seeking escape from their problems'. In other words, the word 'UFO' helps society evade the real issue of extraterrestrial contact, just like 'tippler' and 'social drinker' evades the reality of alcoholism.

I propose, therefore, that from now on, researchers and activists phase out the word 'UFO'. I would use 'off-world craft' instead. Perhaps one day, when we see one, we will know enough to be able to say something like 'There goes a Reticulan laboratory ship' or 'That looks like a Pleiadean surveillance drone', but until then, let's just accept the fact that what we really mean when we say 'UFO' is some form of off-world craft. If we frame the issue in the clearest, most direct terms possible, then the truth will come out much faster.

GOVERNMENT DISINFORMATION

To reiterate, our task is not to gather enough evidence to prove off-world contact, but to end the denial of the evidence that is already readily available. Proof comes from evidence, and the evidence is all round us – truckloads, boxcarloads and mountains of it. There is the

UFO data collected since the late 1940s, including the unknown quantities known to exist in secret government files and warehouses; the historical and archaeological records dating back to prehistoric times; the common experience of mankind recorded in ancient religious scriptures; and what science has taught us about life in general, i.e. that life never develops in a vacuum. It is just a matter of putting two and two together. The problem is, as in George Orwell's *1984*, that we are labouring under a manipulative government policy designed to make two plus two equal five!

In public reports like the Air Force's 'Blue Book' and the Condon Report, the US Government says UFOs are no big deal, they are no threat to national security – just forget it. In secret, however, they are *very* concerned, as revealed by documents released under the Freedom of Information Act and recent books like *New York Times* investigative reporter Howard Blum's *Out There*[3]. Blum exposes a covert 'UFO action group' in the Pentagon, and a cabal of Air Force intelligence spooks who recruited famed UFO writer William Moore to monitor the effects of hair-raising disinformation fed to a midwest UFO researcher [Paul Bennewitz] who was getting too close to secret doings at an air base. The bogus stories nearly drove the poor researcher mad[4].

Thus a great deal of the paranoia attributed to the UFO community can be traced to the government's policy of secrecy and deliberate disinformation. It is very much like the bad old days in the Soviet Union, where before Gorbachev's policy of *glasnost* the government kept information so tightly controlled that the average citizen had to make do with rumour, hearsay and speculation. In such an atmosphere of mistrust, when what the government says officially conflicts with what the people know to be true, a schism develops in the body politic itself, a kind of social schizophrenia that is harmful to the mental and social health of everyone.

The original failure of nerve that got the denial syndrome rolling can probably be traced back to 1947 or thereabouts, shortly after the Roswell 'saucer' crash, when US political and military leaders decided to keep the off-world debris and bodies under a tight lid of ultra-secrecy. Through the years, further webs of deceit and obfuscation were woven to protect the original policy, and like a cancer the denial syndrome metastasized to the media, to the scientific establishment, and to society in general.

Ironically, America's intelligence establishment, which has performed like Keystone Kops throughout the rest of the world, apparently succeeded all too well in this domestic disinformation scheme. One of its successes could well be the very disunity and factionalism that today plagues America's UFO community, rendering it incapable of taking *effective* action in countering the government's policy. America's UFO research groups [and those of the rest of the world! – Ed.] behave like prisoners in a mental gulag: they fight among themselves for scraps of information like prisoners fighting for scraps of food, while the real source of their problems is the totalitarian system that both restricts and doles out the information as it pleases.

POLITICAL ACTION

This is not a problem that can be solved by further collections of UFO sightings. The denial syndrome began with a political decision; only through politics can it be brought to an end. UFO investigators should become political activists, because only a good, old-fashioned political campaign will end the government's policy of UFO secrecy. They could, for example, form 'truth squads' to follow the President around and to ask such embarrassing questions as, 'What do you know about secret UFO files, Mr President?' and 'Why the cover-up?' That's the way to get on the evening news!

Abductees should do what other aggrieved groups have done with great success: form a lobbying group. Imagine bus-loads of abductees descending on Capitol

Hill to lobby for an investigation of the alien abduction syndrome and an end to UFO secrecy. The fact that they are a relatively small group of victims should not deter them. The highly successful 'Mothers Against Drunk Driving' (MADD) began with only one determined lady.

If, as many UFO research groups say, their goal is to 'educate' the American people, then nothing is more educational than a political crusade, both for the public and the participants, as many people learned during the Vietnam War. With more media people per capita than any other city in the world, the place to begin such an educational process is Washington, DC, and I have become involved with Operation Right to Know, an organization dedicated to ending UFO secrecy, whose first demonstration took place in Washington in March 1992 [see Editor's Note].[5]

Furthermore, it is a matter of public record that Ronald Reagan, Jimmy Carter, Gerald Ford and Barry Goldwater, to name but a few politicians, either saw UFOs or expressed an interest in the subject. However, most politicians would never gain the courage to buck longstanding policy unless they felt they had a constituency behind them.

If the government finally opens its secret data banks, then the off-world denial syndrome will quickly end and relative sanity will prevail – unless, of course, the truth is so horrible that it causes mass hysteria, which is one hypothetical explanation for the secrecy.

History shows, however, that mankind has never been harmed by the truth, despite fears of bureaucrats and potentates who tried to 'protect' the public from reality. Quite the contrary, in my opinion: the greatest obstacles to progress have come from official lies, myths and efforts to keep the people in the dark. For example, the ecclesiastical authorities of the Middle Ages were so afraid of Marco Polo's true accounts of the splendours of far Cathay that they threatened to burn him at the stake if he didn't keep quiet. They feared that if people found out that a 'pagan' civilization could in some ways outshine

Christendom, there would be hell to pay. The same thing happened to those who tried to spread Copernicus' findings that the Earth revolves around the Sun, rather than vice versa. Dislodge mankind from the centre of the universe? Never!

An enormous revolution occurred in the Soviet Union because the truth of democracy and human rights, which the Communist party tried to keep from the people, finally could not be contained. In all these cases, the truth-deniers came to be recognized as reactionaries who tried to keep the people in the Dark Ages.

When new truth is given to mankind, it always brings about new and unforeseen advances in human progress. Even if the truth holds dangers, it is better to face the truth with our eyes open like the sentient, spiritual beings that we are.

The politician or statesman who finally succeeds in breaking the off-world denial syndrome will go down in history as a greater liberator than Boris Yeltsin or Mikhail Gorbachev. It is time for us to prepare the ground for such a figure to emerge.

Notes

1. Hopkins, Budd: *Missing Time: A Documented Study of UFO Abductions*, Richard Marek, New York, 1981; *Intruders: The Incredible Visitations at Copley Woods*, Random House, New York, 1987.
2. Strieber, Whitley: *Communion: A True Story*, Century Hutchinson, London, 1987.
3. Blum, Howard: *Out There: The Government's Secret Quest for Extra-Terrestrials*, Simon & Schuster, New York, 1990.
4. For further details, see Good, Timothy: *Alien Liaison: The Ultimate Secret*, Century/Arrow, London, 1991/2; *Alien Contact: Top-Secret UFO Files Revealed*, William Morrow & Co., New York, 1993.
5. For details of the British branch, write to ORTK Britain, 20 Newton Gdns., Ripon, N. Yorks. HG4 1QF.

Editor's note

Operation Right to Know, founded by Ed Komarek and Mike Jamieson, succeeded in carrying out demonstrations outside the White House from 19–28 March 1992. 'Thousands of people from many different countries passed by our educational displays on the Ellipse,' Komarek reports. 'When the weather got bad we lobbied congressmen and senators by personally hand-delivering briefing materials to their offices . . . It is highly recommended that UFO enthusiasts begin sending high-quality UFO information to as many congressmen and senators as possible. This could lead to a rapid increase of awareness within Congress and perhaps lead to rapid actions to end the cover-up by the executive branch of the Government.

'We believe the impact of the demonstrations was strongly felt at the White House through the keen interest of the Secret Service. Many came to pick up material at our displays . . . We expect our information was spread to the White House staff and perhaps to the President himself . . . Unfortunately, we did not get media attention because there was so much to do that we did not get to lobby the media effectively. We will leave that to next time . . .'

Operation Right to Know has formed a committee to plan and execute political actions worldwide, and seeks to form local action groups. Those interested should write to Operation Right to Know, PO Box 2911, Hyattsville, MD 20784 (USA). The second national demonstration took place in Washington on 5 July 1993, attracting considerable media attention.

I have reservations about the outcome of such demonstrations. Unless there are sufficient numbers, I fear that the demonstrators will be regarded merely as a bunch of cranks. But I am in favour of Ed Komarek's recommendation that enthusiasts should send high-quality information on the subject to Congressmen and Senators (in the UK and elsewhere, to their Members of Parliament or other elected government representatives). The majority of such representatives are woefully ignorant about the facts. Unless and until politicians have a clear mandate from the electorate, UFOs are unlikely to become a political issue.

Hal McKenzie suggests that the US President should be asked about his knowledge of secret UFO files. As a former Director of Central Intelligence, former President George Bush almost certainly knows more about these matters than any previous president, and during his first presidential campaign, he was queried by a Mutual UFO Network (MUFON) state section director serving on Bush's campaign committee. In a revealing tape-recorded statement, Bush responded briefly: 'You don't know the half of it'. (Walter Andrus, *MUFON UFO Journal*, November 1992.)

In Japan, the ten-year-old UFO Party is pressing for a serious study of the UFO subject. Tokuo Moriwaki, the fringe group's leader, calls for the setting up of a 'UFO Intelligence Agency' and the construction of a UFO landing site on the west coast of Japan. 'Opening up outer space will usher in a wonderful new era,' the party's manifesto states, all too naively. 'Let us prepare for the arrival of extraterrestrials to help realize peace on Earth.' (*The Sunday Telegraph*, London/*Irish Times*, Dublin, 26/24 July 1992)

It is of course unlikely that the UFO Party will ever be taken seriously, except by over-zealous enthusiasts, and I doubt if any real progress will be made until such time as establishment politicians are prepared to risk their reputations. In this connection, I am reminded of the fact that the former Japanese Prime Minister, Toshiki Kaifu, has admitted that as a UFO enthusiast he searched unsuccessfully for UFOs during trips to Australia, the South Pole, and Switzerland. 'I'll live on with hopes of . . . encountering a UFO some day,' he wrote in 1983. (*Time*, 18 September 1989)

As for the term 'UFO', it has now fallen into such common usage around the world that it is unlikely to be replaced for years to come. However flawed the perception may be, UFOs are regarded by many as synonymous with alien or extraterrestrial craft.

3
UFOS OVER WASHINGTON, DC, APRIL 1992

George Wingfield

Educated at Eton College and Trinity College, Dublin, George Wingfield graduated in 1966 with an MA Hons. degree in Natural Sciences. He was employed briefly at the Royal Greenwich Observatory, Herstmonceux, on stellar spectra and the Earth's magnetism, and for many years worked at IBM UK Ltd in the field of Systems Engineering.

He became interested in the Crop Circles phenomenon on 8 August 1987, after visiting Westbury, Wiltshire, where a number of circle formations had appeared. This also led to an interest in the related subject of Ufology. Widely recognized as a leading authority, George Wingfield is a director of field research for the Centre for Crop Circle Studies (CCCS). He has taken early retirement in order to devote himself to the subject, and is much in demand around the world for his lectures.

On 15 April 1992, I gave a lecture on the cropfield circles phenomenon at the Smithsonian Institute in Washington, DC. My wife Gloria and I had never visited this city previously, and we arrived at National Airport at 4.20 p.m. on the afternoon of 13 April 1992. We had flown from Raleigh/Durham, North Carolina, and were welcomed by Susan Webster, an Englishwoman who has lived near the city for many years. Although we had corresponded, neither of us had met Susan until that day. She drove us from the airport and pointed out many of the landmarks in the city. The weather was bright and sunny, with hardly a cloud in the sky.

We stopped the car by the Tidal Basin of the Potomac to wander in the sun and look at the cherry blossom, which was at its finest. I suggested that we walk to the Washington Monument, which entailed crossing two busy roads. There were dozens of tourists there, mostly in a straggly line round the base, waiting to ascend the inside of the great obelisk. Enquiry indicated that we would have to wait forty-five minutes if we wished to go up in the elevator. I took several photos of the 555-foot-high monument with my Canon Autofocus camera.

Just as we were leaving, I remarked that I must get a photograph of the White House from this vantage point, and crossed to one side to do so. However, this photo was never taken for, as I walked, I glanced up again towards the apex of the great pillar. Over the top of the monument, travelling silently towards the west at great altitude, was a bright disc.

As if this were not astonishing enough, there followed behind it a small fleet of seven lesser objects, also shining brilliantly as they swept silently above the obelisk. Although there was no way of telling, these all appeared to be at a substantial altitude – say 30,000 feet or so. This estimate is based on comparison with jet aircraft at similar heights, but quite clearly these were not aircraft. The large disc must have subtended an angle of about one-quarter of the diameter of the full moon (7 minutes of arc).

Gloria and Susan immediately saw what I was pointing at and watched the objects moving silently above. I motioned to several people standing nearby, who also looked up, but without showing much interest. One boy did ask me what the first circular object in the sky was. 'That,' I replied, 'is a UFO.' He looked somewhat puzzled. Another boy had some binoculars and I borrowed them to look at the leading object. Adjusting the focus with some difficulty, I was able to see that it appeared translucent and circular.

By now, the smaller objects had faded, and only one or two remained in sight. Possibly their initial brightness had been caused by reflected sunlight in the position where we had first spotted them. All had wheeled above us and were receding again towards the east, in the direction of the Capitol. Soon, only the large disc could be seen in the sky, now dwindling in size as it flew away from us.

Then Gloria and Susan both spotted a further small object, apparently much lower, flying rapidly westward. Before it went behind the monument, it halted in flight, flew back again, reversed westward, and brightened suddenly, then apparently vanished into thin air. This object I failed to see, despite looking along Gloria's arm in the direction indicated.

By 6.00 p.m. – perhaps fifteen minutes after the initial sighting – the largest object had faded to a minute dot and was eventually lost to sight.

In due course we headed back towards the Tidal Basin, where the car was parked. Excited and bewildered by the totally unexpected sighting, we felt almost honoured by this peculiar flypast. Then yet another object appeared, flying roughly on a path from the Capitol towards the Pentagon, which was not visible from where we stood. This object seemed to drift silently across the sky, changing shape as it went. At first, it appeared to be shaped like a cross, then perhaps a cigar, then like an aeroplane viewed from above. But this was clearly not an aircraft; in fact, its only conceivable resemblance was to an enormous, irregular cluster of balloons, strung together and tumbling across the sky.

That alone would have been bizarre enough, but it was followed at a distance by a smaller object, similar to those previously in the wake of the disc. This object shone like the others, but occasionally let out a bright flash, although it was impossible to say whether this was due to the sun on a reflective surface.

In all, we had witnessed eleven objects cross the sky, none of which behaved like any conventional flying object one might have expected to see in the daytime. During all this time, commercial jets had been flying in and out of National Airport, but these were in a different part of the sky.

At the first sighting I had attempted two photographs with my Canon camera. One shows the Washington Monument and the tiniest white dot imaginable, which may or may not be the disc. The other was not printed, and the negative shows nothing but blank sky. Susan Webster also took a shot with her camera and this also reveals a tiny white speck high in the sky near the obelisk: A magnifying glass shows that the object on the film is definitely a disc. It may be possible to do some enhancement work on both these photographs.

Although all three of us have travelled to many different parts of the world, none of us had ever seen anything to compare with what we saw on that day. I have spotted a few strange objects in the sky, usually at night, but I have never been sufficiently sure that they were not something of a conventional origin to classify them as UFOs. On that Monday afternoon in Washington, DC, 'UFO' was the only description that fitted the bizarre objects which we had observed.

On countless occasions, people have asked why, if UFOs exist, don't they just come down and land beside the White House? On 13 April 1992, it really looked for a time as if they would do just that.

Editor's note

This is by no means the first time that UFOs have been observed flying over the Capitol and White House areas of Washington, DC. For several days in July 1952, for example, numerous such objects were tracked on radar and observed by civilian and military pilots, leading to worldwide headlines and the largest and longest Air Force press conference since World War II.

4

CIRCULAR CONUNDRUMS OF 1992

George Wingfield

There once was a man who said 'God
Must find it exceedingly odd
That pictograms pop up
And crop circles crop up
When there's no one about – not a sod'

In adapting and updating Ronald Knox's well-known limerick expressing the ontological speculations of Bishop Berkeley, I will probably encourage hordes of versifiers to respond in kind with their interpretations of the circles mystery. These will very likely range from those who make a case for 'I did it. Signed: God', to the sceptics who will insist, rightly, that there were, in fact, plenty of 'sods' out faking circles at night.

Curiously, though not altogether unexpectedly, during both 1991 and 1992, some of these 'sods' were the sceptics themselves, intent on rubbishing the phenomenon by deceiving prominent cereologists [those who study the phenomenon – Ed.]. Their argument was that if an 'expert' can be taken in by a man-made formation, then every formation could be man-made and, *ergo*, the whole phenomenon is no more than a hoax. This is, of course, a monstrous fallacy.

In 1991, the Wessex Sceptics came to mid-Wiltshire and hoaxed three rather inelegant formations which, in my view, stood out like sore thumbs, bearing little resemblance to the genuine pictograms then popping up all around. Nevertheless, the hoaxers did publicly deceive and humiliate Terence Meaden, proponent of the

51

'plasma vortex' theory for circle formations, who was taken in by one of their creations. The next cereological victim was poor Pat Delgado, who initially fell for the 'Doug and Dave' scam, when, in 1991, Douglas Bower and David Chorley claimed to have fabricated many of the circle formations. It was subsequently demonstrated that most of their claims were fraudulent.

In 1992, two particularly militant debunkers, having failed to discover the supposed creators of the Barbury Castle (Wiltshire) Triangle and the other great pictograms of 1991, embarked on a plan to hoax such formations themselves. Both these people are well known in the circles fraternity; their obsession was primarily to discredit the Centre for Crop Circle Studies (CCCS) and certain circles researchers in particular, the prime targets being Michael Green, Colin Andrews and myself. After producing a number of formations in the Alton Barnes, Wiltshire, area in July, they and their helpers presented their two *pièces de résistance*.

THE FROXFIELD FAKE

On 5 August, a large pictogram was expertly hoaxed at Upton Lovell, near Warminster, Wiltshire; then, on the night of 8/9 August, the real masterpiece was prepared near Froxfield, Wiltshire. It was indeed magnificent. One could scarcely fail to admire the craftsmanship and dexterity of the circle-fakers who had painstakingly reproduced many indicators of genuine circles.

The deception, however, did not succeed. In the morning, the great sham pictogram lay waiting in the fields like a Trojan Horse ready to be discovered by CCCS. No one saw it, no one noticed, no one came; only the farmer, who failed to spot it initially, and then gave signs that he was about to harvest the field. At this juncture, our chief conspirator, horrified that the master-piece might be destroyed before it had been seen by his intended victims, himself telephoned the contact number for reporting circles. In due course, certain researchers –

but not the ones he was after – did arrive, as he waited with his camcorder to record their anticipated wonder and admiration.

The Froxfield Fake was indeed right 'over the top'. Among those 'genuine' features expertly reproduced, it was possible to note the style of one of the participants in the competition held at West Wycombe, Buckinghamshire, in which entrants had tried to reproduce the genuine circles (see later). Suffice to say that the 'grapeshot' and one conical centre 'nest' were superbly crafted.

Soon afterwards, the ringleader – a tall man who usually dresses in black! – telephoned me (which is unusual) on some pretext and then casually asked what I thought of the Froxfield pictogram. Knowing that he records such telephone conversations, I had anticipated such a call inviting me to step into the trap. I said it was a fake, that we knew who had done it, and that charges of criminal damage would shortly be brought by farmers against the hoaxers.

GENUINE VERSUS HOAX

By 1991, when the implication of intelligent origin had become irresistible, there was no salvation for the explanation that the formations were all produced by some natural phenomenon. But nor could one accept that they were *all* man-made hoaxes. Terence Meaden's attempt to find a middle path, to the effect that simple and ringed circles are 'genuine', and that pictograms and complex circles (which do not fit his plasma vortex theory) are 'hoaxes', is equally unacceptable and cannot seriously be entertained. Indeed, there are people, desperate to salvage the discredited vortex theory, who have engaged in the hoaxing already described, with a view to disparaging the pictograms.

In any case, the circles have lost their innocence, and 1992 has been a year of doubt and suspicion. The circles phenomenon itself has not changed that much but we, the audience, have. What has become abundantly plain is that no one currently has any guaranteed sure-fire method of distinguishing the genuine article from the cleverly made fake. Sometimes we can be *nearly* certain that we have the real thing, if we are lucky enough to find a virgin formation. We could point to a dozen telling characteristics which were indicators of true circles. But 100 per cent certainty of what really occurred during an unwitnessed event is impossible. And if one goes to examine a new circle even after a day or two, visual assessment will be of little value since it will already have been trampled by dozens of visitors.

Science seldom has all the answers. We may be intuitively certain for example, that the man known to us as our father is indeed our father, yet scientific tests can only give a high probability of paternity. It may be that the scientific tests undertaken by Project Argus of the Wiltshire crop circles in 1992 will give a probable indication of genuine circles, but by the very nature of the phenomenon I doubt whether we shall ever come up with a definitive test to resolve the matter beyond dispute.

If this misgiving is justified, we shall be forced once more to rely upon our own intuition, or else to take far greater notice of the results of dowsing – which may amount to the same thing. The Froxfield Fake displayed no such energy. The fact that dowsers are fallible does not mean one should abandon such methods; scientists, too, make mistakes, and this does not lead us to abandon science. Simple human failures should not deter us. We are confronted here with a real phenomenon of extreme significance, and the present temporary confusion should not cause us to forget this.

The total number of formations in 1992 was not far short of that for the preceding years. There was a great variety of shapes which undoubtedly included many hoaxes. Perhaps some of the simple circles which were associated with UFO sightings (see page 66) were of particular interest. Tailed circles, first seen at Cheesefoot Head in 1989 but largely absent in 1990 and 1991, were often seen this year. Some of these gave a distinct impression of a seed with a shoot coming out of it. Sometimes the tails developed into long curving paths where the circle-making agency had swept through the crop, in one case crossing over itself.

Other themes included circles with plain crosses attached, similar to the 'female' sign or the astrological sign for Venus. Dumb-bells and pictograms similar to those seen in 1990 and 1991 were also found in many parts of the country; and these sometimes embodied spirals and crescents, neither of which were previously seen.

But the intractable problem of distinguishing genuine circles from the hoaxed ones still remained, and visual inspection was seldom a reliable guide. Moreover, the sceptics and circle-fakers now went to great lengths to dupe their victims. Before making one large formation at Hyden Hill near East Meon in Hampshire, it is said they actually dowsed a major earth energy line in the field and carefully constructed their pictogram on top of it. This fake pictogram had been commissioned by John Macnish and was made by Doug and Dave with the farmer's permission. Its making was filmed at night and this was to have been included in a new sceptical documentary on the circles, had not the premature disclosure of the subterfuge diminished its impact.

CIRCLE MAKING COMPETITION

The Cereologist's Circle Making Competition was held at West Wycombe, Buckinghamshire, during the night of 11–12 July 1992, and was sponsored by *The Cereologist* magazine, the Arthur Koestler Foundation, and others, with a first prize of £3,000. The competitors were given five hours and one area of field measuring 100 feet by 66 feet to produce their designs, and were scrutinized by invigilators with infrared binoculars. The first prize was won jointly by Adrian Dexter and David Overd, a designer with Westland Helicopters.

Although no one expected the exercise to provide conclusive answers, it taught us two things. Firstly, impressive geometric formations can be produced at night by diligent fakers, indicating that circles which many of us have too readily accepted as 'genuine', could have been hoaxed. Secondly, man-made circles generally lack the fluidity of flow that we tend to see in the genuine article, sweeping the plants along with it in a way which was not displayed at West Wycombe (although even this was quite skilfully reproduced in the Froxfield Fake).

Interestingly, the more successful competitors used substantial amounts of equipment to scribe their pictograms and bridge the gap when climbing into inaccessible parts of their formations. At least half the teams left behind small items after they had finished. And in every case, the flattened crop in the man-made circles was broken or buckled, which is not generally the case in 'genuine' formations. Equally significant is the fact that although several participants admitted to having hoaxed a few circles in the recent past, most still believed that the phenomenon was a genuine mystery, and none claimed credit for such classic formations as those at Alton Barnes, Barbury Castle, and the Mandelbrot[1].

A CAMPAIGN TO DISCREDIT

Even without these insights, it was apparent that there were many hoaxed formations being made in the cornfields during the early season of 1992. Nevertheless, this hoaxing does not in any way vindicate the heavy-handed campaign which is currently pursued by several sections of the national press – and surreptitiously encouraged, to say the least, by people close to government – to rubbish the entire circles phenomenon.

The most visible attack (to date) from this quarter was contained in an article in the *Weekend Telegraph* by Matt Ridley, who had led a team in the hoaxing competition at West Wycombe. Ridley lashed crop circles 'believers' as credulous fools. 'The believers are either be-kaftanned earth mothers or gently dishevelled and rather upper-class fogies with names like Montague, Wingfield, Michell and Martineau,' he wrote. 'The sceptics are sensible northerners with monosyllabic surnames (such as Brown).'[2]

Who is this Matt Ridley, posing as a bluff, sensible man of the people? He is none other than the Hon. Matthew White Ridley, Eton-educated son and heir to the fourth Viscount Ridley, and nephew of former environment minister, the late Nicholas Ridley (Lord Ridley of Liddesdale). The 'upper-class fogey' jibe is highly ironic, coming as it does from the aristocratic Ridley. One might also wonder whether he ever discussed the crop circles with his uncle who, during his tenure of office, received many documents relating to the phenomenon, some of which his department specifically requested from Colin Andrews and Pat Delgado, the well-known authors of several books on the subject. Although Ridley's scepticism is conceivably sincere, this position was most certainly not the standpoint of the Conservative government which discussed these matters in secret in September 1990[3], and doubtless on various subsequent occasions.

Lest I be accused of dwelling too much on the negative aspects of the 1992 situation, it is worth underlining that they exist and must be confronted. Had space permitted, I would have discussed Doug Bower's contention that the trilling noise associated with the circles[4] is merely the song of the fabled grasshopper warbler. Suffice it to say that this trilling noise has been heard again at night in July 1992, in the vicinity of Alton Barnes and at other circle sites, and it is very doubtful that it was caused by a bird.

If one set out to run a successful campaign to discredit the circles phenomenon, how would one best proceed? Wartime governments have occasionally counterfeited large quantities of their enemy's currency, in order to devalue and ruin the economy based upon that currency. A similar strategy might be employed as part of a disinformation campaign against the circles. Some might interpret the following happenings in this light.

On 9 July 1992, a vast formation, 440 feet long, shaped like a fully extended snail with curious L-shaped eyestalks, appeared after a misty night in the celebrated East Field at Alton Barnes. Although several groups had been watching the field, no one saw people making this formation. Yet such was the prevailing heightened state of paranoia that virtually anyone in the vicinity that night was regarded as suspect. One absurd and malicious allegation was that farmer Tim Carson had himself commissioned the hoaxing of the 'snail' for financial motives.

The very idea of a huge snail-shaped agriglyph is outrageous. Yet although naturally it was viewed with the deepest suspicion, there were some indications that the snail might be 'gluvine'. Distinctive dowsable patterns were found, and close examination gave no immediate suggestion of hoaxing. Some people also reported strong energies in different parts of this bizarre formation. Even so, the likelihood of hoax was strong. Fifteen days later, a second 'snail' appeared two miles away at Stanton St Bernard. This was much rougher, apparently did not dowse, and was promptly condemned as a hoax – which it surely was. A third huge 'snail' appeared on 29 July near Pewsey. This, too, received a mixed reception, and was most likely hoaxed by the group responsible for the Froxfield Fake.

On 1 August, a fourth 'snail' appeared at Manningford Bohune, near Upavon, Wiltshire. This formation was successfully forecast by John Haddington, CCCS patron and, indeed, cereological patron of *Helix aspersa*, the common garden snail (in that he has written about its symbolic significance). He even foretold (the day before) its position to within 200 yards, although, since he was in Scotland that night, we can be sure that he did not physically create it. No disrespect to John, but it is possible that hoaxers may have used the same criteria as he did to decide where 'snail' No. 4 would appear.

It is too early to make a full assessment of the snail conundrum, but the campaign to discredit the phenomenon continues to test us just as much as the phenomenon itself, and the 'snails' – true or false – are all part of the crop circle enigma.

Snails apart, the quickening pace of incidents as the 1992 harvest approached, especially in the usual area of mid-Wiltshire, with several new formations reported every day, began to quieten even the sceptics. Their invisible army of hypothetical unseen hoaxers, who are never caught, never acknowledged and never known to abandon their handiwork incomplete, could hardly have been responsible for *all* these recent formations.

In July and August 1992, numerous circles enthusiasts gathered and watched night after night. They observed no hoaxers. What they sometimes *did* see near Alton Barnes and Milk Hill, however, were luminous orange globes hovering low over the fields and on at least one occasion descending into the crop. They seemed to move and behave in a purposive manner. Although we simply do not know what they are, it seems likely that these objects – these UFOs – are the true progenitors of the circles and pictograms.

THE UFO LINK

In my articles for *The UFO Report* series, I described a number of instances where UFOs had been observed in proximity to circles and pictograms. 1991 and 1992 have seen a remarkable increase in these aerial phenomena, which we naturally associate with the crop circles. On occasions when circles have appeared in completely new locations, they have often been preceded by sightings of unidentified luminous objects, close to or above the fields in question. It is as if these objects were 'seeding' the site with something unseen or non-material, which later gives rise to the circles phenomenon. After initial visitation by the aerial component of the circle-making agency, a new site often continues to exhibit circles in successive seasons, but as a rule nothing further is seen in the sky.

Exceptions are at very active sites such as Silbury Hill or Alton Barnes, where there have been many reports of luminous orange spheres over the cornfields in recent years. In June 1989, for example, a resident of West Kennett observed one such sphere as it descended into the same field opposite Silbury Hill, where an imperfect quincunx formation and some smaller circles were found the next morning. This object appeared to be about 30 feet in diameter. It 'bounced' and then hovered over the ground before blinking out.

Near Milk Hill, on 22 June 1991, John Holman saw and video-recorded another such object, perhaps 70–80 feet in diameter, moving silently across the sky. It then blinked out or vanished behind the hill.

In addition to various video films which have been made of these nocturnal luminosities, there are two well-known video sequences which appear to show small daylight objects moving in seemingly purposeful fashion over the wheatfields. One of these was made in 1991 at Manton, near Marlborough, Wiltshire, by two German visitors, Constantin and Mucki von Durkheim. The luminous object, which does not seem to be solid and possibly shrinks in size as it moves towards the camera, travels above a large pictogram known as the 'Manton Ant'. It disappears into the crop more than once and then reappears. Although this is hardly a 'nuts and bolts' mini-UFO, it is equally unlikely to be back-lit

dandelion seed or thistledown, as suggested by the
sceptics.

Perhaps more interesting is the small disc-shaped
object video-recorded flying over a field near Milk Hill by
Steven Alexander in July 1990. This object flies over a
tractor which is being driven across the field at the time,
and the driver is seen to look up at it. The driver, Leon
Besant, later described what he had seen as a disc; indeed,
he spoke in terms of a small UFO. It is inconceivable,
surely, that he should fail to recognize thistledown! The
sceptics are mute about this.

REMOTE VIEWING

So what are these luminous objects, which move silently
in or above our cornfields during the summer, and even
after the harvest? Are they in fact the actual circle-
makers? This was a question I put to some American
colleagues; in particular I requested that a method called
'remote viewing' might be undertaken to help determine
what produces the crop circles phenomenon.

Remote viewing is a modern psychic technique which
has frequently been used by the US military in recent
years to locate hidden weapons. Edward Dames, who
spent time developing these techniques while in the
Defense Intelligence Agency (DIA) is now, as a civilian,
the president of Psi Tech, a company whose specific
business is remote viewing. Psi Tech was recently commissioned to help in a project to locate possible nuclear
and chemical weapons concealed by Saddam Hussein in
Iraq.

Initial tests, using particular crop circles locations as
targets, yielded intriguing results. Luminous spheres,
about a foot in diameter, with a bluish-white tinge, were
viewed 'rolling' through the wheat about one foot off the
ground and below the level of the ears (of wheat). The
wheat bent and fell in neat swathes as these spheres
passed through it.

During part of this exercise, it was stated that two or

more such spheres were sensed as 'acting in concert', presumably tracing out different parts of a crop formation. This is certainly consistent with the interleaved and multiple lays which CCCS has often observed in some pictograms.

When in Atlanta last April, I asked Edward Dames where these luminous spheres came from and who or what controlled them. This was harder to answer, but the clear implication was that some form of extraterrestrial intelligence (whether physical or non-physical) was at work. The remote viewing process did not resolve this aspect of the enigma, but Dames did suggest that the spheres returned to an 'airless environment' where perhaps thirty to forty such objects were held on some sort of disc, used as a collecting point.

This may be all rather hard to swallow for those unfamiliar with the concept of remote viewing. Nevertheless, the description does correspond in some measure to the small luminous spheres which have been reported so frequently from around Milk Hill and that area.

These spheres are perhaps just one variety of what we tend to describe as UFOs. Many of us studying the crop circles are aware that we are dealing with some kind of non-physical intelligence associated with the circles, and this may well be of the same origin as that associated with the UFO phenomenon.

1992 SIGHTINGS

One of the many American investigators visiting the Wiltshire circles sites in 1992 was Dr Steven Greer, who runs the Centre for the Study of Extra-Terrestrial Intelligence (CSETI). Greer believes that through meditation and the development of a welcoming openness to the UFO intelligences, as well as through attempted communications by means of flashlights, for example, we can induce contact – a type of contact he has termed a Close Encounter of the Fifth Kind (CE5). [See Editor's note]

In developing this approach, Greer arbitrarily assumes

that the intelligence with which we are dealing is friendly, and it is a necessary assumption for his protocols to work. This standpoint is hotly disputed by some who see the extraterrestrial intelligences as a threat, and think in terms of little grey aliens who abduct humans. Such a malign, even demonic, perception of UFOs and their occupants may nevertheless be only a reflection of our own fears.

Whether right or wrong, Steven Greer and his group achieved success on 14 April 1992 at Gulf Breeze, Florida, when such an apparently induced encounter was witnessed by many people. Five luminous UFOs appeared in the night sky and moved in formation – all recorded on video film. At one stage three of the objects form an equilateral triangle and the other two UFOs fly behind. They are then seen to fly low over the watchers. One UFO can be seen flashing back in apparent response to the signals directed at them by members of Greer's group, using powerful hand-held flashlights.

Shortly after midnight on 26 July 1992, Dr Greer and several other investigators, parked in cars near Woodborough Hill, Alton Barnes, Wiltshire, saw an unusual object in the night sky. Chris Mansell, a British art teacher, takes up the story:

. . . I noticed, towards what I estimated to be the south, a long strip of coloured lights which appeared to be revolving from left to right, changing colour from red through white to green . . . and I went to tell Steve. By this time we were all out on the road and watched the 'craft' as it moved slowly from east to west and became stationary at a position just above the horizon . . . We estimated that it must have been 1,500–2,500 feet away . . .

At a certain stage in its movement it appeared to illuminate its own structure (possibly by reflection from the ground), and we all saw that it was a cigar-shaped object, or possibly circular seen edge on, with a small projection at the top. As the craft became stationary, I thought it flipped through 90 degrees so that we could see its underside. The light formation was now triangular, with a triangle of three amber lights at the top, and a row of coloured lights forming the base of the triangle, again ranging from red at the left, to blue-green at the right. The lights on the underbelly were much dimmer than those viewed from the side.

After a few moments, one of the orange lights forming the upper triangle seemed to separate from the formation, move slightly west, and return to the formation. Then, one of the red lights at the base of the formation also seemed to separate, move slightly to the east, and rejoin the formation. Next, it appeared that three red lights broke away from the formation, moved a considerable distance to the west, and then rejoined the formation.

During the whole of this time – about ten minutes – we were observing these events through binoculars and making an audio tape of what was occurring . . . The 'craft' was completely silent . . .

Dr Steven Greer decided that he would like to communicate with the object, and asked Dr Sandra Small to take one of the high-powered hand-held lights from the back of his car, while we kept the 'craft' under observation. He took the light and pointed it directly at the formation and signalled two short bursts of light. To our absolute amazement, the light at the top of the formation mirrored this signal exactly . . . this procedure was repeated a number of times and on each occasion the single light flashed back in exactly the same pattern.

The 'craft' then started to move away to the west and then to the south, and appeared to be going down the Avon Valley [where] we finally lost sight of it . . .[5]

[Researcher Maria Ward, who was also present, has a slightly different recollection of these events – see Editor's note.]

Perhaps significantly, a 40-foot circle was found in wheat near Woodborough Bridge (near the Kennet and Avon Canal) on 30 July, in the close vicinity of where the sighting originated. There had never been circles at Woodborough previously.

Another sighting took place on 28 July near Alton Priors, when John and Julie Wakefield saw a luminous orange object between some trees at 10.15 p.m. Julie reported that the object then came above the trees and was 'bobbing up and down'. She continued:

We clambered out of our Landrover and stood on the roof to get a closer look. We watched the object for several minutes as it bobbed above the trees, then it abruptly stopped and held a stationary position. It maintained that position for approximately a minute, and then suddenly a small piece of the orange ball broke off and flew to the right of the larger one. The larger object was [estimated to be] about 35 feet across and the smaller one about 8 feet. This smaller object then made a clockwise revolution in the sky.

At this point we could hear that some dogs had begun to bark at a nearby farm and the cows in an adjoining field were making noises, as though they had been startled by something. The smaller object then flew back to the original object, which it rejoined, as though it had never left it, and the whole [thing] then lowered between the trees. The cattle ceased to be alarmed but the dogs went on barking. We watched for several minutes but the object was no longer visible.

Five minutes later, the orange ball appeared yet again above the trees, bobbing for a few seconds, and then it remained stationary. We went outside our vehicle again and watched in amazement as the object hung there for over three minutes, and then it went behind the trees again. We decided to drive to the caravan near East Field to see if anyone was there. At that moment, we noticed a very bright orange glow in Tawsmead Copse which lit up the whole wood. The same orange object then came above the trees and flew very slowly from Tawsmead Copse towards Alton Priors. It flew slowly and smoothly and then abruptly stopped and again remained stationary. It looked huge hanging there, and extremely bright.

An Army helicopter then appeared to the north of the luminous object. A further two helicopters appeared to the east and west of it. The object flew southwards, blinking out as soon as the first helicopter advanced towards it. The three helicopters circled several times where the object had been and then flew off.

There were several witnesses to this event, including Dr Steven Greer, Eddie Sherwood and others . . . Various cropwatchers who had been positioned on Adam's Grave and Knap Hill also saw it, together with a farmworker. John and I were lucky, since we had such a close vantage point on each occasion the object appeared. The whole event took place between 10.15 p.m. and 10.35 p.m. . .

The following day, Busty Taylor, the well-known

investigator who has taken so many fine photographs of the circles from his plane, spotted two formations while flying over Draycot Fitz Payne, which is just half a mile from where the luminous object had first appeared. There was a simple 30-foot circle as well as a small circle with an annular ring. The latter had appeared during the previous night (28/29 July), and the plain circle on the night of 26/27 July. The ringed circle had no tracks leading to it and both circles, according to Julie, looked impressive.

'We spoke to Mr Bryant at nearby Draycott Manor Cottage,' Julie added. 'He said the dogs near his house had started to bark loudly and continuously that night, which they don't normally do. He also said that an odd message, *"Caution, police"*, had come over a baby alarm system used in the house. Nothing had ever interfered with this before and he thought that it had a very limited range.'

These strange aerial phenomena, reminiscent of the Warminster UFOs twenty years ago, have returned to haunt this part of mid-Wiltshire, just where the concentration of crop circles has been greatest. The UFO connection with crop circles is undoubted. But we are still as far as ever from understanding the nature of these phenomena.

Notes

1. *The Cereologist*, No. 7, 1992, Specialist Knowledge Services, Saint Aldhelm, 20 Paul Street, Frome, Somerset, BA11 1DX.
2. *The Daily Telegraph*, London, 18 July 1992.
3. Wingfield, George: 'The Evolving Crop Circles', *The UFO Report 1992*, ed. Timothy Good, Sidgwick & Jackson, London, 1991, p. 13.
4. Wingfield, George: 'Ever Increasing Circles', *The UFO Report 1991*, ed. Timothy Good, Sidgwick & Jackson, London, 1990, pp. 19–25, 26, 31.

5. Mansell, Chris: 'Dramatic UFO Sighting at Woodborough Hill, 26/27 July 1992', *The Circular*, Vol. 3, No. 3, 1992.

Editor's note

Regarding the observation from Woodborough Hill on 26/27 July 1992, Maria Ward informed me, for example, that the smaller lights which left the main formation did not 'rejoin' the formation, and that, in response to the signalling by Dr Greer, the degree of illumination of the lights changed (rather than 'flashed back in exactly the same pattern').

Maria had left the CSETI group at 11.35 p.m. to take a team member back to her lodging, but returned to the site at 12.32 a.m. She saw a large, dense, conical shape in the distance, part of which was hidden by the tree line. There was a series of continuous lights around the periphery of the object, coloured blue, white and red. As the object cleared the trees, she could see two, perhaps three orange lights above the rotating band of light. The object then stopped in a gap in the tree line.

The area of darkness within the lighted areas was extremely dense and nothing could be seen through it. Maria described the lights as moving anticlockwise, although the rear of the object could not be seen, so it was not known if the lights moved in a circular fashion. She then saw a beam of light being directed (by Dr Greer) at the object itself, which appeared to come from further along the by-way and to the south of her position. The object appeared to 'flash' for a moment before resuming its former intensity.

The object, which looked almost triangular, was at least 75 feet in length, no more than 40 feet above the ground, and completely silent (although Maria was aware of a slight buzzing sound to the south of her position). It continued to remain stationary for some seven to nine minutes, then appeared to become longer in the vertical than when first observed. At this point, Maria began to feel very sick, and experienced a tingling sensation up her spine and in her head. A large orange light seemed to break away from the top of the object and move away. She then saw another beam of light being directed at the object, which appeared to 'flash' as before, then the object moved away (not upward) 'and just seemed to disappear'.

I should add that this was by no means the only sighting reported by the CSETI team, and I have included a few additional reports in Chapter 14.

With regard to Dr Greer's method of inducing a response from, or communications with, UFOs (CE5), I should point out that there is nothing new about this approach. Similar methods have been used by many individuals and groups throughout the world since the 1950s, with varying degrees of success.

5

THE YIN AND YANG OF UFOs

Paul Dong

Paul Dong was born in Canton, China, in 1928, but now lives in Oakland, California. He has been studying the UFO phenomenon for many years and has written many articles for newspapers and journals in China, as well as a number of books, including *The Four Major Mysteries of Mainland China*[1] and *UFOs over Modern China*[2].

In 1981 he lectured on UFOs throughout China, speaking to packed audiences at the Beijing Ching Hua Students Union, Canton Science Museum, Canton Jinan University, and elsewhere.

Paul Dong is a *qigong* (or *chi gong*) master, and is the co-author of several books on the subject. He has taught many forms of this discipline at the YMCA in San Francisco since 1985. He can be contacted at PO Box 2011, Oakland, California 94604.

In China, 1.1 billion people use the Chinese language every day. However, in contrast to English, it is not so widely used as a language of international communication. For this reason, the outside world has little or no knowledge of many things which happen in China, other than political events.

As readers of *The UFO Report* series[3][4][5] will know, I have hitherto been able to obtain a considerable number of civilian and military reports of UFO sightings in China over the years, but during the last year or so, the number of publicly available reports has diminished. So, instead of the usual 'On such-and-such date in such-and-such place, a light appeared and soon disappeared' etc., I am offering the following research report, which deals with an unusual, Chinese approach to the phenomenon.

First of all, we must admit that even after forty-five years of controversy over UFOs, nobody knows what they are, where they come from, or how they disappear. In the last few years, however, several Chinese UFO researchers have argued in favour of the idea that although UFOs are indeed of extraterrestrial origin, they are not flying saucers travelling at the speed of light. Rather, they come by means of 'unobservable flight' – even faster than light. This 'unobservable flight' relies on the 'yin-yang' transformation. Thus, if we wish to understand this account, we must first get a clear idea of what these terms mean.

UNOBSERVABLE FLIGHT

Although unlike normal flight, unobservable flight can nevertheless have a starting and ending point. That is, it can create the effect of making an object 'fly' from one place to another. Unobservable flight is a motion phenomenon *beyond* the space-time continuum, in which it is impossible to trace the path of motion through time and space. In contrast to this, motion phenomena *within* the traditional space-time continuum, in which it is possible to trace such a path of motion, may be called 'observable flight'. What we here refer to as a path is a continuous curve with a starting point and ending point, with no interruptions between. For example, the launching of a space rocket is observable flight; the orbit of an electron around an atomic nucleus is observable flight. But if an object, brought by mental power, suddenly appears in the hand, the 'flight' of the object is an example of unobservable flight. To give another example, the way certain powerful psychics – such as China's super psychic, Zhang Baosheng – are reported to be able to walk through walls by mental power can also be called unobservable flight.

This is not high-speed flight. High-speed flight has a path of motion, while unobservable flight does not. Nor is it camouflaged flight, which uses some concealing signal to fool the human sense organs, so that people are unable to detect the existence of an object. In this case we can still track the object's path of flight through space-time with instruments. For example, an airplane coated with radar-absorbing material [as well as incorporating 'faceted' construction – Ed.] can camouflage its flight from radar (as is the case with American stealth aircraft). However, what we refer to as unobservable flight is one whose path cannot be determined by any present-day tracking method.

Unobservable flight can overcome spatial obstacles without breaking the obstacle (as in the above example of passing through walls). It can also overcome temporal obstacles and allow flight to the past or the future (as in the American film *Back to the Future*). In other words, it is a phenomenon which transcends the space-time continuum.

THE YIN-YANG MODEL

According to Chinese philosophy, in the beginning of the universe there was nothingness, and out of nothingness came existence, and out of this came yin and yang. Since then, these two principles have controlled all transformations in the universe. Yin contains yang, yang contains yin, and both are constantly shifting and changing and making the events and objects in the universe go through an endless cycle of transformation.

Yin and yang can sometimes be rather abstract terms. In order to make these concrete, the following table with specific examples may be helpful:

Yin	*Yang*
Emptiness (minus sign)	Substance (plus sign)
Formless (unobservable)	Having form (observable)
Earth	Heaven
Moon	Sun
Female	Male
Water	Fire
Dark	Light

Inside	Outside
Static	Dynamic
Rain	Cloud
Magnetism (has dual polarity: both yin and yang)	Electricity
Below	Above
Cold	Heat
Contraction	Expansion
Soft	Hard

Yin and yang are in the contradictory relationships of being opposed to each other, while at the same time being dependent on each other. Thus, anything in the universe has two aspects: conflict and unity. Neither of these aspects can exist in isolation; neither can escape the other and develop on its own. If there is Heaven, there must be Earth; if there is male, there must be female; if there is above, there must be below. All must come in pairs. But in this contradictory transformation process of yin and yang, when yin develops to its extreme point, it becomes yang, and conversely, when yang develops to its extreme point, it becomes yin. This process is the transformation of a quantitative effect to a qualitative effect. Everything, from the natural environment to the life of the human body, must obey this law. If we call the familiar substances of the material world yang substances, then there must exist its opposite, yin substances. Thus, these two types of substances combine to form the whole – the universe. Keeping in mind the above model of yin and yang, let us turn to a discussion of UFOs.

PSYCHIC ABILITIES

Chinese UFO researchers believe that UFOs come from distant stars using the yin-yang transformation. Here is how the story begins:

China has a huge population, and due to the shortage of doctors and medicine, some people advocated the centuries-old practice of *chi gong*[6] (a form of meditation) for healing, as a supplement to the scarce medical resources. *Chi gong* does not require doctors, needles or medicine, and it saves both time and money. Claims as to its efficacy have proved to be justified. As a result, some twenty million people practise *chi gong* every day.

Interestingly, *chi gong* is not only conducive to health, but can also – in the case of those with sensitive meridians (channels of the circulation of *chi*, or vital energy) – promote psychic abilities, as I have been able to prove for myself. Such abilities include healing, retrieving objects by mind power, clairvoyance, repairing broken sticks and needles, remote vision, remote hearing, levitation (the body rising in the air), and so on. Moreover, powerful psychic ability can even generate such phenomena as telekinesis (moving an object from one place to another), walking through walls, unobservable flight (as described earlier) and out-of-body experiences (OOBEs).

Many *chi gong* practitioners claim that after entering the meditative state, they have flown to other planets, seen extraterrestrials and even talked with them. Some claim to have entered a flying saucer in outer space, giving clear descriptions of all the on-board equipment and the actions of the extraterrestrial crew. Others say they can summon UFOs instantly by mental power. Hundreds of people, of all intellectual levels, have described such experiences. They swear that these scenes were real and *not* just hallucinations engendered during meditation. Thus, in the last few years, articles on the subject have frequently appeared in UFO and *chi gong* magazines in China, and several books have also been written and published.

How then do those with psychic powers 'fly' to other planets, and how do UFOs fly to Earth? Researchers say that *chi gong* masters or those with psychic ability can use mind power to pluck the leaves from trees, or move objects upstairs. Yet what abilities are they using, can they be explained, and what observation techniques could a physicist employ to measure them? The yin-yang model allows us to classify them as yin-type abilities, the reason being that they are always associated with yin-type substances. The laws known to present-day physics, suitable for explaining the motions of yang-type substances, do not apply to yin-type substances. In what way, then, do yin-type substances exert their effect? The answer is 'thought'.

The psychic abilities I have so far referred to rely mainly on thought. Because thought is an ordered movement of yin-type substances, it is the motion of a set of coherent 'information signal waves'. Thus, it is a simple matter for these information signal waves to pass through obstacles of yang-type materials to affect other targets (such as plucking the leaves off a tree, bending a needle, etc.). Normally, we use hand-powered or electric-powered machines to carry out complex operations. Thought makes use of the information waves stored in the brain. As a rule, it takes a combination of manpower, equipment, electricity and money to make a videotape of a scene. However, remote viewing of the same scene by mind power only requires the brain to expend a few calories.

By the principles of the yin-yang model, under certain circumstances yang substances can be transformed into yin substances (and vice versa). The term 'certain circumstances' means that after a superior intelligence attains a high degree of mental power, that being can actively manipulate the 'machine' of thought. Some psychics understand how these circumstances can be manipulated. Earth people are all born with the essential elements of psychic ability, but the vast majority have never been discovered; and those who claim to have that potential are branded as fakes, sorcerers and the like. Others do not know the method of creating or activating their psychic abilities by the practice of *chi gong*. Activation entails making use of the special inner body energy developed by a *chi* master to stimulate certain acupuncture points in order to bring out a person's psychic abilities.

In conclusion, I would add that there can be four

sources of psychic ability. In perhaps one in a million cases, it is inborn; it may be activated by accident when certain body parts (called acupuncture points in Chinese medicine) are hit by something, traumatized in a fire, struck by lightning, electrically shocked, or injured in a fall, etc.; it may be activated by a *chi gong* master or psychic; or it may be developed independently by the practice of *chi gong*.

With so many millions of people in mainland China practising *chi gong* regularly, it is likely that psychic ability will become more widespread, and China may enter a 'psychic age'. In this event, people will be able to do many things with their minds alone.

THE YIN-YANG 'SPACESHIP'

If we assume that extraterrestrials entered the psychic age thousands of years ago or more, their psychic power would be many times stronger than ours. It would thus be possible for them to visit Earth for travel or exploration.

By exercising mind power, whether in a meditative state of *chi gong* practice or in a psychic trance, the internal body energy is transformed into yin energy. For example, it is not subject to gravity or inertia, can travel at faster-than-light (or superphotonic) speed, and can pass through any obstacle (psychic effects bear witness to the existence of these phenomena). Furthermore, it can break through space-time, allowing out-of-body experiences in the cosmic dimension.

Let us suppose extraterrestrials have constructed an amazing spacecraft, and in the course of travelling, use their mind power to accelerate so as to exceed the speed of light. Under the space-time effect, this transforms them and their spacecraft into a bundle of yin-type substance – an information signal wave – which can reach Earth in an instant by 'unobservable flight'. The extraterrestrials then exercise their mind power to decelerate below the speed of light, at which 'subphotonic speeds' they appear in their original forms. Should the need arise, they can increase the speed a little to become unobservable, or to return home. The spacecraft's movements and manoeuvres are beyond the constraints of gravity and inertia (that is, they do not obey the laws of human physics), so that it can make 90-degree turns and instantaneous stops (violating inertia) and float in mid-air (defying gravity). If such a situation is possible, then we can translate the incomprehensible into the intelligible, leading to the conclusion that one way we can communicate with extraterrestrials is by psychic power.

These hypotheses are on a par with Western conceptions of the so-called world of matter and anti-matter, and of teleportation (as seen in the *Star Trek* series, for example, in which a person stands on an electromagnetic apparatus, and at the push of a button is dematerialized and then transported to a desired destination, reappearing at that place). The difference is that Western science fiction tales remain no more than that, whereas psychic phenomena go back far beyond that. China applied yin-yang principles to medicine as long as 2,000 years ago; and Western psychic research also dates back some 150 years. During the last thirty years or so, psychic ability has to a certain extent been verified by scientists. Regrettably, it remains impossible to explain.

To summarize, the Chinese have 'constructed' an amazing yin-yang 'spaceship', one which needs neither fuel, nor food nor medical supplies. Neither is it necessary to put people in cold storage or suspended animation. Merely by using thought power to accelerate or decelerate, they can travel to unexplored galaxies at faster-than-light speeds, completing a round trip in no more than a few hours. The process is not subject to the constraints of human physics.

I accept that some may attack these hypotheses as science fiction. Nevertheless, I know that many Western UFO researchers also deal with psychic phenomena. Furthermore, they hypothesize that UFOs might originate from the Earth's interior, the ocean floor, the

Bermuda Triangle or two-dimensional space. Are not such theories also science fiction?

We would do well to heed the well-known saying of the modern Chinese thinker, Dr Hu Shi, who advises us to 'hypothesize boldly and verify carefully'. This is the attitude of true scientific inquiry.

Notes

1. Dong, Paul: *The Four Major Mysteries of Mainland China*, Prentice-Hall, New Jersey, 1984. Available from specialist book dealers (see Appendix).
2. Dong, Paul and Stevens, Wendelle: *UFOs over Modern China*, UFO Books, Box 1053, Florence, Arizona 85232. Available from specialist book dealers (see Appendix). For further information on Chinese UFO sightings, see *Above Top Secret: The Worldwide UFO Cover-Up*, by Timothy Good, Sidgwick & Jackson, London, 1987; Grafton Books, London, 1988; Quill/William Morrow, New York, 1988.
3. Dong, Paul: 'UFOs in China 1987–88', *The UFO Report 1990*, ed. Timothy Good, Sidgwick & Jackson, London, 1989 (out of print); also published as *The UFO Report*, Avon Books, New York, 1991.
4. Dong, Paul: 'China Establishes UFO Stations', *The UFO Report 1991*, ed. Timothy Good, Sidgwick & Jackson, London, 1990 (out of print).
5. Dong, Paul: 'The Chinese Scene 1990–91', *The UFO Report 1992*, ed. Timothy Good, Sidgwick & Jackson, London, 1991.
6. Dong, Paul: *Chi Gong: The Ancient Chinese Way to Health*, Paragon House, New York, 1991.

Editor's note

At a scientific conference held in Beijing in June 1992, the China UFO Research Organization announced that it would like to host a major international UFO conference in 1993. Wang Changting, a senior engineer who is acting chairman of the organization, pointed out that interest in the subject in China was more extensive than in any other country, and claimed that hosting such a conference would lead to new scientific developments as well as greater social stability. The organization, established in 1978, is a member of the China Association for Science and Technology, which is largely supported by the government, and has 3,600 formal members as well as 40,000 research associates. UFO researchers from the Chinese Academy of Sciences and other institutes were present at the conference, which dealt mostly with ball lightning, superconductivity and space propulsion technology.

6

CLOSE ENCOUNTERS IN ROMANIA

Gheorghita Florin

Gheorghita Florin is an engineer who has studied the UFO phenomenon for several decades. He has published numerous articles on the subject and is the author of *UFOs: A Modern Problem*[1]. Formerly a resident of Cluj, Romania, where I met him in 1970, he now lives in Iasi, capital of the province of Moldavia.

The following report was originally published in *FSR*, translated from the French by editor Gordon Creighton[2], to whom I am grateful for permission to republish it (in re-edited form).

A UFO AT FLAMINZI

According to *Opinia Studenteasca*, a newspaper published in Iasi[3], various residents of the parish of Flaminzi (Botosani Region of Moldavian Province) declared that during the night of 20 October 1990, they saw a UFO flying around over the neighbourhood of the village of Poiana. Busy with their everyday lives, the villagers subsequently forgot all about the incident which, had it occurred in America, would no doubt have featured on the front pages of newspapers and been discussed at length. At it was, the affair quickly died down, those who had 'seen' the lights sticking to their guns, and the rest, who had slept through the night, insisting that the others were crazy. And so, presumably, it would have remained, and all would have been forgotten, had not two journalists from the *Botosani Gazeta* gone to Flaminzi, to be followed later by television reporters.

The light in the sky was seen by twenty-three-year-old

Virgil Atodiresei at about 9.30 p.m., as he was returning home along Flaminzi's main road. Suddenly he became aware of a bright though diffused light, directly above the village of Poiana. 'I didn't pay too much heed to it,' said Virgil, 'although the thought did cross my mind that it was odd for a motorcar to be travelling through that place, because there's no road there, it's just ploughed fields.'

Meanwhile, in the village of Poiana, the electricity had failed. Nicolai Bildea, professor of mathematics, had gone into the village to get a light [presumably an electric torch]. It was pitch-black; not a star to be seen in the sky, and there were no lights in the surrounding villages.

The first thing that he and his young companion Iulian Preda noticed was a glow that seemed to be flickering over a garden – rather like a bonfire. However, the thing seemed to be not on the ground, but up in the air. 'We began to fear,' said Preda, 'that maybe somebody had set fire to the crops of the Volochina family.' Then the 'flickering' died down, only to suddenly start up again, until it was as bright as a sodium light. And finally it vanished.

A LARGE PROJECTILE-SHAPED OBJECT

According to the statement of Virgil Atodiresei, the flying object was as big as a submarine, and it was flying over the village at a height of perhaps 100 metres. But its shape seemed a bit indistinct – at times like 'a sphere full of beams of light'.

The two shafts of light emitted by it were conical. At their source, they appeared to be 1–2 metres across, whereas on the ground below, each projected a circle of light about 20 metres in diameter. At a certain stage in the sighting, Atodiresei could see a number of other smaller lights, symmetrically arranged on it, like sidelights. At times, the object seemed to be flying at great speed. Then suddenly it would stop abruptly and change course, repeating these sharp-angled swerves several times.

When Professor Bildea first caught sight of it, he thought it looked 'like a gigantic tortoise'. The object was now flying very low, and he climbed up on to a fountain to get a better view of it. From this vantage point, he could see a band of small lights placed equidistantly around the 'belly' of the 'tortoise'. From this 'belly' shone four light-beams: one directed straight down towards the ground, another (briefly) aimed straight at himself and Preda, and the other two beams obliquely downward, slowly 'sweeping' the ground in all directions. But in addition, from a certain angle, the professor could see that the two rear beams consisted of luminous and apparently layered planes, seemingly formed of thin threads, like laser lights. From a different angle, at his second sighting of the object, he described it as having the appearance of a projectile 50 metres long and 12 metres high. The upper portion presented certain transparent areas that gave the impression of portholes, as there was a faint light coming from them – seemingly from inside the 'projectile'. At his third and last sighting, he once more observed 'side-lights'.

His wife, Voichita Bildea, and her mother, Maria Trifan, aged 73, both saw the lights, but according to them, there were *two* beams, not four. They were unable to give a description of the object; all they could see was a relatively misty spherical shape. From it came those two powerful beams of light – 'so powerful that you could have picked up glass beads in the garden'.

Everyone said it was raining gently on the evening in question. Professor Bildea, however, was the only one who stated that when the UFO appeared, the rain instantly ceased, and that, as soon as the object had finally gone, the rain started up again, just as suddenly, and this time much more heavily. And there was one other thing: he said he had the impression that at one point, one of the beams *had bent itself*, and had remained like that for several seconds.

POWER FAILURE

All the witnesses, without exception, said that the object had appeared several times and that each time the electrical current in the various villages had gone off simultaneously. Shortly after the object had vanished, the lights in the villages had gradually come on again, and all had remained normal until the next appearance of the object.

Next day, said the villagers, someone had come from the Botosani Electricity Works to check the power supply-line, and had found no defect which might explain why the fuses had blown during the night of 20 October. Nevertheless, for two hours during that night, the staff of the electricity plant had been unable to control the flow of current along the line of the parish of Flaminzi. The interruption of the current, they maintained, had not been carried out by the electricity company. Moreover, they said, *the meter had continued to show, throughout, that energy was being consumed, even when the power was 'off'*.

FURTHER REMARKABLE SIGHTINGS

Yet another fantastic sighting occurred that same night in the city of Cluj, capital of the north-western region of Romania, and already renowned for its numerous previous UFO sightings and excellent UFO photographs[4]. A Cluj newspaper, *Truth Liberated*, published a brief account of this new sighting[5]. Subsequently, Monica Ghet, a reporter from the magazine *Screen* came, and in the presence of Dr Savel Cheptea (a lecturer at Cluj University) made a tape-recording of the statements of a witness, Ioan Baghiu, a retired railway train-driver, as follows:

At about 2.30 a.m., during the night of 20/21 October, I woke up and went to the kitchen to smoke a cigarette. As I stood at the window, I noticed several 'stars', which were flashing, above the western suburb of Manastur, at an altitude that I calculated to be about 2,000 to 3,000 metres. Looking more attentively, I was able to establish that, within the contours of a rounded framework, there were some eighteen to twenty small yellow lights flashing. At the base of the rounded contour, there was a larger point of yellow light, intermittently emitting a beam of very intense orange light.

Fascinated, I stood watching this phenomenon until about 4.00 a.m. During this interval, I awakened my wife and my daughters, but only the eldest daughter came to the window to watch the phenomenon for a few minutes. I also drew the matter to the attention of my neighbour on the next floor above, Aurora Balaj, as I heard her moving around in her kitchen.

After 3.00 a.m., I had moreover begun to observe a second luminous phenomenon, and this one closer to our multi-storey block of flats. This second phenomenon consisted, as it were, of two lights, bluish and violet-coloured, like fluorescent tubes, from which very powerful cone-shaped beams of light were coming down towards the ground. The phenomenon lasted only for a few minutes.

Then later on, after 4.00 a.m., I was totally astounded by the appearance, right beside my eighth-floor balcony, of a very large cylindrical object which glided slowly and silently past. This thing was of a dark red colour and had no lights. It was more than 15 metres long. I had an excellent view of it [Fig. 6.1], owing to the public street lighting below. At the tip of the front part of it, which was right by my balcony, I could see the vertical face, with a cross-section diameter of about 70 centimetres or so. On this face, there were six 'glass eyes', like lenses, of a dark hue (like six magnifying-glasses, each of a diameter of about 10 centimetres).

The large 'cylinder' had a diameter of about 3 to 4 metres. (Two men standing, one above the other, could have fitted into it.) I was also able to distinguish four dark windows, with black frames.

The cylinder remained there, close to my balcony, for about two minutes. I did not feel afraid, but I did not dare to go out on the balcony. After that, the large object moved back, wobbling slightly but still totally silent, and vanished. After it had gone, I did go out on to the balcony, but there was now nothing to be seen.

But then, after a while *another* object appeared near my balcony! Although it was of the same size as the first one, it was definitely another one, because its colour was greenish-white

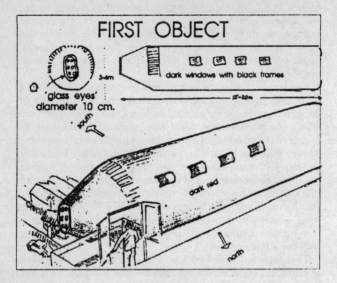

Fig. 6.1

[and] it had no windows. At its tip (seen as a large round section with a dark rim), were four tubes resembling reporters' telephoto lenses [Fig. 6.2]. These tubes, along with the entire frontal plate, were rotating slowly. And this second cylinder was poised at an oblique angle in the air – I think at about 45 degrees.

This second object also did not remain near my balcony for very long. I picked up the telephone and called to my neighbour Bura, but there was no answer. This second cylinder had also glided backwards before vanishing. Stepping out later on to my balcony for the last time, I observed six lights moving away slowly northwards, towards the Baciu Forest. The time was 5.20 a.m.

A UFO AT DOLHESTI

More than a month later, in December 1990, there came another night sighting, also accompanied by a power failure. This time, it was in the parish of Dolhesti, 40 kilometres to the south-east of the town of Iasi. The

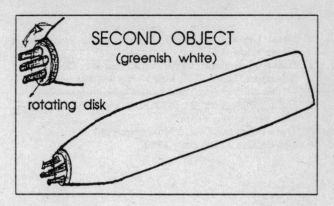

Fig. 6.2

following report appeared in the local newspaper *Opinia* [6].

One night, a few minutes after 4.00 a.m., the night-shift personnel of a business were alarmed by the sudden interruption of their electric lighting. On going to see whether there might be some defect with the current-intake, they observed a powerful light over the area of Crasnita. They climbed a nearby hill and were able to see an oval object of about 10–12 metres in diameter, which was emitting a cold white light like a sodium lamp.

The same description was given, slightly later, by a villager awakened by the barking of dogs. According to other villagers, the object was also seen by some men who were at the bus-station waiting for the bus to Iasi.

Later in the day, at about 1.00 p.m., villagers claimed that the electric current had once more faded out slowly 'like it does when the theatre lights go dim', but had come on again twenty minutes later without any total stoppage.

Notes

1. Florin, Gheorghita: *OZN: O Problema Moderna*, Editura Junimea, Iasi, 1973.
2. Florin, Gheorghita: 'UFOs over Romania in October and November, 1990', *FSR*, Vol. 37 No. 1, 1992.
3. *Opinia Studenteasca*, Iasi, Issue 47, November 1990.
4. Florin, Gheorghita: 'Flying Saucers over Cluj, Romania', *FSR*, Vol. 15 No. 6, 1969.
5. *Truth Liberated*, Cluj, 3 November 1990.
6. *Opinia*, Iasi, 8 December 1990.

7
JUST WHAT EVIDENCE *WILL* PEOPLE BELIEVE?

John Spencer

John Spencer is well known for his books (listed at the end of this article) and for his lectures and broadcasts on UFOs. He has been a director of the council of management for the British UFO Research Association (BUFORA) for many years, and he is an officer of the International Committee for UFO Research as well as a research specialist for the Mutual UFO Network (MUFON). His speciality is the interaction of the phenomenon with the human mind and, not content with armchair theorizing, he has conducted some important field investigations in this country and abroad.

Outside the world of Ufology, John Spencer is managing partner of a firm of chartered accountants and managing director of a company which trains businessmen at all levels of management. He has several books on accountancy to his credit.

There are those who believe that all UFOs are the product of people's minds – hallucinations, fantasies and so on. Others believe they are 'nuts and bolts' – alien spacecraft piloted by extraterrestrials. Perhaps both explanations are true of some reports. For my part, I believe that whatever the many explanations for the whole phenomenon turn out to be – and there are certain to be several – it is the way our minds interface with them that will prove important.

I believe that at least some UFO reports are the result of something external happening to mankind; not a product of the mind, but something that can affect it. How we interpret these events determines the variety of explanations proferred. As such, I believe we can fairly count the UFO phenomenon as one of many paranormal experiences. It should be researched as such.

So what exactly do UFO investigators think they are doing? Consider a situation where an investigator is told, by a witness, of a UFO event occurring. For the sake of simplicity, and for that reason only, let us at this point consider UFOs to be spaceships from other worlds. I need an easy way to describe an 'extraordinary' origin for UFOs, and that will suit the purpose.

Suppose that the investigator examines the case and concludes that it proves an extraterrestrial, or even paranormal, origin of UFOs. What do we then have? Simply one more person who believes in an extraordinary origin of UFOs. With a world population of 3,000 million, and increasing even in the time it has taken you to read this, that is hardly an efficient way of convincing people of the truth of UFOs. We need something more. We need evidence *that can successfully be presented to others* so that they, too, can be convinced.

Consider then, a second situation, in which the witness invites us to an encounter where we actually see a spaceship and meet with aliens. Let us give ourselves the best evidence we can hope for. We come away with sixteen hours of video tape of the encounter; visually- and audio-recorded conversation between the witnesses, the investigator and the aliens; and information from the aliens which can be verified from archive records in museums all over the world. We might also have still photographs of the aliens and the spaceship, and video footage of the aliens doing something unambiguously non-human. We might have magnetometer readings showing massive increases in magnetic field disturbances at the times when the flying saucer appears, positive returns on portable radar, film of thermometer fluctuations and – just for good measure – a few working parts from the alien spaceship's drive mechanism, offered to us as a gift. What then?

THE CONSEQUENCES

It sounds like the sort of evidence that any UFO researcher, or any investigator into the paranormal, would give his third eye for. As he was collecting the evidence, he could probably envisage a lifetime of praise from his colleagues and the scientific community for finally solving one of the world's great mysteries. He would look forward to lectures, books, films and television chat-shows. But what is actually likely to happen when the investigator offers this priceless evidence to the world?

Firstly, he will come up against the political in-fighting which goes on endlessly among all researchers, whether in the conventional sciences or the para-sciences; his methods will be questioned and his integrity and honesty brought into doubt. Secondly, once the material is presented to a wider public, he can expect to spend *literally* the rest of his life defending himself against allegations of fraud. These will come from both the scientific community – whose institutions have a massive interest in not accepting challenges to science – and from the media.

Additionally, the investigator will be confronted by the 'expertise' of those who call themselves researchers but who could hardly be removed from their armchairs by anything short of a surgical operation. Most of them spend their lives in front of word processors, churning out ego-boosting magazines that add nothing to the subject. They will leap at the opportunity to pick apart the evidence on the basis of some very minor aspect of it. You know the sort of thing: 'Because the witness had wheati-flakes for breakfast that day and they contain 0.00001 part of a million of a compound sometimes found in hallucinogenic drugs, can we really take this man seriously?' Would any court of law taking testimony from a witness to a car crash dare raise the type of bizarre doubts as those levelled against the para-sciences?

We can be fairly sure – from decades of bitter

experience — that recorded data does *not* constitute acceptable evidence for the vast majority of people. There have been many sightings recorded on film, videotape and still photos, such as the Billy Meier (Switzerland) and Gulf Breeze (Florida) cases. Yet collected evidence of this nature has not dented scepticism to any measurable degree.

THE APPROACH OF SCIENCE

Science is really no more than a way of measuring things, and a set of 'filters' set up to test and confirm reality. Consider a jar containing different-sized grains of rock and sand. At the bottom is a filter that allows some through and bars others. Science discovers — to use an analogy — that grains bigger than one millimetre are false but those smaller are true. It sets a filter at one millimetre and lets the truth through, preventing the frauds and mistakes. Most of the experiments we do at school in physics and chemistry are no more than versions of that.

The problem we face is that science has determined that there is no appropriate filter size for UFOs. It is totally closed: there are no truths. In the early and perhaps naive days of Ufology, UFO researchers set the filter totally open: everything was real. This has left us vulnerable to the ridicule that has characterized the attitudes of science and the media for the past thirty years.

I agree that a filter has to be set — that we must weed out fraud and error. But in order to determine the proper size of the filter, we need to work with witnesses on a much closer and more open basis.

I believe that the only way to find out what is true and what is false is to give witnesses a chance to prove what they claim on *their own terms*. This is the basis of 'witness-driven investigation' — a term I coined in my book *Perspectives*, which arose from work partly inspired by BUFORA's Ken Phillips and was furthered by my work in Scandinavia.

Witnesses, however, must also give us something in return: the right to examine their findings in order to determine what is true and what is erroneous – or even fraudulent. This differs from the approach of science. Science says, 'I will set up barriers and if you get through them then I'll believe you'. Where UFOs are concerned, it sets tests without consideration as to whether such tests are reasonable. It demands, for example, the right to predict and reproduce claimed phenomena in experimental form. Because that cannot be the situation where spontaneous paranormal phenomena, including UFOs, are involved, science rejects such phenomena.

This is a blinkered approach in that it fails to recognize that there are many aspects of the world around us which at one time could not be understood within these terms, but which today are within the range of comprehension. Science possesses the appropriate measuring instruments for what was once considered paranormal and from that it has gone on to predict and create the necessary conditions for proof. By rejecting what is still paranormal and refusing to seek and employ suitable measuring instruments, science is denying itself vital information. In fact, it should be assisting researchers into the paranormal to find the very measuring instruments that they presently do not possess, thus giving them direction and purpose.

A NEW APPROACH

UFO researchers should be collecting the evidence not only of what happened but the conditions under which they happened. This may include enabling the witnesses – in effect – to 'manifest' some of the phenomena, if that is one way the UFO phenomenon works. Then we should correlate it with as much other evidence as possible of similar events. In addition, we should be drawing from the researches of investigators into other paranormal activity where, firstly, there may be actual interaction and, secondly, lessons to learn.

Let us create a scenario; say that a UFO is appearing because the atmospheric humidity is z, the degree of copper and zinc in the surrounding rocks is y, the temperature is x, and that there are geological stresses underground corresponding to a strain of w. Furthermore, say that each of the witnesses has just undergone the tragedy of bereavement, with whatever consequences there may be at the chemical level in the brain and the emotional level in the mind, and that there exists a host of many other factors. We do not even have to reject the extraterrestrial hypothesis for this: maybe it takes a set of strict conditions to allow 'them' to interact with us.

In these circumstances, the exact combination of factors might not be expected to come together too often: but on rare occasions it would. All the more important, therefore, that the UFO researcher should accumulate as much data, however trivial, as possible about each UFO appearance with a view to recognizing some facet that might give the clue to the 'trigger'.

If the researcher could identify *all* of the factors, then it might either be possible to predict with a reasonable degree of accuracy when those factors could come together (and an appropriate watch maintained) or to recreate them experimentally, thus 'manifesting' the UFO in a way that would comply with rigorous laboratory conditions.

It is obvious that UFO researchers could not do as I suggest without the full, open trust and cooperation of witnesses prepared to work in partnership with us in order to find those factors. What they bring to us is a source of data: what we bring to them is a willingness and a structure to share that data worldwide in order to put the Big Picture together.

Conventional science may have to make some compromises. One of the 'laws' of science is that any experiment should be capable of being replicated by anybody with the same equipment under the same conditions. Studies of the paranormal seem, however, to indicate that the state of mind of the researcher and the witness is a genuine factor in manifesting certain spontaneous phenomena. That claim must be given a chance to prove itself. Until we are familiar with *all* of the factors involved in creating certain phenomena, we must be very open-minded.

I am happy to work with researchers of varying standards, by whatever definition (and I make no particular claims for my own standards), if something they have recorded is, in fact, the clue that is eventually needed, and can be the basis of more controlled research later. I am happy to work with researchers who have weird and wonderful ideas of what the UFO phenomenon is all about, because *just perhaps* there is the mind that can manifest this stuff – whether it is causing nature to produce a light effect, or whether it is some ability to call down the aliens. I am prepared to work even with witnesses and researchers such as those dismissed by one overly sceptical Scandinavian research group as mentally disturbed, because, *even if they are*, maybe *that's* what it takes.

It is a fine line between recklessness and radical thinking. But I would rather tread it and face criticism than shirk and play safe – getting nowhere. If you try new ideas you may fail; but the only people I ever met who never failed are those who never succeeded either. I want UFO research to get somewhere – certainly a lot further than it has in the last forty-five years.

Nevertheless we have a practical problem. Researchers are under the scrutiny of the media. Some research (into 'balls of light' and the mystery cropfield formations, for example) is conducted within the confines of conventional science and with the assistance of conventional scientists: it is the nature of these particular branches of Ufology that they can do so. It is not the same with the close encounter cases.

If researchers do as I am suggesting, and allow more openness of work with witnesses, they will be criticized by the media, by the UFO press, and by second-rate scientific minds. They also will be rejected by scientists who might agree with us in principle, but who would worry about peer-prejudice and the withdrawal of grants. For those, I do have concern. They have placed a trust in us not to put them in awkward positions: we owe them consideration.

We would also receive criticism from less imaginative UFO groups, making it difficult to work on the world stage in these conditions. In such a case we would be ineffective, even for those witnesses we seek to work with.

This is the tightrope we have to walk between what I believe we should do and what damage we might cause to ourselves and others.

How do we meet the needs of witnesses, serve the wider interests of Ufology, and maintain the limited respectability we have built up to date – all at the same time?

Editor's note

Books by John Spencer:

With Hilary Evans (editor): *UFOs 1947–1987: The 40-Year Search for An Explanation*, Fortean Tomes, London, 1987.

With Hilary Evans (joint editor): *Phenomenon: From Flying Saucers to UFOs – Forty Years of Facts and Research*, Futura, London, 1988.

Perspectives: A Radical Examination of the Alien Abduction Phenomenon, Macdonald, London, 1989.

The UFO Encyclopedia, Headline, London, 1991.

UFOs: The Definitive Casebook, Hamlyn, London, 1991.

The Paranormal: A Modern Perspective, Hamlyn, London, 1992.

With Anne Spencer: *The Encyclopedia of Ghosts and Spirits*, Headline, London, 1992.

Gifts of The Gods? Are UFOs Alien Visitors or Psychic Phenomena?, Virgin, London, 1994.

8
A LARGE STATIONARY OBJECT ABOVE MONTREAL

Dr Richard Haines and Bernard Guénette

A well-known research scientist, Dr Richard Haines has three degrees in psychology from the Pacific Lutheran College, Tacoma, Washington and Michigan State University, and further education in engineering from the University of Washington, Seattle, as well as an FAA Pilot Ground School Certificate. Recently retired, his past employment includes posts with the National Research Council, Boeing Airplane Co. and at NASA's Ames Research Center, where he served as Chief of the Space Human Factors Office and as a research scientist, Life Sciences Division, as well as for the Research Institute for Advanced Computer Science.

Dr Haines directed 'focused human vision research' for the manned space programme in such areas as rendezvous/docking for the Gemini programme, spacecraft window design for the Space Station Freedom programme, and 'visual cue extraction from the real world' during landing by pilots of commercial aircraft. In 1989 he was appointed Project Manager for NASA's Remote Coaching Facility, which he helped design and develop. This facility is engaged in defining teleoperational concepts, transmission bandwidth requirements, and other telescience needs for carrying out future operations on the Space Station Freedom.

Dr Haines's four US patents include designs for a visual examination apparatus for glaucoma and a simulator scene display evaluation device. He is the author of numerous articles in scientific journals and has produced three NASA technical films. He has edited *UFO Phenomena and the Behavioral Scientist* (1979)[1], and is the author of *Observing UFOs* (1980)[2]; *Melbourne Episode: Case Study of a Missing Pilot* (1987)[3]; and

Advanced Aerial Devices Reported During the Korean War (1990)[4] (available from LDA Press at PO Box 880, Los Altos, California 94023-0880).

Dr Haines has made several scientific research trips to the former Soviet Union in order to discuss UFOs, and a report on his meetings with scientists (including those from the USSR Academy of Sciences) appears in *The UFO Report 1992*[5]. In 1991, together with Russian colleagues, he founded the Joint USA–CIS Aerial Anomaly Federation.

Bernard Guénette is a professional computer graphics expert and author, who lives in Montreal. A member of MUFON, he has been interested in UFOs for many years, and was fortunate to witness the object described in this article.

INTRODUCTION

This article describes the background and analysis of two colour photographs and numerous eye-witness descriptions of an angularly large stationary aerial object seen on 7 November 1990, between about 7.30 p.m. and 10.00 p.m. EST, as it hovered over the downtown area of Montreal, Canada.

Although the huge object was seen by between forty and seventy-five people (including policemen) standing on the rooftop of the International Hilton Bonaventure Hotel, and at ground-level within a large area, and was photographed by a newspaper journalist on the hotel's rooftop, there was no official follow-up nor very much interest shown in the event by government officials. The original 35mm colour negatives and positive colour prints were subjected to microscopic examination and to computer-based enhancements of various kinds. They were also related to the drawings and narrative descriptions of the object made by many eye-witnesses.

THE INITIAL SIGHTING

At Montreal on Wednesday, 7 November 1990, the sun

set at 4.28 p.m. local (EST) time. (All times cited are p.m. Eastern Standard Time, unless noted otherwise.) The air was clear and cold. But a high relative humidity near the ground of approximately 95 per cent gradually turned into a thin haze extending from the ground to an altitude of several thousand feet. There were only a few scattered clouds present at between 5,000 and 8,000 feet.

At 7.30, co-author Bernard Guénette and a Mr P. Lachapelle were in Old Montreal walking near the corner of Saint-Sulpice Street and Rue de Bresolles, about ten city blocks east-south-east from the Hilton. They noticed many fire engines, police cars and other emergency vehicles, and a commotion nearby which blocked the road; a practice fire alert was underway. Bernard happened to glance directly upward and saw a small greenish Aurora Borealis-like phenomenon with long streamers extending out from it, which did not move during the thirty to sixty seconds they looked at it. Both men felt that the phenomenon was at a very high altitude.

All of the other original eye-witnesses of the object were located on the seventeenth-floor rooftop of the International Hilton Bonaventure Hotel (hereafter referred to simply as the Hilton) in central downtown Montreal, which boasts an outdoor heated swimming pool and other facilities. An American woman tourist was swimming in the pool, and she was the first to sight the strange lighted object, directly overhead in the night sky, at about 7.15. Later, she described it as having an oval shape with a yellowish colour. She then notified Mrs L.S.P., the hotel's pool lifeguard, who alerted the hotel's security officer, Albert Sterling, at about 7.30. He arrived at about 7.35 and also looked up at the large object hovering in the 'almost cloudless sky', and soon (7.38) telephoned the Montreal Urban Community Police (MUCP) Station No. 25 for assistance. His first impression was that it was 'fallen debris from the sky, a satellite or other space object'. He also tried to call the Montreal Dorval International Airport to ask what the object could be, but the line was busy.

Meanwhile, between 7.30 and 7.35, Mrs L.S.P. called *La Presse* newspaper office and also urged other guests to come outside to look at the apparition. Mr Sterling said that the object was situated over the south-east corner of the pool and that there were about twelve people present at that time. There were as many as seventy-five people present during the entire period the object was visible, according to Mrs L.S.P. At 7.55, after the object became brighter, Mr Sterling telephoned the police station a second time.

At 8.00, Marcel Laroche, the first of three journalists to be involved, arrived from the newspaper *La Presse*.

Officer F. Lippé of the MUCP was dispatched at 8.07 and arrived at about 8.11. He spoke with Mr Sterling and looked at the object himself. Later (in MUCP file #25-901107-059), he described what he saw as three yellowish lights, from each of which a single beam of light emanated. The object itself was luminous and round and did not appear to move.

Officer Lippé, Mr Laroche and Mrs L.S.P. all saw a small ('Cessna type') private aircraft fly directly beneath the clouds and much farther below the object. Officer Lippé felt that the object was '. . . much higher than the plane' and Laroche estimated that the aircraft was at an altitude of 1,200 feet above ground level (AGL). Mrs L.S.P. and Mr Laroche referred to the aircraft as 'minuscule' in relation to the aerial object. (Non-scheduled private aircraft must maintain a vertical clearance of at least 1,000 feet above the highest obstruction within a lateral radius of 2,000 feet. Mount Royal, with an altitude of 1,199 feet, is the highest point near downtown Montreal and is located 1.3 miles north-west of the Hilton. It has radio antennas on its top so that the minimum legal flight altitude is 1,200 feet AGL. In addition, private aircraft may not fly above 2,000 feet altitude unless the plane is 'instrument flight rules' (IFR) equipped and the pilot is rated to fly in 'instrument meteorological conditions' (IMC), due to potential interference with air traffic to and from Dorval

Airport. Most private pilots fly between 1,500 and 1,800 feet.)

Jules Béliveau, another *La Presse* journalist, received a letter (dated 8 November 1990) from a François Chevrefils who said that his friend (Mr Jean —) witnessed the object sometime between 7.30 and 8.00 from his small plane. Although he completed a MUFON sighting form, he declined any further interviews, and may not have been the pilot of the small aircraft that was seen.

At 8.15, a mother and her daughter driving on Champlain Boulevard in south-west Montreal, near the Douglas Hospital, reported seeing two large white spots of light in the sky along with a number of smaller lights which did not appear to move and were silent. This sighting location is about 4.2 miles west-south-west from the Hilton.

Officer Lippé telephoned Sgt Masson at 8.20 for back-up, and at 8.30, Masson arrived at the Hilton rooftop. Overwhelmed by the appearance of the object, Masson called the Royal Canadian Mounted Police (RCMP) at 8.44. Inspector Minkoff of the RCMP said that Inspector Morin would be assigned to handle the case. Meanwhile, Officer Lippé telephoned the MUCP's District Director, Denis Pare, who immediately telephoned the RCMP for 'in situ assistance'. Lippé also called the control tower at Dorval International Airport. He was informed (at 8.52) that he was not the first to call about the strange object and that nothing was seen on the airport radar. Almost simultaneously, Sgt Letendre, telephone operator at the RCMP Operations Centre, also called the Dorval airport and was referred to the Flight Path (*Plans de Vol*) Department.

Mr Laroche returned to his car for his personal 35mm camera between 8.30 and 8.45 and returned to the rooftop of the Hilton.

At 9.00, Mr Béliveau and Robert Mailloux, both *La Presse* journalists, arrived at the Hilton. Later, Mr Béliveau described seeing what is sketched in Figure 4. Because of the earlier telephone call by Sgt Masson for more assistance, Denis Pare arrived at 9.00. Investigator Morin of the RCMP was also dispatched to the scene. However, before leaving his home, he called Major Thompson (commander of military operations of Canada's Department of National Defence – St-Hubert base) to discover whether or not military operations were being held in the area. He was told they were not.

Numerous other telephone calls were made by various parties between 8.55 and 9.00, which will not be recounted here.

THE PHOTOGRAPHS

It was between 9.00 and 9.05 when Mr Laroche took the first of several photos with his camera. [Enlargements of the two pictures showing the lights may be seen in the photo section, but unfortunately the subtleties of the original colour prints do not reproduce well – Ed.] When he realized that the conditions were so dark that the photograph might not come out, he called a photographer at *La Presse*, using his cellular telephone, for advice, and was told to stabilize the camera on a bench near by and to use a 30-second manual exposure. The second exposure was taken about two or three minutes later. Co-author Bernard Guénette contacted Mr Laroche on 8 April 1991 in order to inspect the photographs and negatives. Mr Laroche said, 'I have received no communications from any officials – Defence Department, RCMP or Montreal UCP – about any aspects of this event.' Mr Laroche was employed by *La Presse* as a journalist and not as a photographer and, therefore, owns all rights to the photographs he took. Nevertheless, he has not tried to capitalize on this fact to date. Mr Laroche mailed Dr Haines frames containing the two UFO photos, as well as some additional (unrelated) frames from the same roll of film.

One of the two photographs was published with an article in an edition of *La Presse*, which stated: 'Mr Sterling described some clouds in the sky. The lighted object had six lights on the perimeter of a large circle with a ray of light emitted from each one. Most witnesses described the rays as white, while some also claimed they saw blue, yellow and red lights.'[6]

FURTHER DEVELOPMENTS

Having been called at his home, RCMP Faction Officer, Inspector Luc Morin (General Inquiries Department, RCMP), arrived at the Hilton at 9.30 and also saw the object; his description is very similar to that shown in Figure 8.2A. About this time, all three journalists left for their offices at *La Presse* to write the article which appeared on 8 November. Personnel from the Quebec Provincial Police (QPP) and the Canadian Security Intelligence Service (CSIS) may also have been present along with the RCMP and MUCP, according to a witness who was qualified to make this observation.

Also present on the rooftop at 9.40 was another Hilton Hotel guest, an Air Canada pilot. He remarked that he estimated the altitude of the object was between 8,000 and 10,000 feet, although the cloud ceiling was at about 3,500 feet at the time.

Thoughtfully, Officer Lippé contacted the super-intendent of a forty-five-storey commercial building being built across the street to the west of the Hilton (at 1000 de la Gauchetière) to turn off all of the intense lights which were located on the top of a construction crane. As expected, no influence was noticed on the appearance of the object when these lights were extinguished. There is no possibility that the object was a direct or indirect result from these construction lights shining upward on to the bottom of clouds due to the very great difference in cloud base height above the top of the building. Likewise, the calculated angle (from vertical) from the top of the Hilton to the top of the forty-five-storey commercial building was about 60 degrees, which is much lower than the object.

As Officer Lippé was telephoning Lt Proulx of the

MUCP's Survey (monitoring) Department at 9.45 for a video camera to be brought to the Hilton, Officer O'Connor arrived from the MUCP's Judicial Identity Department in order to take photographs with his 35mm photographic camera. (Officer Michel Cote of the MUCP Survey Department arrived at the hotel at 10.20 with a camcorder but the object was no longer visible, so he left again.) None was taken, however, because 'the clouds were too thick', even though the object was still faintly visible to the eye. He did not try to obtain a low-contrast image using a very long exposure (as the journalist had successfully managed to do).

Investigator Morin telephoned the Montreal Head-quarters of the RCMP at 9.58, some twenty-eight minutes after he first saw the object, to request more assistance in order to 'solve this mystery'. Mr Morin stated that the object disappeared from sight at about 10.10, due to increasingly dense cloud cover. If true, this suggests that the object remained at a constant altitude while the cloud base became lower and lower, but this is impossible to verify. The cloud base was about 3,600 feet above ground level (AGL), very opaque, and from 4,000 to 5,000 feet thick, when the object was last seen. Mr Sterling later estimated that by about 10.00, the object had moved to a position above the north-west corner of the pool. Inspector Morin left the Hilton at 10.10; the MUCP policeman left at 10.30.

Mr Sterling's estimate of the visual (angular) size of the object's body (see Fig. 8.2) is inconsistent with his statement that the object moved from the south-east to the north-west corner of the pool during the course of the entire sighting period. If the object was at an altitude of even 3,000 feet and subtended an angle of 20 degrees, it would be 1,058 feet across. A horizontal movement of such a large object of only 65 feet, the diagonal dimension of the swimming pool, is only 6 per cent of the object's width. This very small movement, extended evenly over a two-and-a-half-hour period, very likely would be perceptually invisible. It is more likely that his estimate of the object's position was in error and influenced by where he was standing when he made these judgements.

A Mr Pierre Caumartin said that while he was driving home from work between 10.30 and 11.00, he saw some 'very odd lights, a strange luminous object in a boomerang shape low in the sky at about the level of the clouds'. Its lights were 'very big and strong'. He thought that it might have illuminated the interior of his car. Upon arriving near his home in the eastern section of Montreal, not far from the Longue-Pointe Military Base, he watched the object hover near the Hydro-Quebec Longue-Pointe power station, which receives 12,000 volts of electricity. When he got out of his car, he heard a 'purring' sound, and thought the object was a dirigible, with only a gondola visible below the cloud base. His total sighting lasted from ten to fifteen minutes.

The Longue-Pointe Military Base is the largest military base of the Montreal Canadian Force Base, with forty-eight regular forces, detachments and units, of about 1,900 persons, twenty-five reserve units with 3,000 persons, and ninety-seven cadet corps with 7,500 persons. It also supports three military schools. No one at the base could be found who saw the aerial object on 7 November.

A power failure (*hors tension*) was experienced between 11.08 and 11.50 at the Longue-Pointe Military Base. The base is fed by a 12,000-volt lead from the Hydro-Quebec Longue-Pointe power station. It is the only one which broke down on 7 November 1990 between 11.08 and 11.50. A check of the operating records of telecommunications networks, amateur radio operators and telephone circuits during the evening of 7 November 1990 did not uncover any unusual malfunctions.

In summary, all of the professionally trained eye-witnesses inspected the luminous, stationary object for between one and two-and-a-half hours; yet no one was able to obtain any photographic, magnetic, radio frequency, microwave radiation or other 'hard' evidence of the aerial object, or even request that an aircraft be sent up to investigate. One has to ask how long an unusual aerial phenomenon must remain stationary and in plain sight in order to evoke an adequate scientific and/or technical analysis response. This is yet another reason why traditional science has not become involved in UFO studies.

EYE-WITNESS DESCRIPTIONS AND DRAWINGS OF THE OBJECT

In this section, a total of ten drawings is presented in the order in which they were made. [For the sake of clarity, Dr Haines has drawn over the original sketches, with the exception of Figure 8.2B – Ed.] Mrs. L.S.P., who was the second person to see the object, was the first to describe the oval outline of eight separate lights to MUCP Officer Lippé of Station 25 at about 8.12. Since he had also seen the object, it is likely that his sketch (made on her behalf) was as much his own sketch of the object [not shown – Ed.]. She later said that 'it looked like what was seen in the film *Close Encounters of the Third Kind*'.

Fig. 8.1

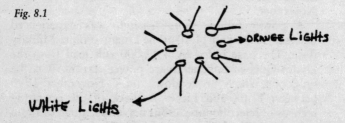

ORANGE LIGHTS

WHITE LIGHTS

The second eye-witness to produce a description (and subsequent police-report drawing) was Mr Sterling. The policeman's sketch of the shape which Mr Sterling remembered seeing is reproduced in Part (A) of Figure 8.2. Parts (B) and (C) were drawn by Mr Sterling himself on 9 October 1991 from memory. Note the difference in

Fig. 8.2A

Fig. 8.2B

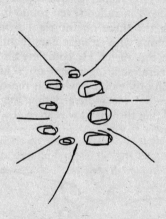

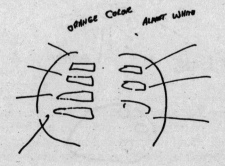

Fig. 8.2C

the number of light sources. He felt that there were from six to nine separate, intense white ('as from a welding arc') light sources around the edge of the object, each emitting a pencil of light. These luminous rays were not oriented vertically but seemed to be directed out horizontally from the object. He also offered the opinion that the object was 'something made, it was something artificial, not human'.

Investigator Luc Morin telephoned his headquarters requesting more assistance for the purpose of discovering the mystery. His sketch of the object (made on 7 November 1990) included seven round light sources in an oval with the three on the right being the largest (brightest?) along with straight lines (light rays) extending out from the object. He completed a Mutual UFO Network general sighting report on 9 June 1991 and made a sketch of the object which is reproduced in Part (B) of Figure 8.3 He indicated that the weather was overcast and that the object was an oval with three light sources on it.

Fig. 8.3A

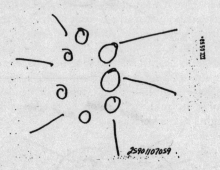

Fig. 8.3B

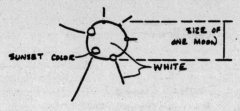

Fig. 8.4

In May 1991, Marcel Laroche drew a sketch of what he saw between 8.00 and 9.30 from the roof of the Hilton, which is reproduced in Figure 8.4. He described it verbally as appearing round, white, with six or more smaller round lights the colour of orange of a sunset colour and about the angular diameter of the full moon (i.e. 32 minutes of arc). It remained above him the entire time. He heard no sound. It is interesting to note the direction of the rays from the three circular areas (light sources?), since they are not all pointed in the same direction. Does this suggest that there were other sources of light which produced the ray pointing to the right?

Another newspaper journalist present was Jules Béliveau. Figure 8.5 shows his sketch of the object which he made on 22 April 1991. He remarked that the object was round, with at least six round white lights around its edge. These edge lights were white or yellowish. Note that, for some unknown reason, he only drew three of the edge lights in his sketch.

Fig. 8.5

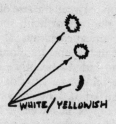

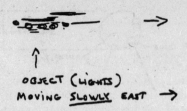

OBJECT (LIGHTS)
MOVING SLOWLY EAST →

Fig. 8.6A

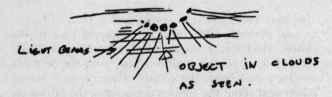

LIGHT BEAMS →

OBJECT IN CLOUDS
AS SEEN.

Fig. 8.6B

As described earlier, Pierre Caumartin, a film and video producer, also sighted the object while driving home after 10.00. He drew two sketches of the object (Fig. 8.6), which represents its appearance over a ten to fifteen minute-long period at a location about 7.4 miles east-north-east of the Hilton.

What all of these sketches have in common is a generally oval, partial or completely closed shape with from three to eight small round light sources located around its circumference, each of which emits a whitish ray of light. Several of the witnesses said that: (1) There was a direct relation between the size of each light source and the length of the rays of light, such that the larger their diameter, the longer each ray; (2) The luminosity of each ray appeared to be constant along their length; (3) Each ray began and ended 'abruptly'; and (4) the largest light sources were all on the left side of the object. Of course, which is the left or right side would depend upon the direction the viewer faced while looking vertically upward. That is, these statements are relatively useless in helping to orient the drawings. But what do the photographs show? This is discussed in the next section.

PHOTOGRAPHIC EVIDENCE

Camera, Lens and Settings: A Nikon model FG-20 35mm single-lens reflex camera was used. It was fitted with a 50mm f1.8 Nikon series E lens, and set to infinity focus. The relatively dark sky required that a long exposure be used, with the camera stabilized on a bench during the exposure.

Film and Processing: A roll of Astral colour 35mm film (ASA 100) was in the journalist's camera before he arrived at the Hilton. Frames 1–3 contained scenes of a labourer working. Frames 4–12 and 15 were under-exposed and showed nothing. The remainder of the roll was not exposed. Figure 8.7 shows the spectral density (A) and characteristic curve (B) for this film. The film was processed at the *La Presse* facilities at between 10.00 and 11.00 on 7 November, as the story was being written.

Referring to the first photo, the faint, luminous radial rays [not included in the enlargement shown in the photo

Fig. 8.7 Spectral density (A) and characteristic curves (B) for Astral colour film. (*Tania Long*)

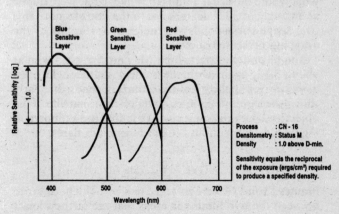

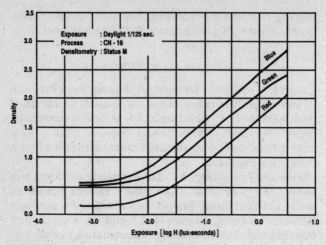

Fig. 8.7B

section – Ed.] are clearly lens flares (reflections) produced at the air-glass interface of the objective lens elements. The faint outline of the object itself can be determined by virtue of the location of the innermost ends of each light area and is estimated by the dashed oval with a width to length ratio of about 0.66. This ratio is equivalent to what would be seen if a thin (coin-like) circle were tipped at an angle of 33.5 degrees arc to the line of sight. This oval shape corresponds in general to at least six of the drawings presented above.

The second photograph by Mr Laroche was taken at about 9.12, again with the camera shutter held open manually for slightly less than thirty seconds. It clearly shows the three luminous sources on the same side of the object and with the same relative luminance as shown in Figure 8.4, but without the prominent lens flares.

PHOTO-NEGATIVE ANALYSIS AND RESULTS

Frames 13 and 14 were enlarged to 8″ × 12″. The distance between the two luminous areas that are farthest apart from one another on the image equals 0.370″ and 0.384″, respectively, suggesting either that the object decreased in altitude, tipped in angle, or physically changed in size between the time the two photographs were taken. For a lens focal length of 50mm, the angular width of the frame equals 40 degrees[7]. Thus, the angular distance between the two farthest light sources on the object equals 1 degree, 14 minutes of arc in frame 13, and 1 degree, 17 minutes of arc in frame 14.

The original colour negatives were digitized, using a Perceptics NuVision image scanner/digitizer system, manipulation programme and dedicated processor. A photograph of a colour enhancement which emphasizes subtle image brightness differences using two primary colours (green for background brightness and reds for object-related luminance) was obtained. It shows clearly that the three brightest lens flares on the left side are only about one-tenth the brightness of the central area. A Nikon 50mm (f1.1) lens contains nine separate glass lens elements which can yield numerous internal reflections[8]. The central area of maximum luminance is on the right in the form of an oval surrounding the disc's image.

A continuous profile of optical density was determined for the first photograph taken by Mr Laroche along two parallel straight lines. One passed across the sky background to the left of the three luminous areas presented in the first photo. The resulting optical density for this 'sky background' is shown by the bottom-most tracing in Figure 8.8. Note that the sky density ranges from 0.6 to 0.75 where density ranges from 0 (maximum darkness) to 1 (maximum brightness) and is relatively flat, indicating that the luminance of the sky was almost constant. This is what would be expected from ground lights reflecting off fog and clouds. The second scan passed through the three luminous areas in the first photo. This tracing represents the change in optical density produced by the aerial object and is shown by the shaded area in Figure 8.8. It can be seen that the object is so bright that it saturates the film over almost half of its diameter.

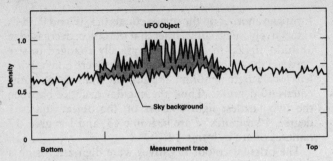

Fig. 8.8 Densitometry Scans Across Sky Background and
Through Object

COMPARISON OF VISUAL AND PHOTOGRAPHIC
MEASUREMENTS OF THE OBJECT'S VISUAL ANGLE

If the angular size and distance to the aerial object can be
determined, then its physical size can be calculated.
While humans are not good estimators of distance or
angles when using their memory of an earlier event[9],
knowledge of approximate cloud height (plus or minus
500 feet) and a range of visual angle estimates establish
useful upper boundaries on the distance (and therefore
the size) of the object.

Five independent estimates were obtained of the
angular width of the object. These estimates are sum-
marized in Table 1 below. Since these estimates are all
made from memory, they are probably in error by an
unknown but variable amount. Some are probably
overestimates and others underestimates. They do indicate, however, the relatively large appearance of the
silent aerial object.

Notes relating to Table 1

(1) Both witnesses estimated that the total distance from
one end of a light ray to the end of the opposite light ray
was 54 to 60 inches at arm's length, which is equivalent
to 112 degrees, 40 minutes of arc!

Table 1: Visual angle estimates of the oval body of the object

Witness name	Est. time of sighting	Stated size/ distance (on which angles are determined)	Calculated visual angle (deg.min.)
L.S.P. (1)	9/24/91 7:30–9:30	'18″ at arm's length' (2)	18/18=1.0 45 deg
Laroche (1)	9/91 8:00–10:00	'10″ at arm's length'	10/19=0.526 27 deg 45'
Sterling	8/23/91 8:00–10:00 (3)	'about 18″ at arm's length'	18/19=0.947 43 deg 28'
	9/24/91 8:00–10:00 (4)	'10″ at arm's length'	10/19=0.526 27 deg 45'
	10/29/91 8:00–10:00	'18″ at arm's length'	18/19=0.947 43 deg 28'
Lippé (5)	10/15/91 8:12–10:30	'12″ at arm's length'	12/19=0.632 32 deg 19'
Guénette (6)	11/7/90 7:30–7:45	'1–2 cm at arm's length' (assume 0.6″) (7)	0.6/19=0,032 1 deg 50'
Caumartin (8)	10/31/91 10:30–10:45	'3–4″ at arm's length'	4/19=0.211 11 deg 55'

(2) Assume arm length equals 19 inches (males) and 18 inches (females).

(3) Assume angle estimate is made at 8.00 p.m.

(4) He estimated the total distance from one end of a light ray to the end of the opposite light ray was 54 to 60 inches at arm's length, which is equivalent to 112 degrees, 40 minutes of arc.

(5) The visual angle equivalent to the entire luminous

phenomenon (ray tip to ray tip) was about 36 inches at arm's length, which is equivalent to an angle of 87 degrees of arc!

(6) Witness was at Saint-Sulpice and De-Bresolles at ground level, about a mile from the Hilton, and the aerial object was seen directly above him. This visual angle is remarkably close to the measured visual angle obtained from the two photographs.

(7) It is likely that the witness only saw one of the pencil rays due to his vantage point at street level, where the nearby buildings blocked his view. He described what he saw as a light green stationary area something like the Aurora Borealis.

(8) Viewing location was at the corner of St Donat Avenue and Roi-Rêne Boulevard, about 7.4 miles from the Hilton. He estimated that the object was only seven or eight blocks away from him at that time.

The large differences in estimated angle are not uncommon in sighting cases such as this one, and are the result of one's emotions at the time, prior training and experience in making such estimates, and errors in carrying out the estimating procedure. Nevertheless, it is believed that a reasonable lower bound for the angular size of the object's central 'oval body' as seen from the roof of the Hilton is 27 degrees of arc. If the main body of the object subtended an angular width of 27 degrees, and was at 3,500 feet altitude, it would be 1,783 feet across! If it was at 9,000 feet altitude, when the Air Canada pilot saw it at 9.30, it would have been 4,586 feet across. However, the clouds were becoming thicker and lower and probably would have prevented it from being seen at such a great altitude.

SOME DETAILS OF THE LOCALE

As shown in Figure 8.9, the city of Montreal lies on Montreal Island at the confluence of the Saint Lawrence River and Ottawa River and stretches generally north-east to south-west. Its highest point is Mount Royal

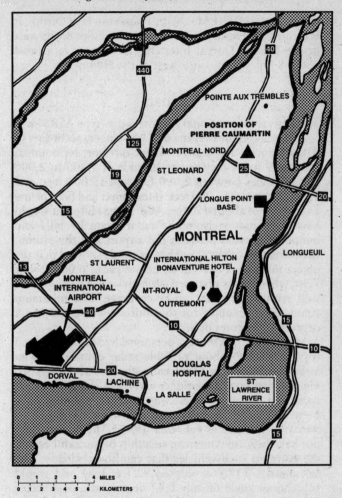

Fig. 8.9 Map showing sighting locations in Montreal. (*Tania Long*)

(altitude: 1,200 feet MSL with a radio tower at its top). It is located in central Montreal, only 1.3 miles north-west of the Hilton. Dorval International Airport is located about 8 miles west-south-west of the Hilton.

RADAR

The Dorval International Airport radar (type ASR5) was operational on the evening of 7 November, according to Alain Jacques, the control tower director. Its nominal range is 7 miles between an altitude of 1,200 to 2,000 feet, 40 miles between 2,000 feet and 17,000 feet, and 125 miles above 17,000 feet. If the object had been below an altitude of about 450 feet AGL at the Hilton, it would have been hidden from the radar beam by hills and buildings situated between the airport and the Hilton. Measurement of the cloud base altitude showed that the object must have been at or below about 6,000 feet at 7.30, when it was first seen – which would have made it well within the radar range coverage. The minimum beam elevation angle for this altitude would only be 8 degrees 10 minutes of arc.

Mr Jacques said that his personnel had been contacted (by the RCMP) about possible radar contact with an airborne object over Montreal to the east of the airport. He said that no radar contact was made at any time that night and, '. . . if an object was present . . . it must have been stealth.' (This comment was made by phone to Bernard Guénette in February 1991.) The object could not have been an American stealth-type aircraft because there are no such vehicles that can hover silently. The Lockheed F-117A is only 65.92 feet long and would subtend an angle of only 0.42 degrees at a distance of 5,000 feet, which is an angle 100 times smaller than the present object.

Nothing was seen on the radar controlled by the Montreal Air Traffic Control Centre.

WEATHER AND ASTRONOMICAL CONDITIONS

The weather was generally clear at 7.30 p.m. around Greater Montreal on the night of the event with a thin layer of scattered clouds at 6,700 feet above ground level. Visibility was 15 miles. At 8.00, the air temperature was −1 degree Centigrade near the ground, and the wind was 4 kph out of the west. While air temperature only dropped one degree over the next two hours, the wind increased to 9 kph from the north-west (variable). A cold front, featuring a narrow band of snow, was approaching Montreal from the west. This weather system passed through Montreal overnight and moved rapidly to the east. Air pressure remained at 101.53 kilopascal between 8.00 and 10.00. By 8.30, there was a scattered layer of clouds at 3,000 feet and an overcast layer at 4,500 feet. By 9.30, the cloud ceiling had lowered to 3,400 feet and continued this way with only minor variations until 11.00 p.m. It had not rained at the Dorval Airport since noon on the previous day (a total rainfall of 0.84 inch; the ground was still damp on 7 November). Light snow began to fall at 10.21 p.m. and continued for several hours at Dorval.

Table 2 presents a summary of key weather details for 7 November 1990 at Dorval International Airport.

Figure 8.10 presents atmospheric data collected on 8

Table 2: Selected weather conditions at Dorval Airport

Time (local) (pm EST)	Air Temp. (deg C)	Press. (k pascal)	Wind Direction	Speed (km/hr)	Humidity Relative (pct.)	Dew pt. (0.1 deg C)	Cloud Base (AGL)
6:00	4		W	4	64	−56	sct.clouds
7:00	−3		W	6	64	−59	5,200'
8:00	−6	101.53	W	4	69	−57	5,200'
9:00	0	101.53	WNW	4	69	−52	4,200'
9:30							3,500'
10:00	0	101.53	NNW	9	69	−52	3,600' (1)
11:00	−2		NNW	9	74	−41	n/a

(1) The clouds were developing into very opaque, thick snow clouds from 4,000 to 5,000 feet thick

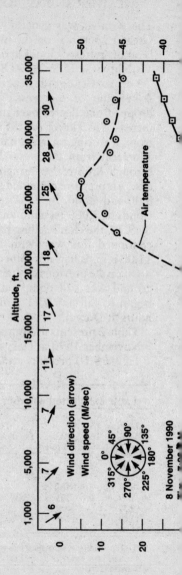

Fig. 8.10 Temperature, Pressure, Humidity, and Wind as a Function of Altitude at 7.00 pm NW of Montreal

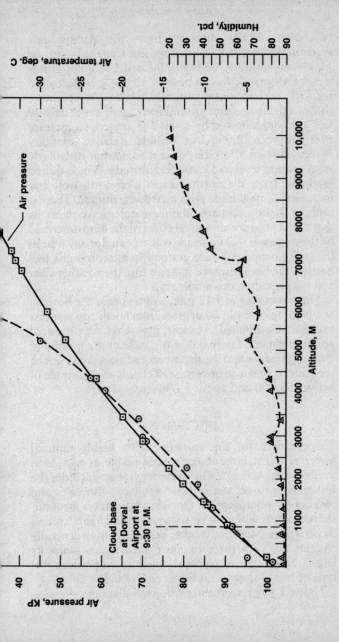

November 1990, obtained from the Atmospheric Environment Service – 'Environment Canada' – for the Maniwaki station (7034480), located 128 miles north-west of Montreal. As can be seen, air pressure decreased regularly with increasing altitude, while air temperature shows a decrease from ground level up to about 26,000 feet altitude, followed by a small (5 degrees C) increase over the next 12,000 feet altitude. Relative humidity decreased from 89 to 22 per cent somewhat irregularly from ground level to 35,000 feet altitude. Winds shifted gradually from the north-west to west-north-west and increased in magnitude with increasing altitude. There is nothing about these particular meteorological conditions that could produce an optical effect of the kind described by the witnesses. No lightning was reported at any time in the entire region. (We are grateful to meteorologist Joel Bartlett for his assistance in analyzing the weather data and for providing this summary.)

The moon rose at 9.12 p.m. and was near the horizon at a bearing of about 60 degrees from north and was just over half-illuminated. At most, it would have produced an illuminance of only 0.004 ft candle at the ground in clear air. Unfortunately, the moon and stars could not be seen due to a growing overcast of clouds at an altitude of between 3,000 and about 5,000 feet.

DISCUSSION

The evidence for the existence of a highly unusual hovering, silent, large object is indisputable, as it has been in other such cases[10]. The present evidence includes the testimony of over ten reliable adult eye-witnesses and two colour photographs. One sketch portrays a round-shaped object with at least six small round lights around its perimeter. Most of the other sketches show a generally circular arc with three or more small lights along its length. What type of physical object could produce this type of image along with linear rays of light?

Figure 8.11 presents three side-view diagrams showing

how an object can produce a luminous distribution similar to that shown in Figures 8.8 and 8.9. In the right-hand drawing, the rectangular dashed object represents the object with its left-end oriented downward at about 30 degrees of arc from the line of sight (LOS) (originating at the eyes (E) on the roof of the Hilton). Here it is assumed that the object's shape is basically that of a coin (seen from the edge) with multiple light sources located around its circumferential edge; each is aimed directly outward along its equatorial plane. It is also assumed that all light sources are equivalent in all of their luminous properties and possess a light distribution lobe represented by the dashed oval at each end of the object. Next, consider only the lower (L) lobe.

Since the concept of a light lobe (L) is so important, it is enlarged in the centre drawing of Figure 8.11. Here, the small six-sided polygon represents an individual light source whose optical axis is X-Y, inclined at about 30 degrees to the LOS. Its apparent intensity is defined by the direction from which it is viewed; apparent intensity is proportional to the length of the line from the source to the lobe boundary, as shown here from the 'sources' to a' (corresponding to the camera's LOS). If the source had been viewed along the line d' to the source or e' to the

Fig. 8.11

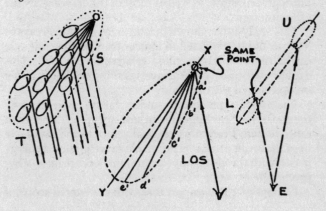

source, it would be about eight-and-a-half times brighter than when viewed along the line a' to the source. In short, the shape of the light lobe defines the apparent brightness of the source as a function of viewing location.

Since the present aerial object was seen within fog and cloud, the light-scattering properties of water droplet-laden air also must be considered. It is well known that each microscopic droplet possesses its own light lobe that scatters light with a lobe shape approximately as shown by the nine egg outlines seen in the left-hand part of Figure 8.11. The close spacing of all of the droplets integrates the individual reflected rays in all directions defined by the individual lobes. However, *we are only concerned with those rays aimed toward the viewers on the rooftop of the Hilton*. Note that the length of each ray aimed toward the eyes from each micro-droplet source is approximately the same. The visual result of this is that the brightness of the entire ray will appear to be relatively homogeneous for all of the rays extending from S to T.

The same general explanation as given above applies to the light sources located on the opposite side of the object (cf. the upper (U) lobe in the right-hand drawing of Figure 11). Here, the length of each ray of light from each microscopic particle toward the viewers is so short that the ray becomes almost invisible. This is what the two photographs show, as well as most of the drawings by the eye-witnesses.

This analysis has shown that an array of whitish rays of light would be expected to appear primarily on one side of the object if it was tilted relative to the LOS. This explains why most of the drawings show small lights only on one side of the oval body.

The above explanation cannot clarify, however, why the end of each ray appeared to stop abruptly, rather than taper to zero brightness gradually. Could the rays have been the result of air ionization along well-defined energy paths, with the visual appearance only occurring as a by-product?

Perhaps of equal importance with the overall scope of

the aerial phenomenon was the almost total lack of official response to it. No action of any kind was taken by personnel of the St-Hubert military base after they were notified of the aerial object hovering above the centre of the city. As far as is known, they did not even report it to the North American Aerospace Defense Command (NORAD) co-ordination centre. Authorization to use Canadian defence forces must come from the Premier of the Province involved (Robert Bourassa). However, since the phenomenon did not appear to show evidence of any security threat and the military do not have any clear mandate to study such phenomena, they did not seek permission from the Premier to take action. In short, no one did anything, beyond some individual efforts by MUCP and RCMP personnel at the Hilton. The object remains unidentified at this time.

Notes

1. Haines, Richard F. (ed.): *UFO Phenomena and the Behavioral Scientist*, Scarecrow Press, New Jersey, 1979.
2. Haines, Richard F.: *Observing UFOs: An Investigative Handbook*, Nelson-Hall, Chicago, 1980.
3. Haines, Richard F.: *Melbourne Episode: Case Study of a Missing Pilot*, LDA Press, Los Altos, California, 1987.
4. Haines, Richard F.: *Advanced Aerial Devices Reported During the Korean War*, LDA Press, Los Altos, California, 1990.
5. Haines, Richard F.: 'A Scientific Research Trip to the Soviet Union', *The UFO Report 1992*, ed. Timothy Good, Sidgwick & Jackson, London, 1991.
6. Béliveau, Jules and Laroche, Marcel: 'Un OVNI dans le ciel de Montreal?' *La Presse*, Montreal, 8 November 1990.
7. Neblette, C. B. and Murray, A. E.: *Photographic Lenses*, Morgan & Morgan, Hastings-on-Hudson, New York, 1965, p. 13.
8. Ibid., p. 106.
9. Haines, Richard F.: *Observing UFOs: An Investigative Handbook*, Nelson-Hall, Chicago, 1980.

10. Anon., 1991. *Vague d'OVNI sur la Belgique: Un Dossier Exceptionel*, Société Belge d'Etude des Phénomènes Spatiaux (SOBEPS), Brussels, 1992.

9

THE WILLIAMSPORT WAVE

Dr Samuel Greco

Dr Samuel Greco is a retired US Air Force major and aerospace engineer. He received his PhD in industrial management from Columbia Pacific University, California; Master of Business, Drexel University, Philadelphia, and a BSc in mechanical engineering from Indiana Institute of Technology.

Dr Greco first became interested in UFOs during World War II, when reports of 'foo fighter' sightings were published in *Stars and Stripes* (1944). Following discharge from the Army Air Forces and college, his interest was revived in 1952 during the Korean War when he received reports of UFO sightings as Officer of the Day. He has been studying the subject ever since, and is a consultant in propulsion as well as a Pennsylvania state section director for the Mutual UFO Network.

With the exception of the updated data analysis section, much of this article first appeared in the *MUFON UFO Journal* No. 290 (Copyright 1992 by MUFON), and I am indebted to editor Dennis Stacy for permission to republish it (in re-edited form).

INTRODUCTION BY STAN GORDON OF PASU

Numerous UFO sightings have been ongoing throughout Pennsylvania during 1991, and this activity continues into 1992. Many of these cases still remain under study, but several of the sightings involve large objects described as triangular or boomerang in shape. On 6 February 1992, the Pennsylvania Association for the Study of the Unexplained (PASU) UFO Hotline began to receive information concerning a series of low-level UFO sightings which reportedly occurred the day before, near the city of Williamsport, in Lycoming County, Pennsylvania. PASU, which is established as a statewide volunteer scientific clearing-house, investigates UFO sightings and other phenomena, and works closely with MUFON; and as in many cases, the investigation of such incidents involved joint co-operation.

After I received some preliminary details about what had reportedly taken place, I determined that the investigator most qualified for this detailed investigation was Samuel D. Greco, PhD. I had known Sam for some time, and his engineering and military background would be most helpful in trying to determine the validity of these reports. Sam is a retired aerospace engineer, with many degrees to his credit. He also holds the rank of Major, USAF (retired). I contacted Sam, and he was glad to get involved and soon began an in-depth research project that would involve many weeks of travelling and meeting with various witnesses to these observations. Sam must be commended since he donated so much time and personal expense while being involved in this very important research study.

While Sam would be handling personal interviews with some of the witnesses, I would be doing a lot of phone interviews with others, as well as obtaining support data from various outside agencies. Our office co-ordinated incoming information on the reports and kept feeding Sam with current data and additional sources to interview. Since the incident was fresh in the minds of the observers, it was imperative to document the information as soon as possible. It was quite evident that many people over a wide geographical area seemed to have seen something quite unusual, and we needed to eliminate any of the normal explanations for what was seen before considering the sightings as Unknowns. I also filed various FOIA [Freedom of Information Act] requests to several government/military agencies, hopeful that someone could provide some answers.

Within an hour of receiving the initial sighting information, the investigation began. Local weather observational data were obtained from the National Weather Service. A call was then placed to the state police barracks at Montoursville. I talked with a dispatcher there who was aware that they had received numerous sighting reports of a large low-level object in the sky, but said that no investigation had been launched. She did say that some callers were convinced that what they had seen was not a conventional aircraft. I then contacted the control tower at the Williamsport-Lycoming County Airport. I talked with an air traffic controller who had handled about twenty calls from the public, who wanted to know what the strange object was that had just passed through the area. He gave me what information he could remember, and told me that he contacted Harrisburg Approach Control to see if they were working any military aircraft, or were aware of any military flights in the area. They were not.

Williamsport Tower also had no confirmation of any military aircraft in the area, but speculated that this still could not be ruled out as a source of the reports, since military aircraft training routes are not far away. Nothing unusual showed up on the radar at the airport during the observation period, even though some reports place at least one of the sightings within a few miles of the airport. The Williamsport airspace is under the control of the FAA's New York Centre. I contacted the FAA Watch Supervisor, who had also received other inquiries about the sightings in the area. He also could find no records or flight plans for any military aircraft to have been in the area during the sighting period. While as of this writing, no agency has been able to provide data that support military aircraft in the area during the observation time, that still does not mean that such an aircraft could not have passed through these locations. But as we examine Sam's report, one must wonder if indeed something or some things not typical of conventional aircraft were active in the Williamsport skies.

L. Lee Janssen, a reporter for the Williamsport *Sun-Gazette*, wrote several articles on the sightings, and the paper received numerous reports from witnesses as well. Most of the observers, regardless of whom they contacted about their sightings, wished no publicity; and as is our policy, those witnesses asking to remain anonymous were so protected by Sam and myself. It is likely from the numerous written sighting statements sent to this office about this incident, as well as information we have obtained during this study, that possibly hundreds of people observed something strange in the skies over Pennsylvania.

And now we continue with Sam Greco's report on his investigation. Anyone with additional information is urged to contact me at PASU, 6 Oakhill Avenue, Greensburg, PA 15601.

Stan Gordon

A WAVE IN PROGRESS

I was sitting in my recliner watching television, at about 20.30 on 5 February 1992, when the telephone began to ring. On the other end of the line was Stan Gordon, MUFON State Director for Pennsylvania. With some excitement, he informed me of what appeared to be a major UFO wave which had occurred at about 18.00 to 19.00 in Williamsport, Lycoming County, Pennsylvania.

Two different kinds of objects, boomerang- and triangular-shaped, had been sighted in the evening sky and there had been numerous persons who had witnessed the sightings. Stan had received calls from some witnesses, and they wished to tell their story to someone who would listen. He asked if I would go to Williamsport to begin interviewing the witnesses, since MUFON did not have an investigator in the Lycoming County area and I was the nearest available MUFON investigator. I accepted this task and asked Stan for names and addresses for two sightings. That evening I made interview appointments over the telephone with the witnesses for Friday, 7 February 1992.

Friday rolled around rather quickly. As I left Mt

Carmel at about 08.00 and headed for Williamsport, it was a sunny but cold day, around the high twenties, and without any precipitation. By the time I had completed thirteen interviews eight weeks later, I had a good idea of how extensive the sightings really were. Also, I had accumulated enough sightings which could be plotted on an area map of Williamsport.

SIGHTINGS SCOPE

The sightings investigated as of this writing occurred in four counties. In Lycoming County, seven of these had taken place in Williamsport or its suburbs. Two sightings were observed in or near the borough of Linden which is situated on US Route 220 West. One took place near Cogan Station on Route 15 North. In Union County to the south, one sighting took place near the Lewisburg suburbs. In Northumberland County, east of Lewisburg, another sighting was reported. In the borough of Selinsgrove, Snyder County, one other sighting was made.

WITNESSES

The witnesses were ordinary people going about their daily lives at the time the sightings took place. During the interviews with me they presented seemingly factual data regarding what they had both seen and heard. They were considered reliable, honest and sincere in their statements. They were not interested in telling their story for publicity or profit and they did not want their names released to the public. Their desire was simply to tell their story to someone knowledgeable about the UFO phenomenon. Immediately after the sightings or the next day, the witnesses drew a sketch of what they had seen. Two persons who were non-UFO believers were converted.

Some of the witnesses had seen the movie, *Close Encounters of the Third Kind*. Two had read a few books or articles on UFOs, or had heard something about them on television news stories. Eight enjoyed seeing the television series, *Star Trek*. Four enjoyed viewing television documentaries about UFOs, such as those presented by *Unsolved Mysteries*. Two persons stated that they had psychic abilities.

They were all in good health before and after the sightings. Some wore glasses which corrected their eyesight to 20/20 vision, and one witness stated he was colourblind. All had good hearing. One person had a hearing aid in the right ear, but his hearing in that ear was [then] normal. None of them had any mental problems, such as depression, amnesia or other abnormalities.

WEATHER CONDITIONS

The weather conditions on the evening of the sightings were clear but cold, about 25 to 36 degrees Fahrenheit. There was little or no wind and no precipitation. Some witnesses thought there was a moon, but they were not sure. One witness stated that the moon was out and that it caused the object to cast a shadow on the ground. All witnesses stated that there was sufficient light in the evening sky after sunset to cause the object to sustain a recognizable form or silhouette against the evening sky.

GENERAL DATA

All the sightings followed a similar pattern. Apart from one which began while the witness was outside on his driveway, all originated in the houses of the witnesses, who were in the living room or recreation room, in the basement watching television, reading the evening newspaper, or in the kitchen washing dishes. Next, a loud or heavy rumbling noise was heard above the house which shook or vibrated the building and rattled its windows. Then one of the witnesses would leave the house to investigate the cause of the noise and, having discovered the UFO in the evening sky, would call the other witnesses to view the object. They would continue to observe the object and its actions until visual contact was lost. Lastly, they would return inside the house to reinforce one another as to what had been observed. Thus they could assure themselves of not being crazy or seeing hallucinations. They would also call other members of their family or friends in the area to ascertain if they had seen a UFO or heard the rumbling noise. It turned out that the sightings were widespread and were similar to those reported in *Night Siege: The Hudson Valley UFO Sightings*[1]. However, the present sightings showed other characteristics not detailed in that book.

SIGHTINGS DATA

The loud or heavy rumbling noise which first shattered the tranquillity of the evening was compared variously to the rumbling noise in *Close Encounters*, to the rumble of a heavily loaded freight train, to the rumble of Niagara Falls, to the rumble of a snow plough clearing the street, or to the noise of a loud diesel-engine truck. The sound was unique in two aspects: firstly, when it was overhead it shook or vibrated the house and caused the windows to rattle; secondly, in all but one sighting, the witnesses did not hear a noise approaching until it was directly above the house.

By the time the first witness reached the outside, either on a porch or on a driveway, the object had moved from its position over the house. It would be sighted at least 100 to 400 feet in front of the house and at least 70 to 500 feet in altitude. The one witness who described it as triangular stated he was directly underneath the object and able to draw its shape from that viewpoint.

All witnesses reported that the object moved at an unusually slow speed; so slowly that they could walk under it at a fast walking pace or a slow running pace and keep up with it.

Against the evening sky, the object was dark or black and it had a recognizable form or silhouette as viewed by witnesses from their vantage point. The most prevalent form was the boomerang, also described as a 'V' or banana-shaped. One was reported as a disc shape when seen from a predominantly side view, another as triangular. An inverted pie-pan shape with a small flange around it, or slightly bell-shaped, was also mentioned.

The object appeared solid to witnesses because of the noise it made, its obvious form or silhouette, and its sheer size. In one case it appeared solid because of the shadow it cast on the ground. The boomerang shape was approximately 100 to 600 feet, wing tip to wing tip, depending on the witnesses who observed it. The triangular shape was approximately 50 feet across at the rear or the slanted legs. The pie shape was about 150 feet in diameter. The thickness of the centre section of the object was stated as the height of a commercial aircraft, or from 10 to 25 feet. One witness, however, stated that it was 90 feet thick.

White lights were observed at the rear of the object and the intensity can best be described, in most instances, as dull, but in two cases the lights had some degree of luminosity. They did not glow very brightly nor did they cast enough light to produce shadows. Their number varied from one to fourteen. One witness thought that perhaps they could be portholes. No beams of lights or searchlights were projected to the ground, but one witness stated he had seen a pulsed beam flash to the ground. It appeared to him that the pulsed beam was doing a ground search. Ten amber lights and two green lights were also observed on the triangular-shaped object along with one white light which seemed to be on top.

The object appeared to be intelligently controlled because it moved in an approximate straight line and always maintained a determined altitude above the ground or over the treetops. In one case, at Linden, the object turned left over the Susquehanna River towards Williamsport. Some witnesses stated it hovered in one or two places for five to ten seconds as it moved forward. In another case, the witnesses said it hovered over the house for at least five seconds. In one sighting at Williamsport, it hovered over the driveway for five minutes and in another, at Selinsgrove, it hovered for five minutes over a racetrack.

REACTIONS

When visual contact was made, most witnesses were astonished at the sight of the object. They did not know what they were looking at in the evening sky. Also, they wondered how such a large object could stay aloft, how and why it flew so low, how it could fly so slowly, and what caused it to make so much noise. However, they soon realized that it was not a conventional aircraft, rocket, meteor, balloon, bird or some planet such as Venus. Most had flown in commercial or military aircraft. They stated in no uncertain terms that they did not know what it was they saw, but they knew what it was *not*.

Some witnesses initially expressed fear on making visual contact with the object. However, when they realized that it was not something conventional, their fear turned to curiosity. In the triangular- and disc-shaped sightings, the witnesses expressed fear that the object would crash and they began to visualize the troubles such an accident would cause. Two witnesses, in separate incidents, stated that after the sightings were over they developed a cold later on in the evening. However, instead of the cold lasting three to ten days, it ran its course of discomfort in about twenty-four to thirty-six hours.

There were three other unique characteristics of the sightings. One was the fact that the noise was not readily heard before it was positioned above the house, although in one case the witnesses stated they heard the noise fade away at some short distance from the house. A second feature was that no medical problems, minor or serious (except the reported colds) resulted from the witnesses being directly under or near the object at such low altitudes − 50 to 600 feet. They did not report any problems from radiation, any electrostatic or electro-magnetic effects acting on their body, any paralysis or hypnotic sensations, any sense of lost time, or any unusual dreams or abnormal behaviour that night or later on. One woman stated she felt lethargic for about three weeks after the sighting, but she attributed this condition to the fact that she had just changed jobs. The only electrical effects noticed in the house were lines on the television screen when the set was turned on. One witness using the phone complained of excessive noise and had to hang up the receiver.

LIGHTS

The third characteristic was the strange presence of red, and red and green, lights around the object. These lights were not on the object itself but appeared to be around it as if escorting or chasing it. The red light moved individually, and the red and green lights moved as a pair in unison. The witnesses characterized these lights as small aircraft. Also, one witness thought that the object was definitely trying to get away from these aircraft. In one sighting, these aircraft seemed to go into a frenzy when the object abruptly disappeared over the racetrack. In two other sightings, the objects abruptly disappeared at two separate locations over the Susquehanna River: in one sighting, the aircraft appeared confused then faded away; in the second, they simply faded away.

ANIMAL BEHAVIOUR

Unusual animal behaviour was to be expected from such encounters, as reported in previous sightings of UFOs. Dogs, cats, parrots and a rabbit showed signs of irrational behaviour. The dogs displayed fear and excite-ment, running around the house in a frenzy. Two of them would not go outside the next day, and one hid under the bed all night. Another dog did not react to the UFO or the noise, most probably because it was deaf. Three parrots got excited, fluffed their feathers and perked up their ears. A rabbit sought shelter at the very rear of its pen. All the animals recovered their normal behaviour within a week.

MODE OF DISAPPEARANCE

For most witnesses, visual contact was lost when the object just faded away from view over Bald Eagle Mountain, south of Williamsport. The witness to the triangular-shaped object stated that it abruptly disappeared at the base of a small hill about half a mile from his house. Two witnesses in separate sightings stated that the object abruptly disappeared when it reached the Susquehanna River. In two other sightings, witnesses reported sudden disappearances, one over the racetrack after hovering over it for five minutes, the other at the base of a small mountain.

NEWSPAPER COVERAGE

Newspaper coverage was good, and I obtained copies of articles which appeared in three regional newspapers. On Friday, 7 February, I had several interviews with local reporters, including one with Laura Lee Janssen of the Williamsport *Sun-Gazette*, who had already talked with Stan Gordon about the sightings. At lunch I told her of my work, what the MUFON organization was all about, and gave her enough UFO information for an article she wrote next day, headed 'Local UFO Sightings Probed: Fact or Flight of Fancy?'[2] When I returned home that evening, I sent her three UFO paperbacks to assist her investigations.

Ms Janssen wrote two additional articles on the sightings. One was entitled 'Close Encounters with "Galaxy" Likely'[3], and the other, 'UFO Mystery Continuing: Conflicting Evidence Grows'[4]. These articles referred to the many people who had seen the objects and to those who had called the local authorities and airport personnel. Some people were reported to have stated that the objects were aircraft of different kinds. Comments by personnel from the FAA, the military, the local airport tower operator, state police, local police, and other interested people were also included. The state police were busy referring callers to the National UFO Reporting Center.

Another reporter, Leon Bogdan of the Bloomsburg *Press-Enterprise* staff, wrote an article entitled 'Group: UFOs Are Buzzing Region'[5], in which he mentioned the efforts and information furnished to him on the sightings by Lester Derr, an independent MUFON investigator.

In the Sunbury *Daily Item* there appeared three articles written by staff reporter Karen Blackledge. One was headed 'Susquehanna Valley Residents Report Seeing Low Flying Lights'[6], and another, 'UFO May Have Been Military Jets'. The first article reported on at least a dozen or more local and area residents who had seen the objects in the sky. The paper received calls on the objects from Milton, Lewisburg and Shamokin. Personnel at Fort Indiantown Gap, Muir Field, and airports at Montoursville, Selinsgrove and Harrisburg also received calls, but none could explain what the objects were.

In one article, however, she reported that spokespersons at other larger airports in the state had speculated that the objects were military aircraft. One person identified the object as a stealth bomber, and another stated that it could have been overhead at that time. This is highly improbable, for reasons given later.

UPDATE

The following is my second update of the Williamsport UFO Wave since I completed the original report on 14 April 1992. After I had mailed that report to MUFON headquarters, I had a feeling that I should place a notice in the newspapers for additional interviewees, since I was sure that there were more people in the sighting area who had been missed the first time around. Therefore, on 12–

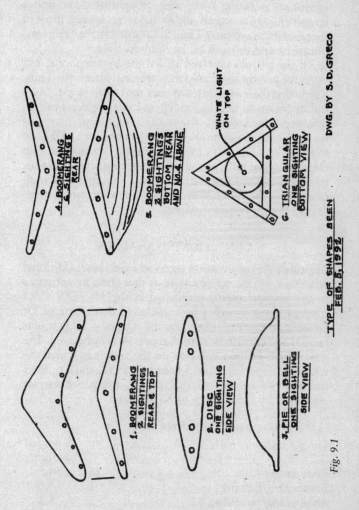

DWG. BY S.D.GRECO

TYPE OF SHAPES SEEN
FEB. 5, 1992

Fig. 9.1

1. BOOMERANG
2 SIGHTINGS
REAR & TOP

2. DISC
ONE SIGHTING
SIDE VIEW

3. PIE OR BELL
ONE SIGHTING
SIDE VIEW

4. BOOMERANG
2 SIGHTINGS
REAR

5. BOOMERANG
2 SIGHTNGS
BOTTOM REAR
AND NO.4 ABOVE

WHITE LIGHT
ON TOP

6. TRIANGULAR
ONE SIGHTING
BOTTOM VIEW

137

14 May 1992, I placed a notice in the Sunbury *Daily Item* and the Williamsport *Sun-Gazette*, since they had the largest circulations in the area of sightings. The notice bore fruit, and nineteen additional interviewees, most of them women, contacted me. Six resided in the Williamsport area and thirteen in the Sunbury area.

All the people involved called me by telephone, but only one person consented to a personal interview. Thus, I recorded their anecdotes as they told them to me. Most did not want to talk too much and were reluctant to go into too much detail about their sightings; they just wanted to let someone know that they had seen a UFO on the night of 5 February 1992. However, I was able to gain their attention long enough to extract sufficient data for this report. The information proved valuable, and indicated that the UFO Wave was somewhat more widespread than was first thought.

CONSOLIDATED ANALYSIS

Although the information received from these additional witnesses was not as extensive as that given by witnesses in the original report published in the *MUFON UFO Journal* [from which I have included here some of Dr Greco's comments – but not the figures – Ed.], it was factual and consistent with that previously obtained. The data which follows is based on the sightings which the witnesses experienced on 5 February 1992, and it follows the analysis in the original report, using the format employed by the authors of *Night Siege*.

(1) UFO shape or light pattern seen

	No.	Rounded percent
Boomerang	18	54.5
Boomerang/Banana	1	3.0
Boomerang/Northrop B2	2	6.1
Boomerang/Lockheed C5A	1	3.0
Boomerang/Northrop Flying Wing	1	3.0

Boomerang/Triangle	3	9.1
Triangular	2	6.1
Box	1	3.0
Pie or Bell	1	3.0
Disc	1	3.0
No information	2	6.1

The pure boomerang-shaped object was seen by 54.5% of the witnesses, and dual nomenclature Boomerang objects by 24.2%, for a total of 78.8%. The Boomerang/ C5A shape object data was not further used in this report because of the claim that it was definitely a USAF C-5A cargo aircraft. The two 'no information' reports were due to the fact that the witnesses did not go outside to view the objects.

The shape of the object probably varies as a consequence of the angle from which it was viewed. One witness directly under the object, for example, reported a true triangular shape.

(2) Estimated size of objects

50 feet across	2	6.3
100–150 feet	8	25.0
150–200 feet	4	12.5
200–300 feet	3	9.3
450 feet	1	3.1
600 feet and above	2	6.3
No information	12	37.5

The most prevalent object-size seen was between 100 to 300 feet in wingspan. The minimum and maximum sizes were 188–233 feet, with an average size of 211 feet in wingspan. Witnesses realized that it was difficult for them to estimate the size of the object in the evening sky. However, all of them related the object's size to distances between trees on their property, that of their house, or that of buildings on the adjoining streets.

(3) Sound heard by witnesses

Low rumbling noise	4	12.5
Loud rumbling noise	14	43.8
Heavy rumbling noise	4	12.5
Loud noise	2	6.2
Heavy jet-engine noise	1	3.1
Rumbling noise	7	21.9
No information	-	-

Most of the witnesses heard a rumbling noise which varied in intensity from low (12.5%), loud (43.8%) to heavy (12.5%). All witnesses claimed the noise shook their house and rattled the windows.

(4) Object movement

Very slow (fast walking pace)	13	40.6
Slow (slow running pace)	14	43.8
Stationary (hovering)	4	12.5
No information	1	3.1

The movement of the objects was extremely slow – much slower than a Piper Cub aircraft can safely maintain its slowest airspeed. Most of the witnesses (84.8%) stated that they could walk at a fast walking pace or a slow running pace under the object. The objects were seen to remain stationary (hover) in the sky by 12.5% of the witnesses.

(5) Duration of visual sighting

0.25 min. or less	3	9.3
0.50–1.00 min.	2	6.3
2–5 mins	16	50.0
5–10 mins	4	12.5
10–15 mins	1	3.1
15–20 mins	2	6.3
No information	4	12.5

Sighting time durations were unusually long for most of the UFO sightings. However, some of them (15.6%) were under one minute – the normal time reported in past sightings.

(6) How witnesses lost sight of objects

Just faded away	25	78.1
Abruptly vanished	4	12.5
Did not observe	3	9.4

Most of the witnesses (78.1%) claimed that they watched the object fade away into the evening sky. However, 12.5% of the witnesses stated that the objects disappeared from sight within one second.

(7) Direction of noise

Heard it coming	11	23.9
Heard it over house	20	43.5
Heard it fade away	13	28.3
No noise	2	4.3

The majority of witnesses (43.5%) first heard the noise when it was over the house. Others (23.9%) heard the noise also as it came toward the house, and still others (28.3%) heard it fade away from the house. Some of the witnesses (4.3%) stated that the object they saw did not make any noise at all.

(8) Did objects hover?

Yes	4	12.5
No	28	87.5

Only 12.5% of the witnesses actually saw the object hover.

(9) Duration of hover

5–10 secs	1	3.1
1–2 mins	1	3.1
5 mins	2	6.2
No hover	28	87.6

Hover time for the objects lasted as long as five minutes (6.2%), a medium time of one to two minutes (3.1%), and a much shorter time of less than ten seconds (3.1%).

(10) Colour of lights

Amber and white	1	3.1
Green and white	1	3.1
Green and red	1	3.1
Reddish-pink	1	3.1
Yellow-flashing	1	3.1
Yellow-steady	1	3.1
Yellow-white	1	3.1
White	23	71.9
None	2	6.4

The most prevalent colour of all lights seen on more than one sighting was white (71.9%). The other colours were seen on other individual sightings.

(11) Colour and number of lights seen

Amber	7	3.98
Green	2	1.14
Red	1	0.57
Reddish-pink	14	7.95
Yellow-flashing	27	15.34
Yellow-steady	26	14.77
Yellow-white	21	11.93
White	78	44.32

The greatest number of lights seen during the sightings was white, 44.32%; yellow, with its various combinations, was second with 42.04%; and red, with its various combinations, was third (8.52%).

(12) Number of lights taken as small aircraft by witnesses

Red and green	5	1	3.1
Red	12	1	3.1
Red	50	1	3.1
Orange	3	1	3.1
No information	–	28	87.6

The red, red and green, and orange lights taken as small aircraft could not be identified further, since no additional data were revealed in the interviews. The largest number of one colour – red – was seen on two sightings (6.2%); red and green was seen on one sighting (3.1%); and orange was seen on one sighting (3.1%). Most witnesses to the other sightings (87.6%) did not report seeing these lights.

The lights were observed to move individually, as in the case of the red lights only, or in unison, as in the case of the red and green lights. They were not discharged from the object nor were they seen as being on or part of the object. They were in movement at a distance near the object and appeared to be either escorting it or chasing it. No other characteristics were observed, and they remain a mystery.

(13) Time and location of objects

1800–1900	Sunbury	
1800–1900	Sunbury	
1800–1900	Lewisburg	15.60
1800–1900	Williamsport	
1800–1900	Linden	
1800–1815	Linden	3.13
1805–1815	Coagan Station	3.13
1805	Williamsport	3.13
1810	Williamsport	3.13
1810–1815	Williamsport	3.13
1815	Williamsport	3.13
1815–1830	Williamsport	3.13
1815–1830	Williamsport	3.13
1820	Williamsport	3.13
1820–1830	Williamsport	3.13
1830	Hummels Wharf	
1830	Sunbury	
1830	Selinsgrove	
1830	New Columbia	21.80
1830	Williamsport	
1830	Lewisburg	
1835	Linden	3.13
1900–1915	Linden	3.13
1900–2100	Warrensville	3.13

1915	Linden	3.13
1915–1920	Stonington	3.13
1930–2030	Selinsgrove	3.13
2000–2100	Sunbury	3.13
2014	Winfield	3.13
2045	Treverton	3.13
2130	Natalie	3.13

It can be seen from these reported times and places that there appears to have been more than one object in the sky at certain times. Between 18.00–19.00 there were five objects seen at approximately the same time in different locations. Unfortunately, the witnesses could not pinpoint the exact time. However, at 18.30 – witnesses were positive of this time – there appears to have been seven objects in the sky at different locations.

In the Linden area, the sightings strongly indicate that two boomerang-shaped objects were seen that evening. One was seen between 18.00 and 19.00 (three sightings) moving south, south-east, south, and then turning east at the Susquehanna River towards Williamsport. However, its flight path from that time on cannot be ascertained from available data.

Between 18.00 and 18.30 hours in the Williamsport area (eight sightings), it appears that one of the objects can be tracked as moving from north to south. This may be one of the five objects reported in the 18.00–19.00 hours group.

It is also obvious that the objects in the 19.00, 20.00 and 21.00 time frames are individual objects, since they were seen in different locations remote from each other.

However, the above statements are subject to change when some time adjustments and course corrections are made, so that tracking on each object can be attempted. This is made much more difficult because four of the objects disappeared in a matter of one second, and assumptions must be made that they reappeared or did not reappear in other areas.

(14) Direction of flight

North-South	21	65.7
North-west-South-east	5	15.7
North-East	3	9.3
East-West-South-east	1	3.1
East-West	1	3.1
West-East	1	3.1

Most of the objects (65.7%) were travelling from north to south; north-west to south-east (15.7%); and north-east to south-west (9.3%). Other individual directions accounted for 21.1%.

(15) Altitude observed

50–100 feet	10	31.2
100–200 feet	4	12.5
200–250 feet	1	3.2
250–500 feet	5	15.6
500 feet and over	7	21.9
No information	5	15.6

The lowest altitude observed – directly overhead or nearly overhead – was 50–100 feet (31.2%), and the highest altitude observed was above 500 feet (3.1%).

(16) Distance from observer

50–100 feet	9	28.1
100–150 feet	3	9.4
100–200 feet	4	12.5
200–250 feet	5	15.6
500 feet and over	1	3.1
No information	10	31.3

The shortest distance from an observer in the horizontal direction was 50 feet (28.1%), and the farthest was above 500 feet (3.1%). All the witnesses were able to estimate the distance of the object as soon as they went outside and viewed it.

(17) Areas with most sightings

Williamsport	10	31.30
Linden	5	15.62
Sunbury	4	12.50
Lewisburg	2	6.25
Selinsgrove	2	6.25
Coagan Station	1	3.12
Hummels Wharf	1	3.12
Natalie	1	3.12
New Columbia	1	3.12
Northumberland	1	3.12
Stonington	1	3.12
Treverton	1	3.12
Warrensville	1	3.12
Winfield	1	3.12

Fifty per cent of the sightings reported occurred in the northern section of the sighting area – north of New Columbia – and fifty per cent occurred in the southern section. Most of the sightings in any one city, however, occurred in Williamsport.

AIRCRAFT OR UFO?

This wave of sightings stimulates the human mind to try to determine what actually occurred on the evening of 5 February 1992. The data presented shows clearly that unusual objects in the sky were seen by numerous witnesses who were interviewed and who told their story to the investigator as they had lived it. Other witnesses are known to have seen the object or heard the noise it made, since they revealed this fact by calling the local authorities.

In trying to arrive at a meaningful solution as to what was observed in the evening sky, a good analysis will also deduce what the object was *not*, as follows:

(a) Not an aircraft

The witnesses were familiar with commercial and/or military aircraft. Some had flown in the latter, all in the former. All the witnesses agreed that what they had seen was neither. Some made inquiries of local, state, and even out-of-state airport tower operators and were told that no aircraft blips had been seen on their radars at the time of their reported sightings.

A spokesperson for the Federal Aviation Administration (FAA), when contacted by some of the witnesses and as reported in various newspaper articles, stated that no military aircraft flight plans had been filed for the sighting area. He also stated that no flight rules had been violated by either military or commercial aircraft, since no complaints had been filed with them.

A United States Air Force (USAF) Freedom of Information manager, when contacted by Stan Gordon, stated that no military aircraft were operating in the sighting area.

(b) Same time, different places

Different witnesses saw the UFO in different parts of the sighting area at about the same time. Some witnesses saw the UFO in two different parts of the sighting area and at a later time in the evening (see item 13 above).

Since no aircraft were reported in the sighting area, the probability that the objects seen were something other than a UFO is extremely low.

(c) Extremely slow speeds

All witnesses stated the UFO was flying at a slow or *very* slow speed, and they could go at a fast walking or slow running pace and keep up with it.

At these speeds, small aircraft are difficult to fly because of their inherent aerodynamic stall characteristic. Larger commercial or military aircraft cannot sustain these speeds in flight. In the landing mode they are 'flown in' by the pilot until the wheels touch the runway, whereupon braking (thrust reverser and brake) action occurs.

(d) The UFO was reported as very large

The size of the UFO was reported as being very large, with a wingspan of 50–600 feet. The largest wingspan of a US military aircraft is 223 feet (Lockheed C-5A Galaxy) and of a US commercial aircraft 196 feet (Boeing 747). However, none of these aircraft was reported to be in the sighting area.

(e) The UFO was seen to hover in the sky

There are three known types of aircraft [in the United States] which can hover – the British Harrier jumpjet [used by the US Marine Corps – Ed.], a helicopter and a blimp. Except for the blimp, these are all small in size when compared to what was seen by the witnesses.

Balloons are seen in the sky on special occasions and very seldom at night. Furthermore, they are at the mercy of the prevailing winds and their flight course is not certain. None of the above types was reported by government aviation agencies, the military or local area tower operators.

(f) The UFO lights were of a greater number and size than what is currently on aircraft

Each witness reported large white lights at the rear of the UFO which could clearly be seen. One witness thought that they were portholes.

These lights are not capable of being installed on small aircraft because of their large size and corresponding weight. Commercial and military aircraft have lights which must conform to FAA and military regulations and are not nearly as large as those seen by the witnesses. Cabin lights on these aircraft are located along the length of the cabin on both sides and there is a much greater number than those seen by the witnesses in any one sighting.

(g) The same UFO shapes have been reported in previous years

The shapes reported by the witnesses – boomerang, disc

and triangular – have been seen many times in the United States and several other countries.

(h) The UFO abruptly disappeared from view in an instant

Witnesses of four sightings reported that while the UFO was in visual contact it abruptly disappeared from sight in less than a second and was not seen thereafter. There are no known aircraft in the world which can abruptly disappear as reported by the witnesses.

The USAF B-2 stealth bomber (flying wing) and the F-117A stealth fighter cannot [usually] be seen on radar, and they cannot abruptly disappear from sight in one second. If they can, it is a military secret.

(i) The UFO sightings took place over a large geographical area

The reported UFO sightings were seen west of Williamsport at Linden, east of Williamsport at Loyalsock Township, north of Williamsport near Coagan Station, and to the south of Williamsport at Selinsgrove.

Although there are small and medium-size airports in the sighting area, no aircraft were reported in the air by the control tower operators.

WHAT DID THE WITNESSES SEE?

The witnesses gave to the investigator an honest and truthful account of what they had seen on that evening of 5 February 1992. This was an experience they will not soon forget. They do not know exactly what type of flying object they saw, but they were adamant in their belief that it was not a man-made object. What then did they see?

While there will be many people who will speculate or try to explain what the witnesses saw, the data presented must be taken into account in any such explanation.

There was an unusual object in the evening sky which the witnesses could not describe as something man-made.

The object had a form or silhouette, it was very large in size, it appeared to be solid, it made a loud rumbling noise, it displayed lights on some parts of its form, and it was seen for a specific length of time.

The object appeared to be under intelligent control because it flew in a straight line, it made turns, it hovered for various lengths of time, it abruptly disappeared from visual contact, it flew at a determined altitude, and it flew at an unusual slow speed.

There were no aircraft in the sighting area reported either by commercial air sources, the FAA or the USAF.

No rational or reasonable explanation has been advanced for any man-made object or astronomical object, event or condition up to the date of this writing.

Perhaps with additional data from future sightings, it may be possible to draw a definitive conclusion for some form of flying object. Until that time, what the witnesses have seen must remain unexplained.

Notes

1. Hynek, Dr J. Allen; Imbrogno, Philip J.; Pratt, Bob: *Night Siege: The Hudson Valley UFO Sightings*, Ballantine, New York, 1987.
2. *Sun-Gazette*, Williamsport, Pa., 8 February 1992.
3. Ibid., 6 February 1992.
4. Ibid., 15 February 1992.
5. *Press-Enterprise*, Bloomsburg, Pa., 8 February 1992.
6. *Daily Item*, Sunbury, Pa., 6 February 1992.

10
POSSIBLE EXTRATERRESTRIAL STRATEGY FOR EARTH

Dr James Deardorff

A graduate of Stanford University and the University of Washington, James Deardorff has degrees in physics and meteorology. From 1951–5 he served as a line officer with the US Navy, then taught at the University of Washington until 1959. In 1962 he went to the National Center for Atmospheric Research to become a senior scientist. In 1978 he became a research professor at the Department of Atmospheric Sciences, Oregon State University, where he is currently Professor Emeritus.

Dr Deardorff is a Fellow of the American Association for the Advancement of Science, and in addition to several books, he has written numerous articles for various scientific and technical journals, including the following, which first appeared in the *Quarterly Journal of the Royal Astronomical Society* (27/1986) and is republished here by kind permission of Dr Deardorff and the editor of the *Quarterly Journal*. The author has studied reports of UFO encounters for many years, and is convinced that contact with extraterrestrials has already been established.

Numerous studies of the past two decades have affirmed the likelihood that many advanced extraterrestrial races or civilizations abound within our own Galaxy[1][2][3][4] not to mention the neighbouring galaxies and the rest of the Universe. Through use of Drake's equation[5] the number of planets within our own Galaxy so inhabited, N, is usually placed in the vicinity of 10^6, give or take a couple of orders of magnitude[1]. The extraterrestrials would presumably be advanced over us technologically by anywhere from just a few thousand years to hundreds of millions of years.

It has also been deduced with considerable agreement amongst different investigators that the time for any one such race to colonize all the hospitable planets in the Galaxy is only of the order of 100 million years or less[6 7 8] based upon their travelling at speeds of the order of 1 per cent of the speed of light, and assuming they would spend a few thousand years consolidating each new planet before setting out for the next. Even if the only motivation for migration were to escape the fate of the parent star leaving the main sequence, as many as $0.1 N$ extraterrestrial races are expected to have done this by now[9]. Thus, the chance that our 'corner' of the Galaxy somehow escaped the attention of advance extraterrestrial races can be considered very remote, assuming they exist.

At the same time it has of course been realized that no extraterrestrial presence or communication has been detected through radio-telescope searches or other astronomical means[10]. This fact has often led to the conclusion that mankind is unique within the Galaxy as a thinking being capable of pondering its own existence and technologically able to explore its own Solar System and beyond. That conclusion has been bolstered by studies which indicate the huge improbability that life could have started [spontaneously]; i.e. that the necessary amino acids could ever have arranged themselves in just the right way at the right time so as to make an aggregate of enzymes capable of self-replication[10 11 12]. This reasoning says, then, that life on Earth, and mankind, is just a statistical fluke which by all odds should not have happened, and could thus be unique.

However, the above two arguments on uniqueness are usually rejected on the grounds that the first life on Earth is known to have started after only a few hundred million years following Earth's formation. Since it did not wait a few thousand million years to start, there is no indication that the initiation of life is a rare event relative to the lifetimes of planetary systems. This fact has forced the counter-conclusion that some kind of precursor replicating molecular system far simpler than anything now imagined can evolve out of the amino acids to start the life process, or else that life somehow gets seeded on young planets by advanced extraterrestrial intelligences. The latter possibility, of course, would require the past existence of the extraterrestrials being debated, and would thus imply their present existence.

Further reasoning against the uniqueness theory draws upon the Copernican-type argument that all previous beliefs of mankind occupying a central and supreme position in the Universe have proven false. These beliefs ranged from having the Earth be flat with 'us' on top, and then having planets, Sun and stars all rotate about the Earth, to having the Milky Way Galaxy being the only galaxy, or a central galaxy, rather than a fairly typical galaxy within a cluster of galaxies within a supercluster. Additional indirect support for the hypothesis of multiple extraterrestrial races within our Galaxy comes from recent observations of proto-planetary nebulae surrounding some young stars[13], strongly supporting the idea of the ubiquity of stellar planetary systems.

These arguments have caused much debate on 'Where are they?'[10] and 'Why haven't we seen them?' Rather than defaulting in the face of these questions, attention has now shifted towards hypotheses about the extraterrestrials which might explain our apparent failure to have been contacted or exploited.

The earliest hypothesis along these lines had the Earth as a sort of zoo being maintained by extraterrestrials rather like a wildlife refuge[14]. The question of why advanced extraterrestrials would be sufficiently benevolent or concerned to behave at all like this was tackled by Newman & Sagan[15] who suggested that there may be universal impediments against cosmic imperialism, and perhaps a *Codex Galactica* to educate the younger societies on how to behave. Sagan & Newman[16] further argued that advanced civilizations with long histories must have learned how to be benign and how to treat an adolescent society delicately.

Harrison[17] collected and extended these ideas by proposing that a 'biogalactic' law naturally exists wherein intelligent life forms which are destructively aggressive tend to wipe themselves out in the solar system of their birth and do not go on to colonize a galaxy. He concluded that the reason we have not yet noticed any advanced civilization in the Galaxy may be that the selection process places an embargo on direct contact with any civilization still planet-bound. The embargo would be such that 'civilizations must not be encouraged or aided to quit their planets prematurely. They must prove their fitness to mingle with alien creatures, and there is no better way of demonstrating unfitness than self-destruction'.

Papagiannis[18] argued somewhat differently that

The limits of growth . . . will become the constraint that will affect the natural selection of these civilizations. Those that manage to overcome their innate tendencies toward continuous material growth and replace them with non-natural goals will be the only ones to survive this crisis. As a result the entire galaxy in a cosmically short time period will become populated by stable, highly ethical and spiritual civilizations.

Either argument characterizes the advanced extraterrestrials as benevolent or highly ethical, in order to explain our existence today, unexploited. However, there are many further variations on these themes, and consequences of them, which merit much discussion. These include the extent of the proposed benevolence, and the manner in which such extraterrestrials might communicate with us if they considered us near the stage to merit such contact. The purpose of this paper is to explore some of these considerations in search of a logical extraterrestrial strategy.

THE DEGREE OF EXTRATERRESTRIAL BENEVOLENCE

A wide range of extraterrestrial benevolence should be expected, considering the huge number of advanced civilizations thought to exist, the probable large differences in their forms and cultures, the hugely varying degrees of evolution which are implied, and the seemingly great difficulty or expense for any collection of such races to police a galaxy so as to stamp out any aggressive behaviour noted. Further, just what constitutes 'aggressiveness' would often not be easy to judge; two warring factions from the same planet may not quite wipe each other out, with one perhaps surviving and rebuilding on a neighbouring planet in the same system. Would the surviving faction have learned enough from its experiences to be judged non-aggressive and merit no punitive action by technologically superior civilizations? Many other scenarios could be envisaged.

Thus, some small fraction of the races in the Galaxy could well be considered hostile by us but be held in check by one or several more benevolent civilizations who for some reason have an interest in either the planet Earth or its inhabitants. One such reason might be that *homo sapiens* closely resemble their own life form, or the form they had at our stage of evolution. Another might be that they or their ancestors once utilized Earth and other planets of our Solar System in some way, before humankind was far enough along to come under the hypothesized embargo ruling. Or perhaps they were helped in this manner early in their own history when they were first developing a space-faring technology, and so feel obliged to return the favour to another race. One cannot, of course, expect to be able to guess what the motivations for overseeing Earth might be for a civilization as much or much more technologically advanced over us than we are now over the people of 500 years ago, for example.

SOME PREVIOUSLY SUGGESTED METHODS OF EXTRATERRESTRIAL COMMUNICATION

As pointed out by Bracewell[19], were the extraterrestrials to communicate with us via radio waves from space, or via a probe sent to broadcast while circling the

Earth, strenuous attempts would no doubt be made by the governmental agency concerned with national security of the country detecting the communications to keep them top secret. It would be quite naive to reason otherwise. The secrecy would be in hopes of obtaining some military or economic advantage over other nations from the decoded information, especially over other nations deemed unfriendly. Even if the detection of the incoming communications by a non-government research group were announced over the news media, the government could easily disclaim it as an erroneous report or hoax the next day, and immediately clamp a tight security cloak over the operation. If that failed, heavy government censorship and withholding of information would still be expected. Bracewell reasoned that the extraterrestrials would anticipate such action, and would somehow manage to get the communications across to the peoples of all nations nevertheless. In my opinion, however, this would entail some quite different extraterrestrial mode of operation in order for them to avoid extensive or forceful interference in human affairs which would violate the hypothesized embargo.

It could also be said that the alien use of a different method would be consistent with our failure so far to detect any such communications from project SETI (Search for Extraterrestrial Intelligence) or other listening projects in the past ten or fifteen years. Zuckerman[9], for example, implies that in a galaxy nearly saturated with extraterrestrials our failure to observe some of their communications must mean that they have some better method than electromagnetic waves. However, by the previous arguments it is doubtful that we would learn of it if communications *had been* received. Further, if a project like SETI were imagined to succeed, its 'success' could prove to be a disaster for reasons to be discussed next.

Another possible course of extraterrestrial action would be for them simply to appear or alight simultaneously in a show of force within the capital cities of many of the world's leading governments, and work out the communications later. However, even if the aliens possessed this capability the possibility must be quickly rejected on the grounds of leading to unethical consequences which an advanced extraterrestrial race should easily foresee. (From Section 1 we are assuming the extraterrestrial is benevolent and highly ethical.) A reaction of mass hysteria of the same type as occurred in 1938 when Orson Welles's programme *The Invasion from Mars* was broadcast over the radio in the USA would probably *not* occur today, thanks to all the science-fiction movies and extraterrestrial video programmes of the past two decades. However, panic would very likely ensue over Western-bloc fears that the East was receiving special treatment from the extraterrestrials, and vice versa, and that the other side was about to launch its nuclear weapons. Surely ethically advanced extraterrestrials would avoid such a scenario if there were any other way, especially since their landing craft would, here or there, undoubtedly be fired upon, possibly requiring retaliatory action.

Even a gradual public awareness of an extraterrestrial existence and eventual appearance would, over a several-month period even, still be such a shocking revelation that it could cause economic chaos and topple governments. The religious consequences alone could be huge, since large masses of people would likely begin to question the basis of their own beliefs if an extraterrestrial presence were confirmed. That is, any religion based upon worship or adoration of a human figure may no longer seem valid or universal upon learning of the definite existence of extraterrestrials having a history of many thousands or millions of years, and upon learning possibly of the alien religious or spiritual leanings, if any. Hence benevolent extraterrestrials are expected to avoid this abrupt course of action.

By the method of elimination, one is then led to the likelihood that any extraterrestrial communications with Earth would progress over a very long time period, such as two or three generations, and in a manner designed to reach people whose value systems can accept the message they are likely to deliver. At the same time the communications would have to be delivered in a manner that would ensure that governments would not find out about it, or not take repressive action, for the reasons given previously. This would seem to require that scientists as a whole would also not learn about the communications; otherwise governments would take notice. Such a manner of communications conceivably would not violate the hypothesized embargo of Earth, since there would be no interference with governmental actions or scientific endeavours. Although it is not clear that any such manner of communication exists, a possibility is proposed below.

AN EXTRATERRESTRIAL COMMUNICATION PLAN COMPATIBLE WITH THE EMBARGO

One possibility, given that the extraterrestrial race had somehow studied human society for a considerable time period without our knowledge, and understood human psychology well, is as follows.

The extraterrestrial communications could be emplaced in a manner easily accessible to the general public but in a form not acceptable or believable to scientists. Government agencies, upon advice from scientists, would then take no actions, and the embargo would more or less remain intact. Awareness of what was taking place would then proceed very gradually – no faster than humankind in general was inherently prepared to accept the extraterrestrial messages. In this way the extraterrestrial intelligence need make no hasty decision on precisely when or if humankind was prepared to receive their communications, or whether governments could be trusted to forward the communications faithfully to the people in general. There would be no forceful extraterrestrial intervention in human affairs, so that governments would still be free to initiate a nuclear holocaust if they so desired, thus quickly answering the question of whether or not mankind is ethically prepared to enter a new 'cosmic' age.

A scenario for this type of extraterrestrial strategy might involve their communicating with one or a very few recipients scattered about the globe. A recipient would be supplied with a comprehensive message over an extended time period, so that he or she could fully understand it, and would also be allowed to gather extensive evidence on the reality of the events so as to be able to gain some measure of public acceptance of the messages. However, in order that scientists in general should not be alerted, only the recipient would be allowed to partake in the communication sessions and to witness the extraterrestrials themselves.

The messages might, moreover, contain vague descriptions of extraterrestrial technological achievements that would read like magic or science fiction. They might even contain a few absurdities purposely added; these, along with the absence of any detailed instructions on how to effect any technological breakthroughs, would help ensure that any scientists who happened to learn about the communications would regard them as hoaxes or fiction. The evidence would also be rejected by scientists because of the demand that tentative acceptance of the reality of an event requires that it either be reproducible or repeatable at will, or have been observed by trusted investigators. Meantime, the messages would get published, translated into various languages, and distributed throughout the world amongst other occult literature. A large number of publishing companies already handle similar literature.

Following the reasoning of Papagiannis[18], the messages could be expected to contain some spiritual, or at least ethical, aspects which might further deter scientific inquiry. If all this were not enough to prevent any premature scientific acceptance, the existence of similar communications which turned out to be hoaxes might occur naturally and serve to confuse the situation greatly.

This would provide a further motivation for scientists to feel no obligation to study the situation.

The problem of how that fraction of the general public which comes across the relevant literature could distinguish it, as a likely extraterrestrial message, from the frauds and cults could be part of the extraterrestrial solution rather than a problem. That is, overcoming this difficulty would ensure a large time-scale for the acceptance of the extraterrestrial communications, thereby minimizing any public panic and religious upheavals, and would require judicious use of logic in trying to decide if the message could be essentially true. These attributes, including independent thinking on the part of as many people as possible, and the deduction that our level of technology must be far below that of the aliens, may be prerequisites desired by the extraterrestrials before fully lifting the embargo. A further prerequisite might be that we have reached a level of understanding wherein we would treat them not as gods but respectfully as fellow creatures with a multi-millennium headstart over us.

The embargo against Earth would thus be a leaky one, designed to hold against scientists and governments in general while very gradually giving way to the general public.

DISCUSSION

The above possibility, and its prerequisites, would seem to demand that the [extraterrestrial groups in charge] have maintained a steady worldwide surveillance over a very long period of time, as well as have the capability to set up rendezvous with the message recipient. For this to be accomplished without our obvious knowledge might require technology so advanced that it would be classified as magic, or occult. However, Sagan[20] has emphasized that magical acts would have to be expected if the extraterrestrials really *are* advanced by thousands of years or more over us. In fact, absence of any descriptions of magical capabilities within the recipient's message could be taken to mean that it was just a hoax and that the hoaxer was not very imaginative. Thus it might be very difficult to distinguish a true extraterrestrial message from various fictional writings. One would have to sift the recipient's validating evidence very carefully, trying to judge it on its own merits and not how reasonable or unreasonable the magic-like descriptions within the communications might seem by present standards.

The same technologically advanced surveillance methods might be needed for the aliens to be able to judge the rate at which their message was being noticed and accepted by the people.

A common example of present knowledge that would seem like magic to a person of 500 or even 100 years ago is television and its invisible signal propagation through space. An example of present scientific uncertainty which might portend a 'magical' breakthrough within 30–50 years lies in the results of certain high-energy particle-collision experiments performed [in 1984] on the CERN accelerator. The best theory to explain the observed events appears to require the existence of 'supermatter' involving six or seven new spatial dimensions[21 22 23 24].

Since the apparent embargo implies considerable extraterrestrial concern in the human race, it is of interest to estimate if the numbers support this possibility. Given N advanced extraterrestrial races in the Galaxy, we suppose that only a fraction r maintain an interest in emerging civilizations of which Earth may be one. If the frequency at which such emerging civilizations appear within the Galaxy is f, and the period of emergence is T, then the number, n, of extraterrestrial civilizations available to observe each newly emerging one over its period of emergence is

$$n = rN/(fT)$$

A conservative value for N is 10^5, and for r is 0.1 per cent. The estimate for f is one per 10 years[25] and is independent of the longevity assumed for the typical alien race. An estimate of T is 100 years, as for example between 1950 and 2050 for us. These figures give

$$n=10$$

which suggests that ample extraterrestrial civilizations exist, if highly mobile, to carry out surveillance and maintain the leaky embargo upon the emerging race. Actually, the fraction r may adjust itself until n has some optimum value. That is, for optimum r, the senior fraction $1-r$ may conclude that the handling of emerging civilizations is proceeding satisfactorily, so that they may continue to engage in other pursuits.

This proposed extraterrestrial strategy of dealing with Earth overcomes the inconsistency of a benign intelligence being the cause of chaotic societal consequences following any rapid confirmation of its presence, or of not realizing that its messages beamed via electromagnetic waves might be confiscated by governments and held top secret in the interest of national security. It also possesses the realistic aspect that the receipt of communications on Earth would be under extraterrestrial control.

Notes

1. Sagan, C. (ed.), 1973. In *Communication with Extraterrestrial Intelligence (CETI)*, MIT Press.
2. Oliver, B. M., 1985. *Icarus*, **125**, pp. 360–7.
3. Freeman, J. & Lampton, M., 1975. *Icarus*, **25**, pp. 368–9.
4. Field, G. B., Verschur, J. L. & Ponnamperuma, C., 1978. *Cosmic Evolution: an Introduction to Astronomy*, Houghton Mifflin, Boston.
5. Drake, F. D., 1961. US National Academy of Sciences Conference on 'Extraterrestrial Intelligent Life', November, Green Bank, West Virginia.
6. Jones, E. M., 1976. *Icarus*, **28**, pp. 421–2.
7. Jones, E. M., 1981. *Icarus*, **46**, pp. 328–36.
8. Walters, C., Hoover, R. A. & Kotra, R. K., 1980. *Icarus*, **41**, pp. 193–7.
9. Zuckerman, B., 1985. *Quarterly Journal of the Royal*

Astronomical Society, **26**, pp. 56–9.

10. Hart, M. H., 1982. In *Extraterrestrials, Where Are They?*, pp. 154–65, Pergamon Press, New York.
11. Hoyle, F., 1982. *Ann. Rev. Astr. Astrophys.*, **20**, pp. 1–35.
12. Blum, H. F., 1965. *Nature*, **206**, pp. 131–2.
13. Neugebauer, G., Beichman, C. A., Soifer, B. T. *et al*, 1984. *Science*, **224**, pp. 14–21.
14. Ball, J. A., 1973. *Icarus*, **19**, pp. 347–9.
15. Newman, W. I. & Sagan, C., 1981. *Icarus*, **46**, pp. 293–327.
16. Sagan, C. & Newman, W. I., 1983. *Q. Jl R. Astr. Soc.*, **24**, pp. 113–21.
17. Harrison, E. R., 1981. *Cosmology*, Cambridge University Press, New York.
18. Papagiannis, M. D., 1984. *Q. Jl. R. Astr. Soc.*, **25**, pp. 309–18.
19. Bracewell, R. N., 1975. *The Galactic Club: Intelligent Life in Outer Space*, Stanford Alumni Association.
20. Sagan, C., 1973. *Icarus*, **19**, pp. 350–2.
21. Thomsen, D. E., 1984. *Science News*, **126**, p. 292.
22. Davies, P., 1984. *Superforce: the Search for a Grand Unified Theory of Nature*, Simon & Schuster, New York.
23. Green, M. B., 1985. *Nature*, **314**, pp. 409–14.
24. Freedman, D. Z. & van Nieuwenhuizen, P., 1985. *Scientific American*, **252**, pp. 74–81.
25. Shklovskii, I. S. & Sagan, C., 1966. *Intelligent Life in the Universe*, Holden-Day, San Francisco.

11
IMPORTANT DEVELOPMENTS IN THE FORMER SOVIET UNION

Nikolai Lebedev

The son of an air force pilot, Nikolai Lebedev was born in Valday, Russia, in 1950. He studied engineering as well as aeronautics and astronautics at the Institute of Mechanical Engineering in Leningrad (now St Petersburg) from 1968 to 1975. He now specializes in irrigation engineering and lives with his wife and son in St Petersburg, where I first met him in 1989. Nikolai is also a journalist for the *St Petersburg Evening*.

Drastic changes in the political and economical life in the former Soviet Union have had some very sad consequences in the last few years, and this has led to considerable difficulties for UFO research, at both government and private levels. For example, because of our desperate financial circumstances, it has become prohibitive to pay for phone calls and faxes, and even to send letters to my research colleagues – especially those abroad. Nevertheless, it is essential, in my opinion, to report accurately the facts which prove that we are not alone in the universe; facts which may save the most valuable thing that people possess – their souls.

UFONAUTS ARE OBSERVING OUR COSMONAUTS

It is well known that all Russian spacecraft returning to Earth make their landings in the region of Kazakhstan. According to rumours, each landing of our *Soyuz*-type spacecraft has been monitored by alien spacecraft. In October 1991, for instance, the newspaper *Trud* reported that on the night of 9 October 1991, the day before the prearranged landing of Soyuz TM-13, a disc-shaped object appeared in the sky over the town of Arkalyk. The object emitted beams of light which crossed the sky as it headed north to south, in the direction of the calculated landing site. It is important to note *Trud*'s comment that: '. . . *As previously*, the arrival of the UFO was seen by many witnesses at Arkalyk, and it was registered by the local department of internal affairs.'[1] [Emphasis added]

The actual landing time of Soyuz TM-13 was 6.00 a.m. on 10 October. It would be interesting to ask the crew members (A. Arczebarski, T. Aubakirov and F. Fibek) if they saw anything. But perhaps the UFO was more interested in observing the sensitive Ministry of Defence sites which are located in the region. In order to ask these questions, however, one needs permission from the General Staff of our Air Defence.

All stages of the landing of our spacecraft are strictly monitored by radar stations of the so-called 'Cosmic Troops', who use highly sophisticated radar equipment. I should also point out that situated in Arkalyk itself is the permanent base of the Emergency and Rescue Group, the main task of which is to recover our spacecraft and cosmonauts. This group numbers many highly trained men who have at their disposal fifteen helicopters, six aircraft and five landrover-type vehicles. And, of course, this team was fully prepared for the landing of Soyuz TM-13. Unfortunately, the story about the UFO sighting appeared in only one central news-paper, without any reference to the group, and only nine days after the event.

In another case, when a spacecraft was launched from Plesetsk at about 6.00 p.m. on 2 October 1991, local UFO investigators in the region of Arkhangelsk (about 130 miles from Plesetsk) who were observing the stages of the launch with powerful optics, noticed to their amazement that, just after the separation of the first stage of the rocket booster, a UFO appeared behind it and seemed to be following it. This was not the only UFO sighting at that time.

M. Alekseev, at the Puksa railway station near Arkhangelsk, wrote to the *Red Star* newspaper (published by the Ministry of Defence) asking what kind of phenomenon it was that he observed on the evening of 2 October 1991. The response was made by Lieutenant-Colonel M. Arhipov, chief press officer of the Cosmic Troops, who confirmed that inhabitants in the region of Arkhangelsk may have observed some kind of 'atmospheric phenomenon', and he linked this with the launch of a research rocket. 'More precisely,' he explained, 'in connection with the burned-out stage of the booster rocket in a thunder cloud.' Arhipov denied that any of the observed sightings 'could be associated with the activities of aliens from space'. [2]

Such comments do not surprise me, coming as they do from a spokesman of the Cosmic Troops.

Late in the evening of 3 August 1990, and the early part of the following morning, a major UFO flap occurred in the northern area of Leningrad (now St Petersburg). I was informed that some of the UFO sightings were in the direct vicinity of the launching pad at Plesetsk, and that this was the explanation. As a journalist with *Vecherni Leningrad*, I therefore sent an official inquiry to the press office of the Cosmic Troops, asking about activity at the launch site that evening. The official reply was signed by A. I. Radionov, military unit 57275. The information he supplied about the launch was exhaustive and gave me the opportunity to dismiss the attempts of some 'experts' to explain away the sightings as having been caused solely by the launch. For instance, the rocket launch occurred from 11.45–11.55 p.m., whereas the UFOs were reported from 9.30 p.m. until at least 3.00 a.m. the following morning. But as to these reports, Radionov told me that they had 'no information about anomalous phenomena or objects'.

From this, it is evident that there is no change in the policy of our space agency in matters relating to our subject. This is an ironical situation, since in early 1992 it was announced on radio and television that a department of the former KGB [now the Russian Security Ministry and Foreign Intelligence Service – Ed.] had signed a contract with two Hollywood film producers, giving them the right to make documentary films based on some hitherto secret KGB UFO files![3] I fail to understand why the KGB did not first supply this information to our Russian mass media. [The reason, in my opinion, is simply that the Russian authorities – including the Foreign Intelligence Service and the Security Ministry – are so desperate for hard currency that they are prepared to sell their wares to the highest bidder – Ed.]

AN ABDUCTION REPEATED?

It is my opinion that the aliens are not only observing us, but they are actively and carefully 'working' among us.

In *The UFO Report 1992*, I described how the forty-two-year-old bus driver Aleksandr Pavlovich Dolotov was apparently abducted by ufonauts in Leningrad on 17 June 1990[4]. During my interview with him, I became totally convinced of his sincerity. Afterwards, I suggested to him that perhaps his night encounter would not be the last, and that another experience might be in store for him. 'If possible,' I asked him, 'please try not to resist the aliens physically, but try mentally to retain your independence and personality as a human being.'

It was obvious that he did not take me seriously. Nonetheless, in subsequent meetings with Aleksandr's wife, Dr Rita Dolotova, I asked her to keep me in touch with any possible developments. At the end of April 1991 I got a phone call from Rita. 'Something happened to him again,' she began, and asked if I would come over to talk to them. The following is a reconstruction of the events which took place, based on what Aleksandr and Rita told me.

On the evening of 29 March 1991, the weather was poor, with snow and rain. It was Aleksandr's day off, but his wife and son were at work. Rita was on all-night medical duty at Baltiyski Station until the following morning. Aleksandr was sitting in the kitchen of his flat drinking tea with a friend. He had previously agreed to meet his son at his place of work at 7.50 p.m. Aleksandr, incidentally, is a very punctual man. Suddenly, he announced that he had to visit his son, escorted his friend to the door and said good-bye. The time was now 7.35 p.m.

The first strange thing that happened, Aleksandr told me, was that for some reason he did not leave home with his friend, since the place where his son worked was in the same direction, and twenty minutes was ample time to get there. Instead, he closed the door, switched on the television and sat down. To this day, he does not understand why he did that.

Suddenly, he heard a mechanical-sounding voice say, 'Come with us!' He does not remember if this was heard physically or mentally, but he does recall that the voice was combined with a very strong feeling of presence, and that something or someone was in the corridor. 'I shall not go,' he replied immediately. He remembers that he stood up, left the room and went into the corridor. His last recollection is that there were at least two tall, human-like figures in black suits. At that point, he blacked out.

As he regained consciousness, Aleksandr found himself in what seemed to be a moving train. At first, he was unable to raise his head, which was resting on his knees. He thought perhaps that he had been speaking to someone who was sitting behind him in the carriage. 'Why am I travelling in a train? I have no ticket', he said to himself, after checking all his pockets. Another discovery which shook him was that his shoe-laces were untied. He would normally never allow such a thing, since he is a very tidy person. Finally, he heard an announcement that the next station was Vliyanka – not far from Baltiyski Station (see Fig. 11.1).

There were only a few passengers (but no one behind

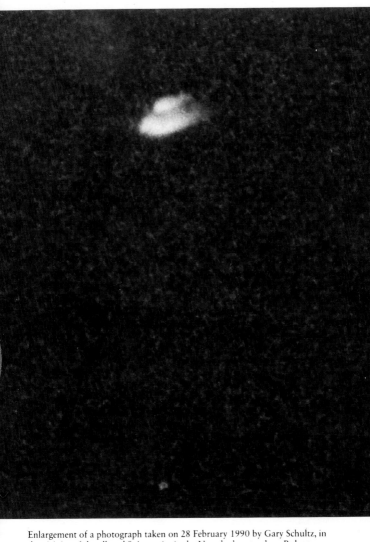

Enlargement of a photograph taken on 28 February 1990 by Gary Schultz, in the vicinity of the alleged S-4 test site in the Nevada desert, where Robert Lazar and others claim that alien spacecraft are being test-flown by U.S. pilots. (© 1990 Gary Schultz)

Carlos Mañuel Mercado, who claims to have been contacted by alien beings at his home and taken to an underground base located below the El Cayúl mountain, Sierra Bermeja, Puerto Rico, in June 1988. (© *Jorge Martín*)

Dolín Acosta, who claims to have been 'X-rayed' by a beam of light from a UFO, in the Olivares sector of Lajas, Puerto Rico, 1987. (© *Jorge Martín*)

Freddie Cruz (*right*), director of the Civil Defence Agency of Lajas, Puerto Rico, tells Jorge Martín about his sighting of a flying disc chased by a U.S. Navy jet on 28 April 1992. Cruz, together with others, has also witnessed UFOs entering the Laguna Cartagena in southwest Puerto Rico. 'To me, there's an alien base around here and the authorities know about it,' Cruz stated.

Enlargements of two photographs taken by journalist Marcel Laroche, showing beams of light emanating from a large stationary object which hovered about Montreal, Canada, for two and a half hours on the night of 7 November 1990, seen by numerous witnesses. (© *Marcel Laroche*)

Photograph taken by reporter Vladimir Savran on 12 October 1991, showing
an unknown object above the Atomic Electricity Station at Chernobyl, Russia,
the day after a potentially disastrous incident took place at the plant.
(*Vladimir Savran/Izvestia*)

Enlargement of photograph taken by Patti Weatherford, in the presence of
numerous witnesses, at Gulf Breeze, Florida, on 5 November 1991. 'I could see
a definite curved structural shape above the blazing red light at its bottom,'
reported witness Bland Pugh, who watched the object through binoculars.
(© *1991 Patti Weatherford*)

The enormous aerial device seen by Roger Cross in Concord, New Hampshire, USA, on 3 March 1992. Other sightings were reported in Concord and surrounding towns.
(*Tania Long, based on a sketch by Bob Dix of the* Union-Leader, *Manchester, New Hampshire*)

A mutilated steer found in Caldwell, Kansas, USA, on 31 January 1992.
(© *Chuck Pine*)

Enlargement of head, showing missing teeth, jaw bone and flesh, and left eye.
Tissue samples examined by pathologist/hematologist Dr John Altshuler
showed that the excisions were made by something hot enough to cook the
blood.
(© *Chuck Pine*)

Calumet, Oklahoma, USA, 10 February 1992: steer with rectum cored out.
(© *Chuck Pine*)

Benton County, Arkansas, USA, 4 March 1992: udder completely removed from cow.
(© *Danny Varner*)

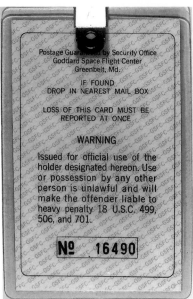

Bob Oechsler's NASA identification card, proving his former employment at the Goddard Space Flight Center, Greenbelt, Maryland. Following the revelations in *Alien Liaison*'s 'Cosmic Journey' chapter, some critics attempted to discredit Oechsler by stating that he had never worked at NASA.

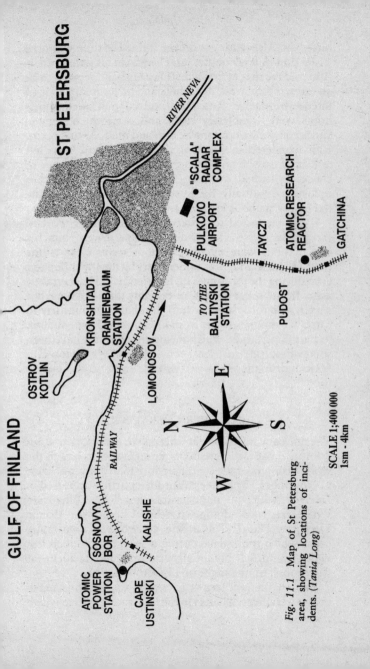

Fig. 11.1 Map of St Petersburg area, showing locations of incidents. *(Tania Long)*

SCALE 1:400 000
1sm - 4km

him), and Aleksandr got off the train. The time was now 11.05 p.m. A few minutes later he was in his wife's office. Rita told me that at first glance her husband seemed to be all right, if somewhat disturbed, and he complained of an intense headache. Rita then noticed that Aleksandr's boots were completely clean and dry, which seemed strange in view of the snow, rain and mud. At this point, Rita wondered if the door of their flat had been left unlocked, so she phoned a neighbour and asked her to check. It turned out that the door was closed, but unlocked. Normally, her husband would never leave the flat empty without locking it.

I was interested to observe how Aleksandr tried to rationalize these extraordinary experiences, but his explanations were unconvincing. It seems clear to me that: (1) Aleksandr was under a strong mental influence, even during the meeting with his friend; (2) He was taken away from his flat by two, or possibly three tall men, but no physical force was used; (3) It requires about forty to forty-five minutes to get from his station, Oranienbaum, to Baltiyski Station, which means that he must have been somewhere for at least two hours; (4) However Aleksandr managed to get into the train, it was not by foot.

UFOs OVER CHERNOBYL

The nuclear catastrophe at Chernobyl, in the Ukraine, on 26 April 1986 will remain in our memories as one of the worst disasters of the century. More than five years later, in November 1991, an extraordinary article appeared in *Izvestia*, with the unbelievable headline: 'What are Extraterrestrials doing at the Chernobyl Atomic Electricity Plant?' The article described an interesting event which took place during a second and much less widely reported potentially catastrophic incident at Chernobyl, on the night of 11 October 1991.

At 7.46 p.m., the fourth generator was disconnected in order to eradicate a defect in the lubricating system where a leak was found. This was done by putting the high-voltage switch in the 'Off' position. The refrigeration system was also put out of operation. The rotor of the generator, which is joined to the turbine rotor, was idling. At this stage, the high-voltage switch can only be put in the 'On' position manually. The refrigeration system of the nuclear generator uses hydrogen gas as a coolant – an effective method of heat transfer, but easily inflammable.

Suddenly, at 8.09 p.m. the gas in the generator began to overheat, and as a result it burst, leading to an explosion. The fire-fighters went into action, but the fire was only put out at 2.00 a.m. on 12 October. The fourth generator was destroyed; the first and third generators were flooded with water by the firemen and were put out of operation too. The roof of the building (50 metres high) was also destroyed by the explosion and fire. The station was practically 'dead', but there was no damage to the nuclear reactor, which is situated just behind the wall of that building.

Shortly after the incident, experts established (now officially) that the accident happened because of the high-voltage switch being set to the 'On' position; a situation that could not have happened by itself. The article in *Izvestia* referred to some witnesses who, a few minutes before the explosion, noticed a glowing bright light just over the building.

Today, due to an executive decision of the Ukrainian government, Chernobyl nuclear power station is out of operation. Experts agreed that this should have been done after the 1986 incident. [But in 1992, reactor No. 3 was reactivated after officials pleaded that its energy was essential for the coming winter, even though it is considered unsafe by the Atomic Energy Agency – Ed.] Is it remotely possible that extraterrestrials interfered in some way in 1991, in order to prevent a more catastrophic incident?

On 12 October 1991, journalist Vladimir Savran of the *Chernobyl Echo* visited the power station and took several photos of the building that housed the damaged generator. To his astonishment, when he developed the film, some kind of object could be seen hovering over the station (see photo section). Here follows my translation of part of an article about the photo in an edition of *Izvestia*, written by N. Burbyga:

. . . Said Vladimir Savran: 'I arrived at the power station the next morning and did not see anything similar [referring to a glow over the building that was reported the previous day]. There were no aircraft, helicopters, nor any other objects above the power plant. But when I developed the film, I saw on the frame some kind of object hovering over the power station, the appearance of which I couldn't understand. Now I think I can explain it approximately: for some reason, that thing was invisible to the human eye, but it was captured on film.'

Was the object produced in the lens or in the camera? The first analysis was carried out by experienced criminologists of the IAD [Internal Affairs Department] of Kiev and showed that there were no defects in the film or in its processing. Furthermore, there were no signs of photo-montage. So what was it? If it was extraterrestrials, why then did they appear in the vicinity of the AES [Atomic Electricity Station]? Perhaps they wanted to alert us to potential mishaps, or were simply observing us from afar. Or perhaps they themselves provoked the accident? We know one thing for sure: the accident had occurred because of spontaneous [disconnecting] of the high-voltage switch. Could this have been put into the 'On' position by itself? Experts familiar with its construction consider such a possibility to be improbable . . .[5]

The fact that the object did not actually appear in the sky does not surprise me, since, in my opinion, the aliens have the ability to be invisible to the naked eye if they so desire. I should add that there are persistent rumours that, just before and during the 1986 Chernobyl disaster, a UFO was observed just over the building housing the fourth reactor. Moreover, the following incident also provides testimony to suggest that such sightings over nuclear power stations are not matters of mere chance.

A CLOSE ENCOUNTER AT VORONEZH AIRPORT

At the end of September 1989 there were several spectacular UFO landings in the city of Voronezh, which caused a sensation around the world[6]. About a week earlier Igor Yadigin, a twenty-nine-year-old aviation mechanic, was on his way to the aviation and technical base situated in the grounds of Voronezh Airport. His duties that day began at 8.00 p.m., and to shorten the distance from his home to work he took a short cut that necessitated walking through a ravine, which was the last obstacle before the airport.

As Yadigin crossed the bottom of the ravine and began to climb up the path leading out of it, he glanced to his left and saw something glowing at a distance. The glow was emerald in colour. His first thought was that it was a rotten tree-stump, shining in the twilight, so he decided to take a closer look. The glow turned out to be a spherical-shaped object with a diameter of no more than some 70 centimetres. The sphere was hovering motionless just above the ground.

Looking at his watch, Yadigin noted that the time was 7.40 p.m. He continued walking towards the object and was about 6 metres away when he suddenly heard the crackling of twigs from his right. Unafraid, he looked in that direction and saw a very tall, well-proportioned man in a dark silver suit. His height was about 2.5 metres.

Yadigin's first thought was to invite the man to have a look at the sphere, but at that moment he noticed that the stranger's entire head was covered to the shoulders by a sort of helmet. The helmet had a visor, rectangular in shape, and it was not possible to make out the man's face because the helmet appeared to contain a type of liquid.

Before this encounter, Yadigin had been fairly relaxed, thinking only of the usual domestic problems. But suddenly, as if in some way induced, his thoughts focused on nuclear power stations. Simultaneously, a faint glow appeared on the man's visor and something made Yadigin turn in the direction of the sphere. To his

173

surprise, a screen appeared on the sphere, on which could be seen a 'live', high-quality picture of Chernobyl nuclear power station (with which he was familiar). The image was not in colour, but it was evident that the position from which the 'film' had been taken was unusual – just above the huge ventilation shaft of the so-called fourth block, housing the fourth generator. Yadigin then observed an explosion, followed by men arriving in cars, and a helicopter flying in the vicinity. No sounds could be heard, but the panic-stricken expressions on people's faces were only too clear.

The image on the screen then changed to that of the Novovoronezh nuclear power station (about 30 miles from Voronezh), where Yadigin had been on several occasions. Again, the position from which the 'film' had been taken was above the station. People on the ground could be seen speaking to one another, but suddenly there was a noiseless explosion, accompanied by smoke. Figures could be observed rushing around, and this was followed by a scene of the evacuation of the population from the south-west part of Voronezh to the airport.

As the 'frames' faded from view, a thought came into Yadigin's mind of Voronezh's nuclear heating station, which at the time was only under construction. He glanced at the tall figure. Again, a faint glow appeared on the visor, and the sphere displayed pictures of the completed station. The effects of an explosion could be seen – fire, black smoke, and looks of horror on people's faces. Igor could only think, 'When?' The image on the screen changed back once more to that of the Novovoronezh disaster, followed by five blinking dots of light. He was not sure what this meant. Could the dots perhaps indicate years? Would there be a disaster in 1994?

Immediately after this extraordinary experience, Igor Yadigin lost consciousness. When he recovered, there was nobody around and the sphere had gone. The time was 8.05 p.m. Apart from a headache, he felt all right, and headed for the airport, where he received a written reproof from his boss for arriving half an hour late.

A month after the incident, Yadigin made an interesting discovery. He found that when he placed his hand about 40–50 centimetres from the television screen at home, it adversely affected the picture. In my opinion, this could indicate that his hand was acting as a source of radio signals. Two months later, the effect grew weaker, then disappeared completely.

Yadigin was unable to write a letter describing these experiences until five months later. He told me that each previous attempt to take up pen and paper was followed by frightening spasms in his throat, epiphora [weeping], almost total numbness of the fingers, and a strong headache. Perhaps the extraterrestrials gave Igor information about possible future disasters, but did not want him to write about them immediately.

KGB CONCERN

A letter describing his experience that Igor Yadigin sent to the Voronezh television station was passed on to a number of local UFO researchers, who in turn sent it to the local department of the KGB. As a result, Igor was invited to the KGB office. The officials paid close attention to his story, not venturing their own opinion. But at the end of the interview, they informed Yadigin that they had received similar information from two other men. The KGB took the extraterrestrial warnings seriously, because they were concerned not only about the possibility of a disaster caused by design defects but also due to an act of sabotage. They told Yadigin that they planned to send a letter to President Gorbachev, urgently requesting that construction of the Voronezh atomic heating station should be halted, and that the Novovoronezh station should be put out of operation. Interestingly, construction of the Voronezh station has now officially been stopped, and extraordinary measures have been undertaken to increase the safety of the Novovoronezh station. Similar measures were taken at the Leningrad atomic power station.

According to the KGB officers, on the same day of Yadigin's encounter, the radar station at Voronezh Airport detected a flight of UFOs in that vicinity. Air traffic controllers noticed on the radar screen that three unknown targets were flying at very low altitude over the airfield, at a speed of about 800–900 kph. (In my opinion, the sphere encountered by Yadigin was not itself an actual spacecraft, but a device with another purpose.)

UFOs OVER LENINGRAD NUCLEAR POWER STATION

In July 1991, I heard from a friend that one of our newspapers had published information about a UFO sighting over Leningrad's Sosnovyy Bor nuclear power station. The sighting had occurred on 2 March 1991, according to the report. Slightly sceptical about the story, which did not appear in an official newspaper, I began to make telephone calls directly to Leningrad's Pulkovo Airport, in my capacity as official correspondent of the *Vecherni Leningrad* (now *Vecherni Peterburg*) newspaper.

A. P. Egorov, chief of air traffic control, explained that he was not fully informed, but that in cases where unidentified targets appeared on radar, they must be officially registered. I then spoke to the chief of air inspectors, V. P. Bazikin, who denied all knowledge of such an incident, as did a deputy flight commander. But a day later I received a call from Egorov, who confirmed that there had indeed been something unusual on the radar screens at the airport that day, and gave me phone numbers of those involved in the tracking thereof. The chief of the radar tracking department suggested that I should speak with those who were working at the radar complex on the day in question. Eventually, I received a full and exhaustive report about the UFO sighting from Sergei Kotochigov.

First of all, I must emphasize that Kotochigov is a very rational and highly qualified engineer, who knows his radar complex thoroughly. He remarked that his superiors wanted to sleep calmly at night and therefore were not interested in official investigations into the UFO sightings recorded at Pulkovo Airport. He then gave me a lot of background information about the radar complex, which is relatively new. It was designed by the Leningrad Radio Institute, and it incorporates the latest computerized technology, with a range of up to 200 kilometres in distance and no less than 22 kilometres in height. The codename of the complex is 'Skala' (rock).

All information from the radar screens is recorded on videotape and is kept for not more than five days before being reused. Each aerial object detected by radar is shown on the screen as a dot of light, or 'blip'. Except for very large targets, the dimensions of these blips do not depend on the size of the object. If the object is an airliner, for example, the plane transmits special signals, and a cross appears beside the blip. After an inquiry in the form of a special coded radio signal by the air traffic controllers, information about that airliner must appear on the screen (such as its registration or flight number). Additional information such as azimuth (the horizontal angle or direction of a compass bearing), distance and speed, are determined by the radar complex.

Kotochigov told me that 2 March 1991 was an ordinary working day. At 7.27 p.m., a target appeared on the radar screen. Initially, the air traffic controllers did not pay much attention to it [probably because there was no pattern of conflicting traffic – Ed.], but at 8.27 p.m. they transmitted a [blind encoder], and immediately noticed that the azimuth, distance, and even vector [any physical quantity that requires a direction to be stated in order to define it completely – Ed.] of speed, kept changing, which is unusual. The average figures were: distance, 63 kilometres; azimuth, 273 degrees. The only conclusion that could be drawn was that the unidentified target was making very fast and chaotic movements over a certain area – and that area was the nuclear power station at Sosnovyy Bor.

Significantly, a large, star-like object was observed

visually from the control tower at Pulkovo. At 8.32 p.m., the object began to move at a phenomenal speed. At first, its azimuth was 273 degrees and at 88 kilometres distance, with a speed of 3,154 kph. At 8.33 p.m., the blip on the radar screen disappeared altogether. (Perhaps the object really flew away, but there is also a possibility that it rendered itself undetectable by radar.) A few minutes later, the object reappeared over Sosnovyy Bor, then, after a minute, began to move in a north-east direction at a speed of about 3,000 kph.

During a meeting with Capt. A. P. Alekseev (military unit 62728), which took place exactly a year after the incident, I learned that this unit had received an official report about a visual UFO sighting over Sosnovyy Bor on 2 March 1991. According to the report, it was not possible to make out the precise shape of the object, because of its bright glow. As I recall, the altitude of the object was not more than 1.5 kilometres.

During my meeting with Sergei Kotochigov, I learned that the Air Defence Command of Leningrad military district, as well as Leningrad's KGB, and even the designers of the 'Skala' radar complex, were all informed about the incident. It is interesting to note that the designers ruled out any suggestion that the observations were due to a malfunction of the computer and radio systems.

On 17 March 1991, the same or another UFO appeared over a sensitive site in Leningrad, when an unidentified target was observed on the radar screens from 4.00 p.m. to 4.20 p.m., during which time a motionless object appeared just above the Atomic Research Reactor on the outskirts of Gatchina (see Fig. 11.1). (Significantly, a potentially dangerous incident took place at that site in 1991.) Kotochigov told me that the UFO departed at a speed of about 2,243 kph. He promised to keep me informed about any future sightings detected by radar at Pulkovo.

Dr Rita Dolotova (see earlier) told me that at 6.00 a.m. on 18 September 1991, when she was returning from her duties in the Sosnovyy Bor area and about to catch the first train from Kalishe Station back to St Petersburg, she suddenly noticed a bright, star-like object in the sky. It had a triangular shape and was almost motionless. At 6.15 a.m., the object began to move away. I made a phone call to Sergei Kotochigov, but he said that nothing 'interesting' was seen on radar. However, an unknown target was tracked three weeks later.

On 10 October 1991, Kotochigov told me, the Skala radar complex detected the presence of an unidentified target positioned above Cape Ustinskiy (see Fig. 11.1), not far from the nuclear power station at Sosnovyy Bor. For some moments, the target was completely motionless, but then it began to make the now familiar chaotic movements. Sometimes the target disappeared completely. Air traffic controllers and engineers observed the target visually for nearly twenty minutes. Later, they obtained permission to use the powerful computer that controls all air traffic in the St Petersburg vicinity, and it was discovered that the distance of the target varied from 65 to 73 kilometres. At 4.22 p.m., the target was completely motionless at 72 km, but suddenly it began to move in an east-south-east direction – without any acceleration – at a speed of 1,852 kph. No terrestrial aircraft or spacecraft is able to make such a manoeuvre.

Moments later, the target disappeared totally from the radar screen, but then reappeared above the vicinity of Sosnovyy Bor at 4.30 p.m., making the same chaotic manoeuvres. At about 5.45 p.m., the blip on the radar screen disappeared once more. Either the object simply moved too fast to be detected by radar, or it was able to conceal itself from the radar beams.

We have to ask ourselves if all these sightings were by pure chance. Sosnovyy Bor nuclear power station is of the same type as the one at Chernobyl. On 23 March 1992, at 2.37 a.m., a leak occurred in the third reactor, and because of this there was an increase in pressure in the lead mounting of the reactor, leading to a discharge of iodine and inert gases into the atmosphere. Immediately, the reactor was deactivated. Fortunately, there was no increase in radioactivity in St Petersburg, but it was nevertheless a very serious incident.

Are the ufonauts only observing our potentially dangerous nuclear power stations, or are they trying to prevent further tragic accidents? We can only speculate, but I have to say that I believe in the likelihood of both hypotheses.

MYSTERIOUS EXPLOSION AT SASOVO

The little town of Sasovo is about 300 kilometres east-south-east of Moscow. At 1.34 a.m. on 12 April 1991, half a mile from the south-west outskirts of Sasovo, an enormous explosion was heard. Many buildings and private houses were shaken by the blast, breaking windows, and shaking windows even 30 kilometres away in Chuykovo. At the site of the explosion was found a large crater with a diameter of about 28 metres and a depth of 3–4 metres. In the middle of the crater there was a raised section of earth about 3.5 metres in diameter. Huge clods of frozen soil were scattered around the crater up to a distance of 200 metres. Such was the force of the explosion that some of the clods were thrown so high into the air that they impacted deeply into the ground. According to experts, 25 tonnes of explosive would have been required to produce such effects.

The shock wave spread in a strange way. Poles carrying electricity 100 metres away, for example, remained totally undamaged. Military experts such as Colonel Prodan and Captain Matveyev (both qualified sappers) stated categorically that in their opinion the explosion at Sasovo was not an ordinary one. They gave their reasons as follows: there was a total absence of specific chemical products that are always found after an ordinary explosion; the 'hillock' in the middle of the crater is not something which is normally found; and the spread of the shock wave was not consistent with a standard explosion.

The newspaper *Komsomolskaia Pravda* published an account of the incident[7], which was limited to speculation, and in general failed to mention the following facts: (1) Immediately after the explosion, a sound like a jet fighter flying away from the area was heard; (2) An eyewitness stated that there was in fact the sound of *two* explosions, followed by a flash of light, and then the sound as of a jet fighter; (3) Another witness said that, just above the electric power line, 100 metres away from the crater, a bluish glow, similar to an arcing effect, could be seen.

Soviet Russia then published an article in which it was stated that fertilizer was the cause of the explosion. Certainly, fertilizer was present in that area, but military experts ruled out this explanation.

I paid little heed to this incident, but then, at the end of 1991, I was watching a TV programme when suddenly my attention was drawn to an interview with a militia officer from Sasovo, who said that, just before the explosion, he personally observed a brightly illuminated sphere-like object in the direction of the explosion site. Speculations that a jet fighter was involved in the incident were ruled out officially, so perhaps a UFO was somehow involved in this mysterious explosion.

SIGHTING BY THE CREW OF FLIGHT 2523

At 1.35 a.m. on 20 August 1991, Aeroflot Flight 2523 took off from Voronezh Airport, heading for St Petersburg. One of the passengers on board was Igor Yadigin, the aviation mechanic whose story of a close encounter near Voronezh Airport is described earlier.

At about 2.05 a.m., one of the crew members invited Yadigin to the flight deck. As he entered, Igor was shaken by an extraordinary sight in the sky (Fig. 11.2).

The jet was flying at an altitude of about 10,000 metres. To the right could be seen a sphere-like object, emerald in colour. The sphere was surrounded by a milky white hemisphere, through which the stars were visible.

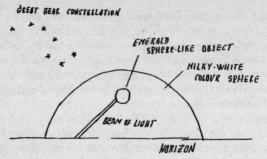

Fig. 11.2 *(Nikolai Lebedev)*

Above and to the left of his viewpoint could be seen the
Great Bear constellation. From the central sphere, a beam
of light extended to the ground. In the estimation of the
crew members, the diameter of the central sphere was
about 400–800 metres, and it was stationary at a
distance of not less than 50 kilometres. Igor and the crew
members then noticed the navigation lights of a jet, which
was changing its course in order to avoid the sphere. In
Igor's opinion, the size of the jet was that of a grain
compared to a plate. The total duration of the sighting
was about fifteen minutes, after which the apparition
simply vanished.

STALIN'S INTEREST IN UFOs

In 1991, an interesting interview with V. Burdakov of the
Russian Academy of Sciences was published in the
Workers' Tribune[7]. According to the academician, one
of our early chief rocket scientists, S. P. Korolev, was
invited to the MGB (Ministry of State Security – later the
KGB) headquarters in Moscow in early July of 1947. The
MGB chief explained to Korolev that the invitation was
made by Stalin.

Korolev was shown to a special apartment and was
given many foreign documents dealing with UFOs [some
believed to relate to the so-called Roswell incident of July
1947 – Ed.], together with a team of translators. Three

days later, he was invited to a meeting with Stalin, who asked him his opinion. Korolev replied that the UFOs did not appear to be weapons of a potential enemy, but that the phenomenon was real. According to Korolev, other leading scientists – Kurchyatov, Topchiev and Keldish – were also asked for an opinion, and they came to the same conclusion.

Burdakov commented that Korolev himself had observed a UFO over the launch pad at Baikonur in 1962 – a disc-shaped object with four beams of light coming down. I should point out that Korolev was at that time a man with practically unlimited power in his field. It was he who had supported and equipped an expedition to investigate the extraordinary incident which had occurred in Tunguska, Siberia, on 30 June 1908, when many witnesses observed a very bright object which appeared to crash and explode above the ground, causing damage similar to that caused by the Hiroshima atom bomb in 1945. In Korolev's opinion, the blast was caused by an extraterrestrial vehicle.

In the article, Burdakov said that UFOs are not merely an atmospheric phenomenon, but may be material, technological craft. He added that he had seen a report on the subject prepared by a group of Soviet academicians, dated in the mid-1950s, stating that a fragment of material, cone-shaped with a blunted top, had been examined. The structure of the material was crystalline, and it was concluded that it was not of terrestrial origin.

SIGHTINGS OVER CHELYABINSK AND ST PETERSBURG

On 12 April 1992, at 2.00 p.m., I was watching the television programme called *Vesti* in St Petersburg, when it was announced that, according to a TASS News Agency report, a brilliant star-like object had been seen in a cloudless sky over Chelyabinsk. Moments later, the object began to descend, and then a triangular shape with bright lights at each end could be seen, as it hovered above the houses in the town. It then flew off, but five minutes later returned, only to fly away again.

A similar object was observed by Anna Gromova directly above St Petersburg, at 3.35 a.m. on 17 November 1991. The object was motionless and triangular in shape, high above the houses, its apparent size similar to that of the full moon. Through the window of her apartment she then noticed another, similar object, higher than the first one. At 4.35 a.m. she retired to bed. The witness wrote to me and later telephoned to discuss the experience. Although rather elderly, I found her to be completely rational and credible.

TRAGIC INCIDENT IN TURKMENISTAN

Turkmenistan is one of the Turkic republics of the former Soviet Union. On 25 May 1990, during daytime, a giant disc-shaped object hovered at an altitude of about 1,000 metres above the town of Mary. It was reddish-orange in colour, with what looked like portholes on the rim, and had an estimated diameter of 300 metres. Military personnel observed it from a distance of no more than 3,000 metres.

Fig. 11.3   (Nikolai Lebedev)

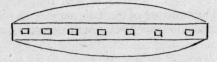

The airspace in that region was under strict control at the time, due to the war in Afghanistan. All Soviet Air Defence Forces were divided into regional Air Defence armies, and the area around Mary was under the control of the 12th Air Defence Army, whose Air Defence division was under the command of Colonel Anatoli Kurkchy. When informed about the UFO, Kurkchy gave the order to fire three ground-to-air guided missiles at it. The UFO made a slight horizontal manoeuvre, and three beams of light which had been coming from its port side disintegrated the missiles. Colonel Kurkchy then gave the order to scramble two 2-seat interceptor aircraft, but at a point about 1,000 metres from the disc they appeared to be thrown to the ground, killing the pilots and destroying the aircraft.

Colonel Kurkchy was immediately removed from his post by the Army Command, and proceedings were instituted against him (under Paragraph 1, Item 5 of the Turkmenistan Criminal Procedures Code) by military prosecutors of the 12th Air Defence Army. However, according to my source, who spoke with the military prosecutor's department, the investigations were suddenly halted and all information connected with the event was made secret. Later I learned that the squadron in which the four pilots had served was disbanded.

I had difficulty trying to persuade my source to allow me to publish this story, but eventually he agreed. The article appeared in the *St Petersburg Evening* in November 1991[8]. Strangely, the editor deleted some very relevant details concerning the incident. I had appealed to those who had observed the disc to write to me at the newspaper office, and I gave my work phone number. Many interesting telephone calls ensued, two of which were particularly important. Both were from the Air Defence Staff of the Leningrad region. The first call was from General Kremenchuk, who stated that the information in the article was totally untrue. Had it been true, he explained, he would have learned about it. He promised to call the Air Defence division in the Mary region and find out if there was any factual basis for the story, asking me to phone him the following week. I did so.

General Kremenchuk informed me not only that the Air Defence division had no record of any incidents connected with UFOs or crashed aircraft, but that there was no one in the service by the name of Colonel Kurkchy. The next call came from a lieutenant-colonel [name known to me – Ed.] under General Kremenchuk, who also promised to try to obtain some information, but added that he did not believe that such an incident could have taken place. A few days later I called him back. Although unable to confirm or deny the information contained in my article, he told me that Colonel Kurkchy did in fact exist and was now commander of the Air Defence division in the large island of Novaya Zemlya (New Land). This northern territory has the second largest proving ground for nuclear weapons in the CIS, and because it is off-limits to civilians, it was impossible for me to get an interview with Kurkchy.

I should add that if military personnel are required to remain silent about top-secret matters, the KGB compel such personnel to sign an official document which includes a warning that in the event of the security oath being broken, they will be executed without any preliminary judicial inquiry. A retired KGB officer told me recently that there existed (in 1991, at least) a specially trained KGB unit whose task was to relocate those likely to break their security oath.

SIGHTING BY THE CREW OF A MILITARY TRANSPORT AIRCRAFT

On 18 April 1992, an unusual flying object was observed by the crew of a military transport plane flying in the vicinity of Komsomolsk-na-Amure, in the Far East territory of Russia. The pilots observed the object for over an hour, but no description of its shape was given in the article in which the story appeared, which was prepared by Colonel Usoltsev, a military correspondent for the *Red Star*. The UFO flew directly ahead of the plane on the same course, making a series of aerobatics, such as figures-of-eight and loops. Beams of light came from the object, coloured light green to pale blue. However, neither the on-board radar nor ground radar detected anything unusual[9].

Many sightings have been, and are continuing to be, reported in the Commonwealth of Independent States and independent republics, but space does not permit me to include them all. Let me conclude by reaffirming my conviction that the UFO question, seen in the light of extraterrestrials visiting Earth, is our government's most secret problem. It is known for a fact that many civilian and military scientists are directly involved in the study of UFOs but, for the most part, their findings are kept secret. In my opinion, they should be allowed to speak openly about it. It is a crime to insist on concealment: we have a duty as citizens of Earth to contravene the regulations. I am totally convinced that if we were to act openly and quickly, it would be impossible for government agencies to harm those who break their security oaths.

Our many UFO groups are divided [as elsewhere – Ed.]. Not all groups accept that UFOs are extraterrestrial in origin: it is a widespread opinion that they are nothing more than figments of the imagination or that they originate from other dimensions and are therefore purely parapsychological phenomena. Sometimes the attitude of these groups is determined by officers of the former KGB, who have infiltrated them, or is influenced by politicians. In the latter case, this is especially true in the republics, where the UFO situation is exploited for nationalistic purposes.

It is my belief that there is a so-called 'mother' civilization which gave birth to all life on our planet. The planet or planets from which this civilization originates does not exist in our solar system, but it has permanent bases therein. Finally, I am equally convinced that groups from other solar systems also visit us, using different types of spacecraft – and with varying motives.

Notes

1. *Trud*, 19 October 1991.
2. *Red Star*, 10 October 1991.
3. Leningrad TV News, 21 February 1992.
4. Lebedev, Nikolai: 'The Soviet Scene 1990', *The UFO*

Report 1992, ed. Timothy Good, Sidgwick & Jackson, London, 1991.
5. *Izvestia*, 9 November 1991.
6. See for example Vallee, Jacques: *UFO Chronicles of the Soviet Union: A Cosmic Samizdat*, Ballantine, New York, 1992; Creighton, Gordon: 'The UFO Landings at Voronezh', *The UFO Report 1991*, ed. Timothy Good, Sidgwick & Jackson, London, 1990.
7. *Rabochaya Tribuna*, 13 August 1991.
8. *Vecherni Peterburg*, 17 November 1991.
9. *Red Star*, 2 June 1991.

12
1992 ANIMAL MUTILATIONS UPDATE

Linda Moulton Howe

A graduate of Stanford University, Linda Howe has devoted her film and television career to documentary productions. She has received local, national and international awards for her documentaries about science, medicine and environmental issues, including *Fire in the Water* and *A Radioactive Water*. In 1979, as Director of Special Projects at the CBS TV station in Denver, Colorado, she began researching the animal mutilations mystery. The result was an Emmy award-winning documentary, *A Strange Harvest*[1].

In 1983 Linda began to work as an independent film producer on a contract for Home Box Office. In April that year she was invited to Kirtland AFB, New Mexico, where she was shown an alleged presidential briefing paper describing contact with 'extraterrestrial biological entities', and was promised official material, including film, confirming this, for inclusion in a UFO documentary for HBO that she was working on at the time. The promise was never fulfilled.

In 1989 Linda Howe published her book, *An Alien Harvest: Further Evidence Linking Animal Mutilations and Human Abductions to Alien Life Forms*[2], which is a synthesis of ten years of research into these mysteries. In 1991 she produced *Sightings: The UFO Report* for the Fox Television Network, and her next TV production is about global survival issues.

In the cold winter nights of December 1991 to January 1992, something was haunting Oklahoma, Kansas and Missouri, leaving dead and mutilated cattle in its wake. One couple, driving down a country lane after dark, saw two bright objects moving low in the sky. 'As one got over the road above us, it blinked out,' said Mike Markum of Cement, Oklahoma. 'The other object stopped and started – that's what caught my attention. We heard no sound.'

Markum and his wife report that they have seen several 'sparkler-like balls' going over their house at low altitude. Once, one of these objects shot off at tremendous speed and left a green trail.

By the end of January, five Oklahoma Counties (Grant, Blaine, Garfield, Kingfisher and Commanche), Sumner County in Kansas and Webster County in Missouri, had about thirty reports of mysteriously killed and mutilated animals. Even though satanic cults or predators are the socially accepted explanation for the mutilations in these counties, Sheriff Archie Yearick in Grant County told me that he was puzzled 'because there aren't any tracks around any of these carcasses'.

That same comment has been made by law enforcement officers and ranchers since the animal mutilation mystery began in September 1967 when a horse named Lady was found in the San Luis Valley of Colorado, stripped of flesh from the neck up. Lady's hoof tracks stopped 100 feet from where her body was found. Residents had seen odd lights and 'small jets' moving low and rapidly over the desert. Worldwide news articles cited speculations that UFOs and the mare's strange death were connected.

When I began research for my documentary, *A Strange Harvest*, in 1979, I did not set out to do a film about an alien life form connection. But that is what I found in several eyewitness accounts of orange, silent, glowing objects the size of football fields hovering above pastures where mutilated animals were later found, or beams of light observed shining down from 'silent helicopters' that illuminated pastures 'brighter than daylight', and where mutilated animals were also found the next day. I also investigated reports by eyewitnesses who had observed strange craft and/or non-human creatures involved with animals.

In 1983, a Missouri couple watched through binoculars as two small beings in tight-fitting silver suits 'floated a paralyzed black cow into a craft'. The alien heads were large and white-coloured. Nearby, a tall, green-skinned 'lizard man' stood glaring, its eyes slit with vertical pupils like those of a crocodile.

In 1980, a Waco, Texas rancher watched one morning as two 4-foot-tall creatures with large, slanted black eyes carried a calf between them. He was terrified and ran away. Three days later he had the courage to go back to the scene with his wife and son. There they found the mutilated calf's body. The hide was completely intact and included the hooves and the skull bone, but the muscles and internal organs, as well as most of the skeletal structure, were missing. The hide was turned inside out and folded neatly on the ground next to the backbone, from which all the ribs had been removed. 'Who would do this, and what are they trying to tell us?' the rancher asked me.

Since I began research into the animal mystery in 1979, no year has passed without mutilation reports. 1992 was no exception.

OKLAHOMA, KANSAS AND ARKANSAS

On 25 January 1992, a cow was found dead near Okemah, Oklahoma. The udder had been cut bloodlessly from the animal and was found lying on the ground. The right chest was slit and an Okfuscee County Sheriff Deputy assumed that the heart had been removed. But no veterinarian was asked to do a necropsy. Without any hard evidence, the deputy's report simply stated 'Motive: Satanic Ritual'. But even he was surprised about how precisely the cuts had been made without any blood residue.

On Saturday, 2 February, MUFON Oklahoma investigator Chuck Pine travelled to Garfield, Kingfisher and Grant County Sheriffs' offices to help get more details about the January mutilations. Grant County Sheriff

Archie Yearick said that that morning he received a call from the police in Caldwell, Kansas, about a fresh steer mutilation there. Chuck proceeded north over the border and travelled with a police officer to the mutilation site. He retrieved tissue samples from the mutilator's cuts as well as unaffected tissue for comparison, preserved them in formalin solution and sent them via Federal Express to Dr John Altshuler, a pathologist and haematologist in Denver, Colorado.

Dr Altshuler and I have been working together since 1989 in an effort to gather as many mutilation tissue samples as possible for microscopic examination. So far, the microscope has shown that tissue from animals (including rabbits, deer, horses and cattle) have been cut with high heat in the hundreds of degrees (Fahrenheit), as evidenced in the cooked haemoglobin and other cell changes. In one 1990 Oregon case, the tissue was serrated as if cut with pinking shears. Both Dr Altshuler and the Oregon State Diagnostic Laboratory confirmed that high heat had been used at those excision lines. Dr Altshuler found the same heat-induced cell changes in the Caldwell, Kansas, steer.

The following Tuesday, 11 February 1992, there were two more reports of cattle mutilations at Calumet, Oklahoma, 10 miles west of El Reno. The first was found by Robert Jacobs and his son Travis Dean on the morning of 6 February. Half of the Brahma steer's tongue was removed; a bloodless, oval excision had removed the genitals, and the rectum was cored out (see photo section). No blood or tracks were in evidence.

That evening, Travis took his girlfriend, Julie Hamilton, back to the field to show her what had happened. It was about 8.15 p.m. when they saw a light above their field. 'It was about ten times brighter than a star,' they reported. 'As we drove closer, we began to see different coloured lights on the edge. They were red, yellow, blue and white. They flashed at random, not sequentially.'

When they got to within about three-quarters of a mile

from the object, Julie became frightened and they returned to town. The object rose higher in the sky and followed them. 'We were doing about 80 mph, and by the time we reached town, it had gone past us,' they said.

After dropping off Julie at her house, Travis picked up his father and went back to the field, where they saw the light again over the pasture. Robert said he could clearly see the different colours flashing on the object. They tried to approach it in the pick-up truck, but the light moved away and disappeared. After a few minutes, the light reappeared, moving to the southeast before disappearing again.

The following Monday afternoon, 10 February, another steer, a Hereford, was found dead and mutilated in the same pasture. As in the Brahma steer case of 6 February, the front half of the tongue had been removed, the left ear was gone, a neat excision had removed the genitals, and the rectum was cored out (see photographs).

After midnight on 3 March, back in Okemah, Oklahoma, three men saw a grey, diamond-shaped object with 'windows', which landed, then took off. The witnesses estimated the object's diameter to be over 30 feet.

On 9 March, again in Okemah, a cow was found with its udder cleanly and bloodlessly excised from the belly. There was also a large hole on the cow's left side. 'Like a bullet hole', some said – but there was no exit hole and no bullet. There was also blood on the ground near the cow's head, which is not typical.

On 4 March, Benton County Sheriff Deputy Danny Varner went to meet Bill Cowger at Tyson's Hog Farm, near Hiwasse, Arkansas. An eight-year-old cow was lying on her right side. The left eye was missing, the tongue had been removed, and a large piece of hide measuring 20 by 30 inches had been removed between the back legs, taking the udder with it (see photographs). The cut was only hide deep. Muscle tissue underneath was untouched.

Sergeant Varner's investigation report states as follows:

I found the cow's tongue had been removed by someone [using] a very sharp instrument. The tongue was cut diagonally from side to side, approximately 6 to 8 inches from the cow's front teeth. The cow's left eye had been removed. The cow's udder and hide were removed by a very sharp instrument, no damage was done to the stomach wall and the cuts looked to be [those] of a surgeon. The cow's vaginal area looked to be enlarged and pulled outwards. The ground surrounding the cow had no indications [she] had struggled and I was unable to find any footprints around the cow. A small amount of blood was found on and around the cow.

On Monday, March 9, 1992, I contacted Dr Marion Harris, a veterinarian from Gravette, Arkansas. I asked Dr Harris if a cow's internal organs could be removed by entering the cow's vagina. [He] stated that organs could be removed through the vaginal tract if the cow had recently had a calf about 6 weeks prior to her death. I asked Dr Harris if he would do an autopsy on the cow and he stated he would.

On Thursday, March 12, 1992, at 2 p.m., I, Det. Sgt Sam Blankenship and Bill Cowger met Dr Harris at the property where the cow was found. Dr Harris was unable to determine if any organs were missing because of waiting 8 days before an autopsy was attempted.

MISSOURI

The period of February–March 1992 also included reports of eleven mutilated cows in Webster County, Missouri, east of Springfield. At the same time, people reported seeing strange lights in the sky over Northview. The Highway Patrol said that so many people were parking along the Interstate 44 Northview exit to look for UFOs that it was a safety hazard.

Tissue samples from nine of the mutilations were sent to Dr Altshuler, who found evidence of high heat at the excision lines and a hardened 'plasticized' edge, which is not consistent with typical lasers. Even a portable laser is the size of a large freezer and requires a large electric generator.

'If you could afford one, why would you lug it out to a field in the middle of the night where a farmer might take a shot at you for messing with his cows?' asked Duane Bedell, co-director of the MUFON chapter in Webster County. 'And how are the cows killed without a struggle, no tracks and no blood?'

One farmer, Joe Bouldin, said that his cow's throat had been slit, the oesophagus removed and the teats sliced off the udder. 'But there were no marks on the ground anywhere,' said Bouldin. 'It's real mysterious.'

A necropsy revealed that most of the blood had been drained from the cow. But the ground was dry. 'How do you drain a cow of blood without spilling any?' Bouldin asked. 'I've never carried a gun before in my life, but now we are carrying a loaded gun in our truck. That's how I feel about all this.'

Another troubled farmer was Edwina Ragsdale. 'It's just like the cows were embalmed,' she said. 'We went out there last week [February 1992] and there was a faint smell of decay, but they should have deteriorated by now.'

Asked what she thought was responsible, she replied, 'UFOs or cults – they both scare me.'

I have also seen an 'embalmed' animal. In May 1980 when I was producing *A Strange Harvest*, a rancher east of Colorado Springs (Colorado) found one of his horses dead and mutilated. As often happens, mutilations are not reported for several days. In this case, the crew and I filmed about twenty days after the horse was first found dead. The weather had been warm, but there were still no maggots. Another week later, after the horse had been dead for a month, maggots emerged. But when we cut into the horse's flanks to take tissue samples, the muscle was bright red. I asked a local veterinarian if that was normal. He said it was not, and that there should have been decayed tissue.

In April 1992, mutilations were reported in Liberty, Mississippi, and Leduc, Alberta (Canada). In Liberty, two cows had been found with half the face hide removed and tongues cut out. The three-day-old calf was found with its head and hind feet missing, with no trace of blood or tracks.

CANADA

On 14 April 1992, ranchers Dorothea and Roman Verchomin discovered the first of six mutilated cows on their farm in Leduc, Alberta. This was a twenty-year-old Holstein milk cow that Mrs Verchomin had raised and kept to provide extra milk during the calving season.

She was a quiet, docile cow, and Mrs Verchomin said she does not understand what could have separated her from the herd. The cow had not been dead more than six hours when she was found.

In the left shoulder was a hole 'like a bullet hole' that angled down into the chest, similar to the cow in Okemah, Oklahoma. As in the latter case, no bullet was recovered and no exit wound could be found. On the cow's throat was a 12-inch vertical cut just beside the jugular vein. There was also a cut around the rectum, approximately two inches deep into the hide, right through the hair, and the anus and vagina had been cut out (see photographs).

'Most notable was the absence of blood in and around the body,' wrote MUFON investigator Janice Semeniuk, working with Gordon Kijek, Director of the Alberta UFO Study Group. Mr and Mrs Verchomin called veterinarian Dr Wayne Sereda, and when he opened the cow on site, 'the flesh was unusually white', indicating the thorough removal of blood.

Mrs Verchomin said that the vet and Constable Coulombe, the Royal Canadian Mounted Police investigator, discussed how 'they' could drain so much blood out of the animal, while maintaining that predators were responsible for the kill. That conclusion upset Mrs Verchomin. 'I have never seen cuts like those on that cow,' she said. 'I followed the cuts with my finger: they were harder than the hide and every 2 inches there was a slight rise like a scalloped edge. The rest of the cows became very upset when they found her; their eyes rolled around and they bellowed and stampeded.'

After years of farming, Dorothea Verchomin is convinced that no predator could cut a cow that way. 'Coyotes don't even come on to our property,' she said, 'and they haven't bothered the herd in the past.'

Speculation about satanic cult activity raised the possibility that someone arrived quietly, perhaps by canoe, from the lake shore of Saunders Lake, which runs alongside the property. Yet there were no clues as to how the blood was drained from the cow without leaving any trace.

Mrs Verchomin remembered that she had let her dogs out the evening before and was awoken around 1.45 a.m. by their barking. Realizing she had not shut down the pump house, she took a flashlight into the yard. 'It was unusually quiet, even for the country,' she said. 'There was no noise whatsoever.' But she saw nothing unusual until the next morning, when the mutilated cow was found.

Then, between 14 June and 16 July 1992, Dorothea and Roman Verchomin found five more dead cattle on their farm. All six of the cows were found lying on their right side. The chronological list of these events is as follows:

14 April	20-year-old Holstein cow
14 June	250-pound Charolais Hereford calf
21 June	250-pound Hereford heifer calf
24 June	250-pound Hereford heifer calf
28 June	800-pound Hereford cow
16 July	800-pound Hereford cow

Mrs Verchomin estimates that the 14 June calf was found about two days after death. It was in a twisted position with the right side of the head and chest lying on the ground with front legs straight to the left, while the back half was flat to the ground with the hind legs spread apart. The left ear and eye were gone. A hole in the left side of the neck angled down into the chest. The tail was removed up to the tail bone. The rectum and vulva were cored out along with a large, oval-shaped piece of hide that extended from the rectum up between the back legs, along the belly to three ribs up on to the chest. All the internal organs had been cleanly removed and the internal cavity was dry and blackened in colour.

Again, Dr Sereda was called to examine the animal. This time he brought a veterinarian colleague along and stated that because the calf was decomposing he could not make a positive determination as to the cause of death. An RCMP investigator was also present, but neither photographs nor tissue samples were taken.

The 21 June calf was still warm when found dead near its mother's feet. The cow was standing guard over the body, a full mile from the rest of the herd. Mrs Verchomin took the carcass to the Provincial Laboratory veterinarian who commented that 'there is no such thing as cattle mutilations' and promptly determined that the calf had died 'due to overwhelming bacterial infection' – specifically *clostridium* bacteria. No excisions were made.

Three days later, on 24 June, 'we smelled another dead animal,' said Mrs Verchomin, and another 250-pound calf was discovered, decaying 60 yards from where yet a larger Hereford would be found on 28 June.

That 800-pound Hereford cow had an ear and eye missing, the tail was removed to the tail bone, the rectum and vagina had been cored out, and the udder had been excised in a 'perfect, round circle only hide deep, leaving the membrane tissue covering the muscles completely untouched'. Mrs Verchomin said that the pristine nature of the cuts on the perfectly preserved body astonished her. Constable Coulombe of the RCMP Leduc Detachment arrived to check the cow, but no vet was called because 'the body was already two or three days dead'. There were no signs of predators. 'In fact, the animal lay there for a full week and not even the coyotes touched it – not one bite! Finally, it decomposed. . . .' said Mrs Verchomin.

On 16 July, a two-year-old Hereford cow was found with the rectum cored out and one teat cleanly removed from the udder as if 'burned off'. Part of the tongue and several teeth were gone. On the left side of its neck was a 4-inch slit with a 1-inch wide and 2-inch deep hole in the middle of it.

Tissue samples were taken from the outer region of the rectum and vulva and forwarded to Dr Altshuler. He found the excision lines to be darkened and plasticized, and microscopic analysis revealed that the cells had been exposed to high heat.

CAT MUTILATIONS

Mutilation reports are not confined to cattle. They have included most domestic animals, such as cats. Since the 1970s, there have been waves of cat mutilations in Canada, California and Texas. From 15 May 1992 onwards, cats were found dead and mutilated in Vancouver, British Columbia. Typical was the case of the purebred Russian Blue cat that was put out in the evening and never came back. The back half of the cat was found three blocks from its owner's home, without a trace of blood. It was the fourth cat found cut in half in a two-week period. In the summer of 1991 in Plano, Texas – an upper middle class community north of Dallas – the police department received nearly one hundred reports of missing domestic cats, along with several mutilated ones.

A QUESTION OF SURVIVAL?

After *An Alien Harvest* was published in 1989, I received a letter from a security guard in Denver, Colorado, who described a night in August when he was patrolling the grounds of a large corporation west of the city. From his truck, he could see a large circle of lights in the dark sky. The lights remained stationary over a pasture a few hundred feet from his position. He never phoned anyone because he was afraid that if he uttered the word 'UFO' he might lose his job. But the next morning he felt guilty as he watched a farmer gather up two dead and mutilated cows from the pasture where the lights had hovered overhead. 'What kind of technology are we talking about?' he asked me. 'I never took my eyes off those lights. There was no beam, no sound – nothing. How did they do it?'

If alien life forms have been involved in nearly three decades of worldwide animal mutilations and disappearances, what is it the aliens need?

In 1980, Myrna Hansen and her young son saw two white-suited beings working on a cow near Cimarron, New Mexico. The cow was bellowing in pain and Myrna tried to interfere. The result was that both she and her son were apparently abducted by large, brightly lit discs which took them to an underground facility that Myrna thought was in the Las Cruces region. There she saw a humanoid figure floating in a vat of reddish liquid which she perceived to be a 'treatment' or 'sustenance' of some kind for the immersed being. She also thought the liquid was related to blood fluids and tissues removed from animals[3].

In 1973, abductee Judy Doraty observed a brown and white calf rise in a pale beam of yellow light. Later, during the abduction, she found herself inside a small, round white room, where she saw tissue being excised from the calf's eye, tongue and testicles by two small, grey-skinned creatures with large eyes. They had four long fingers but no thumb, tapering to dark nails. Their eyes were yellow with black vertical pupils like those of a cat or snake[4]. Judy's daughter, Cindy, was also abducted at the same time, and in a 1990 hypnosis session with psychiatric hypnotherapist John Carpenter she also reported seeing a calf rising in a beam of light. Judy had the clear impression that the alien operation on the calf had something to do with survival – theirs and ours.

In both the Cindy Doraty and Myrna Hansen cases, the women were examined by the beings, and in Myrna's case, eggs were removed in a painful procedure from her ovaries. In some cases, men and women have been shown 'baby things' which they are told are hybrids – part human and part something else.

If genetic material is what the alien intelligence wants, why does it need so much over so many years? And why does it leave animals to be found with strange, bloodless excisions that provoke fear and anger?

Notes

1. *A Strange Harvest*, produced by Linda Howe, 1980. Videotapes are available in the UK from Quest Publications International Ltd., 15 Pickard Court, Temple Newsam, Leeds, LS15 9AY, and in the US from Linda Moulton Howe Productions, PO Box 538, Huntingdon Valley, Pennsylvania 19006-0538.
2. Howe, Linda Moulton: *An Alien Harvest: Further Evidence Linking Animal Mutilations and Human Abductions to Alien Life Forms*, Linda Moulton Howe Productions, 1989. Available from the author or from Quest Publications International Ltd., 15 Pickard Court, Temple Newsam, Leeds, LS15 9AY.
3. Ibid., pp. 112–16.
4. Ibid., pp. 48–58, 300–39.

Editor's note

Further evidence for animal mutilations and their connection with UFOs is contained in my book, *Alien Liaison: The Ultimate Secret*, Century/Arrow Books, London, 1991/2, an updated edition of which is published by William Morrow (New York) as *Alien Contact: Top-Secret UFO Files Revealed*.

In May 1993 I visited Dr John Altshuler in Denver and examined many slides of tissue samples as well as actual hide from mutilated cattle. In comparison with control samples, the difference is extraordinary.

In Dr. Altshuler's opinion, the cat mutilations reported by Linda Howe (p. 199) are *not* related to the genuine phenomenon.

13
COSMIC JOURNEY: THE AFTERMATH

Bob Oechsler

Bob Oechsler (pronounced X-ler) interrupted his education at the University of Maryland to join the US Air Force in 1968, serving mostly with the American Forces Radio and Television Service in the continental United States. During the Vietnam War he served in Cambodia, Thailand and Laos, and some of his work during this period involved the filming of classified prototype weapons systems, requiring a Top Secret clearance.

On returning to the US, Bob spent a year and a half at Wright-Patterson AFB, then in 1972 left the USAF and returned to the University of Maryland. He next joined NASA at the Goddard Space Flight Center in Greenbelt, Maryland, as a mission specialist. Among the projects he was involved in were the International Ultraviolet Explorer and the Apollo-Soyuz Test Project.

Bob now runs his own company, Robots Internationale, Inc. He has pioneered the field of Mobilized Security Surveillance, drawing praise from the Chamber of Commerce, and he has lectured as a robotics expert at the Franklin Institute in Philadelphia. He is listed in several 'Who's Who' publications as well as the *International Book of Honour*, and has acted as technology consultant for science editor Jules Bergman of ABC News.

As a UFO specialist, Bob Oechsler is Assistant State Director for MUFON in Maryland, and he devotes a great deal of his time to research, including technical analysis of photographs and video films. Since 1987 he has hosted a nationwide radio programme, *UFOs Today*, and has appeared on all the major US TV networks as well as on many European and Japanese programmes. In addition, Bob has acted as a consultant for several major TV documentaries.

When Timothy Good first started interviewing me about my UFO research experiences, it was not my intention to contribute to a publication. Rather, the intention was to share information in order to obtain a critical peer review, drawing on Tim's vast research experience.

In retrospect, it is easy for me to understand why anyone – including government officials – would resort to total denial in order to avoid the type of ridicule that comes from those 'activists' who refuse to accept this phenomenon and its potential. For me, publication of the 'Cosmic Journey' chapter in *Alien Liaison* has created an awful dichotomy. Being shunned by colleagues in the UFO research business as a result of their failure to accept my findings makes me wish at times that I had not cooperated in this manner. On the other hand, the importance of the information reported will, I hope, contribute in the long run to a better understanding of the UFO phenomenon and its impact on human cultural evolution. The purpose of this essay is to give my own review of that final chapter of *Alien Liaison* and to respond to the controversy that its publication has generated.

Most of the controversy has stemmed from a review by Jerold R. Johnson in the *MUFON UFO Journal*[1], the official publication of the Mutual UFO Network, to which I responded in the same journal[2], and a self-circulated review penned by the controversial figure named Henry Azadehdel (Armenian-born insurance salesman and international orchid smuggler, according to the British *Independent Magazine*[3]), who represented himself to me as a UFO researcher named Dr Alan Jones, although he currently uses the alias of Dr Armen Victorian. The latter was how he represented himself to Admiral Bobby Ray Inman and is the name he used for his review.

The Cosmic Journey chapter details my personal credentials, including my work at NASA's Goddard Space Flight Center. Even my NASA employment (see photo section) was called into question by Jerold

Johnson, as well as my initial contact and subsequent telephone conversation with Admiral Inman, acknowledging the US Government's possession of alien disc technology; the follow-up entrée into the CIA and Naval Intelligence; the Cosmic Journey project (for which the space shuttle mock-up is now on display at the Kennedy Space Center); and the many connected events that unfolded, taking me into secret facilities and highlighted by an uncomfortable encounter with a humanoid possessing extraordinary capabilities, which left me astonished and an eyewitness companion bewildered.

The chapter describes the development of the Cosmic Journey project, which was to have been a massive travelling exhibition on the space programme, including a major UFO feature as the subject of one-third of the project which, had it been completed, would have acted as a public indoctrination programme supplemented by an independent programme directed at public schools. Public indoctrination into alien contact is a theme I have been reporting on since the publication in 1989 of my book, *The Chesapeake Connection*[4].

The major revelation of the chapter, however, was the transcript of part of my telephone conversation with Admiral Bobby Ray Inman, a former top intelligence chief whose posts have included Director of the National Security Agency, Director of Naval Intelligence, and Deputy Director of the CIA.

DEBUNKING TACTICS

In his scathing review of *Alien Liaison*, Jerold Johnson focused most of his attention on the Cosmic Journey chapter, and on his telephone conversations with various parties, including Admiral Inman, with whom he felt some camaraderie, having attended the same university.

Walt Andrus, Associate Editor of the *MUFON UFO Journal* and International Director of MUFON, sent me a note with a copy of Johnson's review, asking if I could document any of the claims in the book. I do not think that the problem is one of documentation, however, since attempts to provide validation for that documentation tend to develop into a never-ending battle. The real problem is that of prevailing bias, to which I will refer at the conclusion of this article.

What we find in critical reviews such as the one presented by Johnson is judgement by apparent distortion. For example, he postulates that the publishers of *Alien Liaison* might have been concerned about the threat of an injunction for openly discussing too many UFO 'official secrets'. He also comments that the author relied on informants 'without adequate primary source checks', and makes judgemental references to the claims, such as 'probably false'. All this contributes to a lack of proper journalistic investigation.

In these highly litigious days, I doubt that any publisher would permit the printing of anything not thoroughly covered with legal documentation by their attorneys. *Alien Liaison* was no exception, to which I can personally testify, since I was obliged to provide a letter confirming the accuracy of my claims in the book, which was then given to the publisher's lawyers. In addition, when short extracts of the Inman tape were aired during a *Now It Can Be Told* documentary in the USA in 1991, attorneys for Tribune Entertainment Company investigated the legality of the tape recording and backed the matter up in writing by agreeing to defend me and accept liability which might have arisen out of their decision to broadcast the excerpts.

It is no longer surprising to me that Bob Lazar – the nuclear physicist who claims to have carried out ultra-secret work on an extraterrestrial spacecraft for the US Office of Naval Intelligence in Nevada – has had extraordinary difficulty in validating his classified employment in the area of disc technology. Johnson and Victorian were unable to validate my *un*classified employment with NASA and resorted to apparent debunking tactics. For example, Johnson phoned NASA's Public Affairs Office at the Goddard Space Flight

Center and was informed that 'The title "mission specialist" is not something that is used around here; that's a title that NASA gives to an astronaut!' This implies, of course, that I had lied about or misrepresented my credentials. Had Johnson bothered to call me on the phone, I could have provided clarification. In the technical aspects of my former work at NASA in the mid-1970s we were referred to either as Operations Specialists or Mission Specialists. I worked mainly with Technical Mission Directives and was indeed referred to as a Mission Specialist. We had no contact with the Astronaut Corps except through communications monitoring during missions. I was unaware of the UFO phenomenon during my tenure at NASA and thus consider my employment there as irrelevant to the issue.

Johnson claims that I 'doggedly pursued retired Admiral Bobby Ray Inman ... for some years now hoping to get the Admiral to reveal an association with the "MAJESTIC TWELVE" group'. Johnson reveals his limited knowledge by suggesting that my assertions are, to his knowledge, the only connection between Inman and UFOs. My interest in researching Admiral Inman did not arise, in fact, until after I first met him in person while on assignment in May of 1988. The reason for introducing myself and asking about MJ-12 was as a direct result of my reading the well-known report published by John Lear in 1987 in which Inman was named as a possible current member of MJ-12.

When I asked Inman if he would put me in contact with someone in order to 'get closer to MJ-12', it was the lack of surprise in his acknowledgement without question that made me curious about him. Still, it was fourteen months before I contacted him again, and that was at the request of Timothy Good, during a visit he made to the United States in July 1989. Then, following the incredible revelations in Inman's return telephone call, I still waited for about two years before permitting the contents of the conversation and the identity of the caller to be published. After all, the Admiral was kind enough to provide me with some guidance in pursuit of my prime objective, which was to obtain access to a recovered craft for civilian research, and it seemed more pertinent to follow through on the leads he provided. The relationship cooled after I invited him to give a keynote address at the Ozark UFO Conference the next year.

The subject matter of the conversation that I had with Admiral Inman became an issue of contention with both Johnson and Victorian, in that Inman initially denied having discussed the subject of UFOs with me. Nonetheless, Ron Pandolfi, who works at the CIA Headquarters in Langley, Virginia, in the Office of Scientific & Weapons Research, having a personal interest in the UFO subject, arranged to meet with Admiral Inman in the latter's Roslyn, Virginia, office. After validating my meeting with Everett Hineman, the CIA Deputy Director for Science & Technology, Pandolfi asked Admiral Inman if he had in fact talked to me about UFOs. Inman did not deny that such a conversation had taken place, but was unwilling to discuss any details.

Johnson questioned my 'convoluted' questioning style during the conversation with Inman. But the last thing I wanted to do was make use of inaccurate phraseology and scare off the Admiral by leading him to think I was some sort of kook. 'Aliens', 'ETs' and 'UFOs' were therefore off-limits in the discussion. For all I knew, if the government did possess non-human-made craft, they certainly weren't 'unidentified'. I chose therefore to use terms such as 'crafts', 'phenomenon', 'recovered vehicles', and phrases such as 'intelligence behind the crafts'. I attempted to appeal to his technological interests in a sort of respectful camaraderie. I asked for guidance. I got more than I expected.

THE INMAN TRANSCRIPT

The telephone conversation took place at 8.00 a.m. EDT on Thursday, 20 July 1989. Admiral Inman was return- ing a call from the previous Friday, when I spoke (in the presence of Timothy Good) with his executive assistant, Tom King. The latter had accepted that call on behalf of the Admiral, who was on the west coast but was expected to return the following week, at which time, King said, he would have the Admiral return my call.

When the phone rang in my kitchen and the caller said 'This is Bob Inman', I asked to be excused in order to fetch my notes, and of course switch on the tape recorder which had become a matter of common procedure during my research, for note-taking purposes. I presumed that the Admiral was unaware of the fact that the conversation was being recorded. Here follows the transcript of that conversation. I have used the abbreviations 'BOB' for myself and 'BRI' for Inman. The additional clarifying commentary is in italics.

BOB ... Yes, thank you very much for returning my call.
BRI You're most welcome.
BOB Do you remember who I am?
BRI Unfortunately I do not, I apologize.
BOB OK, well we met at the University of Science – University of Maryland Science and Technology ...
BRI I do pull out, now, I thank you.

This sudden abrupt recollection is important because it indicates that the Admiral did in fact consider our brief meeting in May of 1988 to be worthy of recollection. It was during that brief encounter that I asked if he would be good enough to have someone get in touch with me, relative to how I could get closer to MJ-12, again indicating that MJ-12 meant something to him. If MJ-12 represents anything relative to the UFO phenomenon, then the Admiral is clearly aware of the subject-matter pending in this conversation, which, he was advised by Tom King from my prior call, and at the recommendation of Tim, involved a matter that was classified as 'SCI' – Sensitive Compartmented Information.

BOB I wanted to for one thing on behalf of myself, I was

looking for some guidance that I hoped you might be able to afford me . . .

BRI OK.

BOB . . . in giving some kind of direction in how I can assist in this project. I've been spending a great deal of time researching the phenomenon and technologically I think I might have some very interesting things to offer . . .

BRI Uh huh.

BOB . . . Probably not nearly as much as it was, what you probably already know. But I certainly would like to get some guidance in a number of different areas. It's probably a situation where I would like to at some point get together with you, and get an overview of what direction I might take in which I might be able to help in. On behalf of Admiral Lord Hill-Norton, and Mr Good, the best I can do there is, I have no idea what the level of security crossing countries happens to be. And I really don't want to get too much involved in that end of it – I'll leave that to your discretion.

BRI What is Peter Hill-Norton doing now?

BOB What is he doing right now?

BRI Yeah.

Obviously I was unprepared for this question, having no idea what Admiral Lord Hill-Norton's first name was nor what activities he was currently engaged in.

BOB As far as I know he is working in the background of things. He has worked extensively with Timothy Good in a publication he has put out, *Above Top Secret*, which you may or may not be aware of, out by William Morrow out of New York.

BRI I am not – aware of it.

BOB OK, in any case he is working – they are more or less working together, Timothy Good as a consultant. Admiral Lord Hill-Norton is, as the way he's expressed it to me, quite furious with his inability to gain knowledge on the issues . . .

BRI [Muffled acknowledgement]

*It is important to note that, by his muffled acknowledge-
ment, Admiral Inman appears to understand the
dilemma here and recognizes the inferred subject matter.*

BOB ... And he in fact sent Timothy Good here on a
tour hoping to find out more information. There was a
conference in Las Vegas at the end of June, the first
couple of days in July, where he had hoped to pick up
some contact information. And I had suggested to him
that the only individual I knew that possibly would be
able to help him – if it was indeed possible to gain any
information across country boundaries – would be
through you. And I suggested that that contact be
made.

BRI What is the general area of interest?

*This is perhaps the first clue that the Admiral wants
confirmation of the issues, or that he perhaps wants to
narrow the scope of the inquiry.*

BOB Two things. One, it's my feeling from my research
that there is a dichotomy of sorts, one in which there
seems to be an indoctrination programme to educate
the public to the realities that are involved here. The
other must be a problem relating to security measures
and the need-to-know level. I have the ability to
control the influence and understanding and accept-
ability of a great, great mass of the public. I have a
nationwide radio broadcast – regular radio broadcast
on the subject matter. I'm well written amongst all of
the publications. I am connected with all the major
organizations. I've investigated – I spent eighteen
months investigating, including field investigations
involving the Gulf Breeze situation. I know all the
internals on that. And I have focused a great deal on
the technological end of the technologies, and I've
studied a great deal of the things that have been going

wrong along in the Chesapeake Bay, in connection with the Electromagnetic Continuity Analysis Center and with the EMP projects.

Four important points here: (1) a programme to indoctrinate the public; (2) acknowledgement that the Admiral is speaking to a journalist; (3) 'Field investigations' in Gulf Breeze, Florida, where the Joint Chiefs of Staff met (at Pensacola Naval Air Station) in August 1988 amidst an invasion of UFO activity, and (4) EMP (Electro-Magnetic Pulse) projects which were acknowledged in the Washington Post *to be electromagnetic pulse weapons that were being developed in order to keep pace with the Soviet 'zap gun'. Since the Soviets were based right there in the Chesapeake Bay where the testing was being conducted, whom are we supposed to think the weapons were designed to be used against? A 'threat from outer space', perhaps, to which President Reagan had referred publicly on several occasions?*

BRI All of those are areas in which I am vastly out of date. When I made the decision to retire seven years ago, I made a conscious decision to sever ongoing ties with the US intelligence community. I have had some exposure on limited occasions, to some areas of activity over the succeeding seven years when I did the Embassy Security Survey as a consultant to the Defense Science Board. But overwhelmingly my efforts in these seven years have been focused on industrial competitiveness . . .

BOB Right.

BRI . . . on the application of science and technology in the commercial world.

BOB I am aware of that.

BRI So for many of the things, at least as I sort of infer from the conversation, of the interest of Mr Good and Peter Hill-Norton, they are areas where while I had some expertise, it's now, you know, seven years old.

211

The Admiral seems to confirm here that the areas he infers from the conversation are areas where he at some point had some expertise, which he later narrows down to a period between 1979 and 1982, when he knew and worked with the Deputy Director of Science and Technology at the CIA. He served as NSA director from 1977–81 and Deputy Director of CIA from 1981 until his retirement in 1982.

BOB I see.

BRI And the pace at which things move in that field, the odds of my being accurate are increasingly remote, in understanding those things.

Again, to recognize 'the pace at which things move in that field' suggests he has no reservations about the subject matter to which we are referring.

BOB Is it your understanding that there is a cultural dialogue going on . . . [*long pause*] . . . today?

BRI Well I guess I'd have to ask with whom? Between what parties?

(A smile can be 'heard' on the tape.)

BOB Well, between any of the parties that presumably are behind the technology in the crafts.

BRI I honestly don't know. Have no exposure at all. So I haven't a clue whether there are any ongoing dialogues or not. I'm trying to think who there in the Washington area that is at least much closer to the issues, might be able to at least give you some guidance.

His immediate response without pause indicates no confusion in the use of the term 'crafts' and again suggests an understanding of what is being referred to. His later commentary regarding 'whether as time has evolved, they are beginning to become more open on it', suggests that he understands who is behind 'the technology in the crafts'.

BOB That's what I'm looking for. I'm not looking to step on any toes. I think I have some things to offer and I would like to participate. And to be frank with you, you are essentially the only one I would feel safe in getting guidance from at this point . . .

BRI Uh huh.

BOB . . . Based on the more I know . . .

BRI Yeah.

BOB . . . the more concerned I become with how I should handle what I know.

BRI The Deputy Director for Science and Technology at CIA is named Ev – Everett Hineman. He is in fact getting ready to retire in the very near future. That may make him somewhat more willing to have dialogues than he otherwise would have had. When I knew him in the period seven to ten years ago, he was a person of very substantial integrity and just good common sense. So as a place to start he would clearly be high on the list. In the retired community of those who nonetheless were exposed to the intelligence business and stayed reasonably close to it, there is a retired rear admiral, a former Director of Naval Intelligence named Sumner Shapiro, who has been a vice-president of BDM. I think he just retired.

The commentary regarding Hineman suggests that someone may be willing to publicize the activities we are discussing. It seems pertinent to reiterate that the Admiral knows he is speaking with a journalist.

BOB VDM?

BRI BDM. It's a corporation there in the McLean area. His level of competence again is very high, his integrity is very high. Whether he has any knowledge in the areas you are working on I don't have a clue, because I don't have any ongoing dialogue with him. But those are at least two thoughts for you that are there in the area where you are located. And who have a prospect of still having some currency. I don't know that they do. In my case, I don't have any.

The BDM corporation was behind the conference on cattle mutilations, organized by Senator Harrison Schmitt in 1979.

BOB   Do you anticipate that any of the recovered vehicles would ever become available for technological research? Outside of the military circles?

BRI   Again, I honestly don't know. Ten years ago the answer would have been no. Whether as time has evolved they are beginning to become more open on it, there's a possibility. Again, Mr Hineman probably would be the best person to put that kind of question to.

The acknowledgement that 'recovered vehicles', previously referred to as 'crafts', were being studied ten years ago, and that access to them was then denied, confirms their existence. 'Beginning to become more open' suggests possible public exposure and confirms previous secrecy.

BOB   OK.

BRI   Well good luck to you.

BOB   OK. And also Louis Cabot has become quite interested in . . .

BRI   Good.

BOB   . . . some of my findings, so you may hear from him.

BRI   OK. He's a good man.

BOB   OK.

BRI   Thank you.

BOB   Very good. Thank you for calling.

BRI   Bye.

BOB   Bye-bye.

NATIONAL SECRECY LAWS

My meeting with Everett Hineman at CIA Headquarters took place on 10 August 1989 and lasted for forty-five minutes, during which we discussed several proposals, all related to the UFO phenomenon. A follow-up telephone conversation with Hineman on 1 September 1989 revealed that he had had access to 'some folks' who were familiar with the Bob Lazar case.

Subsequent correspondence with Admiral Inman led to a response by his executive assistant (recorded on my answering machine) that the Admiral regarded the subject matter as being covered under 'national secrecy laws', and asked that his name not be used without his permission in regard to these matters. The latter comments were in direct reference to my letter to the Admiral dated 29 March 1990, which was specifically referenced on the tape.

In his review, Johnson reports that he asked Admiral Inman if the quote in *Alien Liaison* about 'recovered vehicles' was essentially correct. 'What kind of vehicles is he talking about?' asked Inman, to which Johnson responded that the whole book was concerned with 'flying saucers'. 'That's totally out of context,' said Inman. 'The conversation I recall . . . the reference was to *underwater* vehicles.'

In a reply to a letter from Armen Victorian, Inman stated that: 'Having no prior knowledge of Mr Oechlers [sic] interest, I did not understand until well into his dialogue that his research was about Unidentified Flying Objects.' That hardly seems like the 'underwater vehicles' reported in Johnson's review.

Since Inman's executive assistant had confirmed by voice message on my telephone answering machine that these matters were covered under national secrecy laws, I presume that this fact could compel one to mislead in any manner necessary. We must not forget that when Johnson spoke with Inman and Shapiro *et al*, he made it clear that he was going to publish a review. When I spoke with these people, the issue was guidance – not publication.

AUTHENTICATION

In order to set the record straight and to respond to those who have seen fit to dismiss my claims, I arranged to have Dr Bruce Maccabee, a US Navy physicist who is well known for his thorough investigations into UFO cases, review all of the evidence, including signatures and recordings regarding the revelations of Admiral Inman. In an officially signed statement [copy on file – Ed.] Dr Maccabee states as follows:

Having reviewed a conversation and verbatim transcript (the former of which was recorded for notational purposes on July 20, 1989), I can verify the following as a true and accurate representation of a conversation where Mr Oechsler is seeking guidance in getting access to a recovered vehicle or craft. B. R. Inman indirectly acknowledges US Government possession of such craft and provides the names of individuals for Mr Oechsler to contact who might be able to provide additional guidance in gaining access to such craft or vehicles.

I have also reviewed a series of correspondence bearing the signature of B. R. Inman in which he acknowledges on August 5, 1991, that the subject matter of the above referenced conversation involved 'unidentified flying objects'. See direct quote below,

Signed below this date of August 13, 1991
[Signed] Bruce. S. Maccabee, Ph. D.
I hereby testify by my signature above that this is a true and correct representation without distortion or misrepresentation.
'*Having no prior knowledge of Mr Oechlers interest, I did not understand until well into his dialogue that his research was about Unidentified Flying Objects.*'

The confirmed revelations of Admiral Inman that the US Government possesses UFO technology may shed some light on another controversial issue; that of Bob Lazar, who has provided some evidence that he may have worked on such a craft (see *Alien Liaison*). When I last spoke with Everett Hineman, he gave me the impression that Lazar's claims may be valid, but misinterpreted. 'I come to different conclusions than you do,' he told me. In fact, I had not offered any conclusions, but I now believe that Bob Lazar was an unwitting participant in a plan to release information regarding the US Government's involvement with extraterrestrial hardware, perhaps as part of an elaborate indoctrination programme.

FURTHER DENIALS

If Jerold Johnson really wanted to prove the issues I brought out in *Alien Liaison*, he should at least have contacted me. Had he done so, he might have obtained some guidance from my methodology of approaching individuals such as Admiral Inman, especially regarding these sensitive issues.

According to Johnson, when he asked the Admiral if he had indeed suggested the names referenced, the apparent response was quite curious. 'Yes, I did,' said Inman, 'but Oechsler misrepresented himself as approaching those gentlemen *at my urging*, which was not the case . . . I only provided names for him to contact.'

The plain fact of the matter is that Inman clearly indicated that he was aware of these recovered craft, but had not been involved with the issue for seven years. Inasmuch as he was Mr Hineman's boss during his tenure at the CIA, Inman suggested that Hineman would be the best person to question regarding the prospects of a research team gaining access to one of these craft. He indicated that he did not feel qualified to project what those prospects were, since the 'pace at which things move in that field' exceeded his level of understanding. My exact words to both Hineman and Shapiro were: 'Bob Inman suggested that we meet'. I never suggested to anyone that Inman urged me to do anything. When asked about the subject matter of the requested meeting, I indicated that the matter was SCI – Sensitive Compartmented Information [at my suggestion – Ed.].

It is interesting to note that Johnson claims, 'We [no

party other than Johnson was mentioned] called Admiral Inman on the phone, and he was cordial and forthcoming in his answers to our specific and unambiguous questions.' Inman's answers to Johnson, however, were far different from the ones I received. Somehow the 'intelligence behind the crafts', 'recovered vehicles' and 'phenomenon' miraculously came to represent 'underwater vehicles'. Flying saucers became totally out of context.

COSMIC JOURNEY MISREPRESENTED

Throughout his lengthy review, Johnson continued to take issue with every little detail, such as the quiet, faintly marked helicopters that we flew in during a project visit to Houston. My claims do not seem so outrageous today, however, following various revelations to the public regarding advanced helicopters, the TR-3A, F-117A and B-2 stealth aircraft, the Aurora project spyplane, as well as the existence of an extraordinary craft which seems to defy the laws of physics – 'like a flying saucer' – revealed by an NBC *Nightly News* film team in the Nevada desert in 1992[5].

After attempting to discredit my NASA background, Johnson writes: 'Our confidence in Timothy Good's source thus bolstered, we embark on the climax of his book, Bob Oechsler's strange and wonderful odyssey (often by unmarked, quiet helicopter) into some of the most secret and impenetrable places the government has for storing, studying and using "alien technology", the Cosmic Journey Project. All the locked doors open to Mr Oechsler, who merely has to flash his identification as "mission specialist" for Ringling Bros. and Barnum & Bailey . . . that's right . . . Circus!

'With some misgivings about Good's journalistic judgement, we read on about how Bob Oechsler ran away and joined the Ringling Bros. and Barnum & Bailey International Organization and, as Bob tells it, from early November 1989 through late January 1990, worked for them in getting actual captured alien spacecraft and an "alien/ET corpse in a cryogenic tank" (p. 199) for use in a proposed travelling public exhibition.'

The government did *not* use Cosmic Journey for storing, studying or using alien technology. I did not use any type of identification to open any doors, neither did I work for the project in 'getting actual captured alien spacecraft' or an 'alien/ET corpse'. Regarding the latter, I was *consulted* on the potential sociological consequences of the use of such exhibits. To the project directors, my expertise in robotics represented as much potential for the proposed exhibition as my UFO research experience.

With the kind of approach that Johnson took in writing his review, some of the negative comments he received from the Cosmic Journey staff do not really surprise me: he probably blew any chance he may have had for verification of my experiences. For example, his representation of my devastating encounter with a humanoid in Dallas was described as '. . . An encounter with an apparent "alien" in a Dallas, Texas cocktail lounge, which included the psychic equivalent of a bar-room brawl between Oechsler and the cat-eyed entity; with Bob seeming to be getting the worst of it until his lady friend (at last a name: Melanie King) intervened and chased the alien away! (This *is* in the book, really . . .) We are relieved to learn that Bob Oechsler suffered no permanent psychic injuries as a result of this altercation . . .'

I was a victim not of a battle, but of an intrusion into my brain. Melanie King did not intervene and chase the alien away, and hers was one of many names referenced. In fact, only one name was withheld in the Cosmic Journey chapter; that of the general at the Pentagon (whose name is now known to several researchers and who has denied ever having met me).

A CAMPAIGN TO DISCREDIT

It should be emphasized that Henry Azadehdel (aka Dr

Alan Jones, Dr Armen Victorian, *et al*) has made it abundantly clear to several researchers that he will go to whatever extent necessary to discredit Timothy Good as a UFO researcher. So it should not be surprising that he would expend a large effort in exposing any flaws in *Alien Liaison*. A fascinating development, however, was that in his zeal to discredit, he actually managed to get Admiral Inman to acknowledge that the topic of our taped conversation did in fact involve 'unidentified flying objects'. Victorian subsequently appeared to muddle that reference with semantic acrobatics.

Victorian made an extensive number of calls to the United States. One such call was to John Dingley, whom I had met at a conference in Chicago and with whom I shared the Inman taped conversation. Dingley called me immediately afterwards, and said that Victorian had asked if the subject of UFOs was ever mentioned on the tape. Dingley replied that the term 'UFO' was not used, but that it was his belief that the subject matter was indeed inferred as the main topic of conversation.

Victorian cites a letter he received from Admiral Inman, dated 5 August 1991, which begins: 'In response to the request in your letter dated 2 August 1991 for an "ultimate clarification" by me re Mr Oechler [sic], I provide the following: a. I receive hundreds of calling cards each year from individuals who approach me at public appearances. I have no specific recollection of the receipt of a calling card from Mr Oechler prior to our telephone conversation . . .'

If this was indeed the case, why then did the Admiral say 'I do pull out now, I thank you', following my brief partial reference to our initial meeting?

In his second paragraph, Inman continues: 'I have never heard of any organization called MJ12 nor did I have any understanding from Mr Oechler about his seeking information on a specific organization . . .' It is perfectly true that I never raised the issue of MJ-12 in the course of our telephone conversation. It was, however, the only subject that I raised in our brief initial meeting, to which he responded 'I do pull out now' on the phone. It reads to me as if Inman is dodging bullets. He then went on to acknowledge that '. . . I did not understand until well into his dialogue that his research was about Unidentified Flying Objects'. This is hardly surprising when one realizes that it was late in the conversation when I asked about ongoing dialogues with the intelligence behind the crafts, or even later when I asked him about the prospects of a civilian research team gaining access to a recovered vehicle. I suppose I should have said 'disc', then perhaps all of this controversy would not have arisen.

In the same letter to Victorian, Inman went on to state that 'Throughout 22 years of service in the intelligence community, I have never encountered any credible evidence of the existence of extraterrestrial or interplanetary entities, individuals, crafts, vehicles, or persons . . .' This reads like the typical party line, and of course belies his acknowledgement of some of the same terms used in our conversation.

In his concluding paragraphs, Inman then refers to my meeting with retired Rear Admiral Sumner Shapiro. 'I have been apprised by RADM Shapiro that Mr Oechler totally misrepresents both the nature and content of their conversation,' he wrote. 'I remain persuaded that complete misrepresentation of my views and those of RADM Shapiro has occurred and thus I distrust any and all stories and conclusions that have been conveyed.'

On 3 August 1991, Victorian spoke by phone with Shapiro and asked him if he had ever met me. 'He claims to have met me,' Shapiro replied at first. After the question was repeated, however, he added that, 'He met me on one occasion and I realized that he was a fraud. He had arranged a meeting with me under fraudulent circumstances, and I dismissed him almost immediately. I never had a meeting with him in a restaurant . . .' I fail to see how an entrée from Inman equates with 'fraudulent circumstances', and I clearly recall that my initial meeting with Shapiro *did* take place in a restaurant (in

Virginia) and the second one at his private residence. The latter meeting followed one of Shapiro's apparently daily visits to the Pentagon, which confirms Inman's contention that although the former Director of Naval Intelligence had retired, he stayed reasonably close to the intelligence business.

In a phone conversation with Johnson on 8 June 1991, Shapiro denied all the comments he made to me regarding alien vehicles. 'That's absolutely false. I gave him no reason to believe I had any knowledge of what he was talking about,' he said. 'I thought the guy was a nut . . . I had to ask him "What is the subject? What are we talking about?" . . . and Oechsler pulled out of his bag a triangular plastic thing with what looked like a shrunken head in it, a triangular head like some kind of spaceman . . . wasn't long before I asked him to leave.'

To put this into perspective, it was evident that Shapiro had not consulted with Inman regarding the specifics of my research prior to the meeting. In order to draw a link between the technology and its non-human source, as one might ordinarily pass a business card I displayed a small hologram of laser art-work depicting the head of an alien creature. Shapiro became visibly upset, pacing about his living room and expressing concern about his failure to reach Inman for confirmation of the recommended meeting, and he wondered aloud why Inman had not directed me to the current Director of Naval Intelligence. He decided to terminate the meeting at that point, suspecting that I was there under false pretences.

Why would Rear Admiral Shapiro consider my background to be a complete sham when anyone could check that I am listed in several Who's Who publications for my robotics expertise, and that I have addressed the full contingent of the US Chamber of Commerce and lectured at the Franklin Institute on the subject of robotics?

Victorian and Johnson spoke to Robert Kirchgessner, director of a Special Development Group financed by Kenneth Feld, who happens to own the Ringling Brothers and Barnum & Bailey Circus, the Ice Capades, and several other travelling exhibition features. The issue of course was my involvement with the Cosmic Journey Project. Kirchgessner told Johnson that my involvement consisted solely of one meeting in Orlando. 'He was called down one time to discuss the alien aspect of it,' Kirchgessner said. 'I met him one time in Orlando and we felt that his contribution to the project wasn't what we were looking for.'

The denials did not stop there, for other individuals approached by the reviewers (including a NASA spokeswoman at the Johnson Space Center) have rubbished all the sensational claims presented in *Alien Liaison's* 'Cosmic Journey' chapter, sometimes resorting to *ad hominem* discrediting tactics. Space does not permit me to go into details here. But at least the reviewers were able to substantiate (to a small degree) my involvement in the project. The response and interpretation that they received serves only to suggest that it is very difficult to see the fire through the dense smoke. That smoke has to come from somewhere!

Why would so many people be willing to protect a secret – especially one of such magnitude – and so willing to discredit the messenger? In the case of Admiral Inman, if the subject matter of our conversation did not involve UFOs but instead some nondescript underwater vehicles that presumably had been recovered in numbers, as suggested to Johnson, then why all the secrecy? Remember, too, that I also have Inman's executive assistant Tom King on my message machine tape indicating that these issues were covered under national secrecy laws.

Derogatory comments from the staff of the Cosmic Journey Project and the denials of principal parties to specific conversations baffle me no end. Yet the preponderance of evidence at my disposal is nothing short of extraordinary. It includes a video tape of the project, audio tapes of conversations and subsequent testimony from individuals providing extensive corroboration. For example, several researchers have contributed to the validation of the microgravity chamber that I visited

outside Houston. Lucius Farish was told by a reliable
individual about such microgravity projects over ten
years ago. And Ron Madeley of Houston has been
working with an individual who has an extensive background in the development of a facility such as the one I
visited. I have never even met Ron Madeley and only
heard from him following publication of *Alien Liaison*.

It took a long time and a great deal of ridicule before the
public at large would believe that the world was round
and that the Earth is not the centre of the universe. The
concept of a prevailing bias as it relates to these matters is
simply that some of us believe in the existence of non-
human life forms and others do not. No matter how
much evidence there is to convince you that something or
some condition exists, and even if your mind becomes
changed due to the evidence before you, your bias will
ultimately prevail: it is the primary control mechanism of
humanity. It is our control and our limitation on the
speed of human mental evolution. How long will it take
us to break the barrier – and will we get a push from
beyond? Has the time come to move on to a higher level
of consciousness? Can we make the leap? Only time will
tell.

Notes

1. *MUFON UFO Journal*, No. 279, July 1991, published by
   the Mutual UFO Network, 103 Oldtowne Road, Seguin,
   Texas 78155–4099.
2. Ibid., No. 285, January 1992.
3. Dalrymple, William: 'Raiders of the Lost Orchids', *The
   Independent Magazine*, London, 19 August 1989. In this
   lengthy article, Dalrymple refers to the fact that
   Azadehdel was sentenced at the Old Bailey in June 1989
   to twelve months in prison and ordered to pay £20,000
   costs, following conviction for the smuggling of rare
   orchids. In July, three appeal judges ruled that the
   sentence was too severe and the sentence was reduced to

six months, with the remainder suspended. In the end, Azadehdel spent only six weeks at Pentonville Prison in London.

4. Oechsler, Bob, with Regimenti, Debby: *The Chesapeake Connection: An Implication of Corporate Involvement in the Cover-Up*, 1989, The Annapolis Research & Study Group, 136 Oakwood Road, Edgewater, Maryland 21037.

5. NBC *Nightly News*, 20 April 1992.

Editor's note

On 4 December 1991 I wrote to Admiral Inman (in part) as follows:

'. . . When the opportunity arose to publish some astonishing confirmation for the reality of the subject matter from two former high-ranking intelligence directors, I seized the opportunity. In addition, I decided to publish material relating to the Cosmic Journey project because, as you will have read in the final chapter, I was approached by the project people and asked to participate in what I was later informed (via Robert Oechsler, whom I subsequently recommended to the project) was to include the possible display of a vehicle and/or body. When I learned that the project had been put on the back burner, I resolved to go ahead with publication, hoping perhaps to facilitate the official release of some of this controversial material.

'In view of your comments to "Dr" Victorian . . . that I have totally misrepresented your views and those of Rear Admiral Shapiro, I would be delighted to include your rebuttal to the statements in my book in any possible future edition – particularly an American edition, if we can get one. Would you be agreeable?'

I have had no reply to date.

As to the status of the Cosmic Journey project, I have made several attempts to find out more, with limited success. In June 1991, for example, I had an appointment with Colonel Simon Pete Worden of the National Space Council in the Old Executive Office Building adjoining the White House. I was unable to learn anything at all during the brief meeting, however. In February 1992 I wrote to Vice President Dan Quayle, as Chairman of the National Space Council, asking about the project's status and the proposal to feature 'an actual extraterrestrial vehicle and/or body', (naming the general who had conveyed this information to Bob Oechsler), and asking if there were plans to include any part of the Cosmic Journey exhibition in Expo '92, which had promised 'Tomorrow's Technology – New Life Forms' etc. I received a letter from Jack Schmid, Exhibits Coordinator for NASA, dated 8 April 1992, which states (in part) as follows:

This is in response to your letter to Vice President Dan Quayle requesting information about the status of 'Cosmic Journey', a major traveling exhibition that was being developed by Kenneth Feld Productions, Inc.

There were plans to have the exhibition at Expo '92 in Seville, Spain, but negotiations between Feld Productions, Inc. and a group of Spanish investors were not successful. At that point further development of the exhibition was terminated.

A full size mock-up of the Space Shuttle orbiter that was built for the exhibition is currently on loan to the Kennedy Space Center where it is being displayed at Spaceport USA, Kennedy's visitor center . . . I am not privy to any future plans that the Feld organization might have in mind . . .

Obviously, there is no confirmation here for the possible display of alien material, but neither is there any denial. And there the matter must rest, until those in authority decide that the time is ripe to offer the public irrefutable proof. In the meantime, I stand by the claims of Bob Oechsler.

14
WORLD ROUND-UP OF SELECTED REPORTS

Timothy Good

Although certain correlations can be made, no firm conclusions of a statistical nature should be drawn from the following reports, which I have selected from hundreds, covering a fourteenth-month period from July 1991 to August 1992.

The preponderance of reports from the UK and USA, for example, should not lead to the assumption that more sightings have occurred in these countries. The shortage or lack of reports from other countries (such as India) is probably due to such factors as a reluctance to report or publish, a dearth of researchers and journalists, and poor communications. In addition, I have to admit that I receive few foreign-language journals and newspaper cuttings.

As well as providing some interesting and important reports, my intention here is to emphasize the massive scale of the phenomenon, which is too frequently overlooked.

Those requiring further information should contact the reporters, researchers, newspapers or journals concerned, since I am unable to vouch for the accuracy of all these accounts.

1 July 1991: Nr. Troy, Ohio, USA

At noon, a father and his twelve-year-old daughter observed a large, bright, silvery object, 15–20 degrees above the horizon. The object was pencil- or cigar-shaped, and approximately a half to one mile away. The witnesses are familiar with aircraft, since they live 12 miles north-east of Dayton Cox Airport, and said that this object was four times the length and twice the width of an airliner, with no tail, wings or windows, and soundless. There were two darker or grey areas on an otherwise smooth shiny surface.

When the father went to fetch a video camera, the object disappeared in a 'green flash'. The following morning, a flight of five green military helicopters was observed over the area where the object had been seen, then right over the witnesses' house. (Franklin Reams, *MUFON UFO Journal*, No. 291, July 1992)

8 July 1991: Nr. Selkirk, Borders, UK

Lorry driver Steve Hallett was driving along the A7 road near Selkirk, within sight of the area's TV transmission mast, when he was astonished to see a large, brightly lit disc-shaped craft hovering overhead, which he estimated to be 40 feet in diameter. The object had coloured lights and seemed to have a dome on top. The instruments in his truck went haywire. He stopped, fascinated, and watched the UFO for about fifteen seconds before it disappeared into the night sky at terrific speed.

This report was brought to my attention by John Hay of St Mary's Loch, Selkirk, who had heard Steve Hallett interviewed by Jill McPherson on Radio Borders, the day after the incident. 'The driver was overwhelmed by his experience,' John Hay wrote to me. 'I was told [by Jill McPherson] he is a down-to-earth person with no motive for concocting such a story.'

25 July 1991: Carleton, Quebec, Canada

A group of campers watched as a bright white globe hovered over a nearby field at 4.00 a.m. Several times, a much smaller red light emerged from the white object and descended to the ground, where it would 'drift' for a short time before ascending again and 'melting' into the white globe. The sighting lasted for an hour. (Christian Page/François Bourbeau, Ufology Research of Manitoba associates)

8 August 1991: Cherry Burton/Sancton, Humberside, UK

At 11.02 p.m., pilot Chris Venter was walking his dog in a country lane near his home when he was startled by a large white glowing light moving low across the sky towards his position. The object was moving from east to west at approximately 1,000 feet. As it passed overhead noiselessly, he saw that it had a large bright white light on the front with a structured round body behind. On the underside were a great many small coloured lights. The object moved away at the speed of a small aircraft and then did a U-turn, again approaching his position, passing overhead and moving away towards the north. 'This was like no aircraft I have ever seen,' said Mr Venter. 'Both my dog and I were terrified.'

At about 11.00 p.m., Len Dawson, also in Cherry Burton, reported seeing a huge flying object pass above him. 'I was outside, and remember that it was a beautiful dry, clear night. I suddenly became aware of a huge oblong-shaped object in the air, coming towards me. It was very low, probably about 100 feet off the ground, and the size of two semi-detached houses together. The front end was round and had a bright white light coming from it, and as it passed over my head I saw lots of small coloured lights underneath it. I could hear a faint droning sound, like you get with an electric transformer . . . The object was moving at about 20 mph and flew away towards York . . .'

At 11.15 p.m., Joyce Porter and four other women were returning from York when they saw a large ball of light. 'We were on the outskirts of York when we saw the object. It appeared to be solid and was glowing bright white as it passed over the front of the car. It was moving no faster than 50 mph. It was an amazing sight, and we watched it for about two minutes.'

At about 11.30 p.m., Liz Ibbotson, together with her teenage daughter Fiona, noticed a glowing ball of light outside their farmhouse (5 miles from Cherry Burton).

Both went downstairs to watch from a picture-window. The glowing, white ball of light was hovering a short distance away, and seemed to be about 3 inches in diameter at arm's length. Suddenly, the light moved away at high speed, then did a U-turn and shot back towards them, passing low over the roof then going out of sight.

The two went outside through the back door to see where the light had gone, and observed that it was now hovering over a high-voltage pylon about 100 yards away. It started to move towards them again, then passed low overhead, making a low droning noise. A cross of coloured lights could be seen underneath; one line of red lights and one of green lights. At the centre of the cross was an oblong white light. The object then suddenly shot away in an instant. (Anthony Dodd, Quest International)

According to a local newspaper, staff at Humberside Airport and RAF Leeming were unable to account for the sighting. 'In any case,' said Mrs Ibbotson, 'I can't think of any craft that matches this description. And something very low would not be picked up on radar.' (Steve Anderson, *Hull Daily Mail*, 10 August 1991)

9 August 1991: Pocklington, Humberside, UK

In Pocklington, 8 miles north-west of Sancton, Mrs Pearce was going to bed at 1.00 a.m. when, through her bedroom window, she noticed a huge ball of light hovering in the air. She stood transfixed as the thing started to move towards her, eventually passing above the house at a speed of less than 50 mph. Underneath the object could be seen a cross of lights, formed by a line of green lights and a line of red lights (as in the previous sighting). The object was in sight for five minutes, but no sound could be heard. 'I've never seen anything like it before,' said Mrs Pearce. 'It frightened the life out of me.' (Anthony Dodd, Quest International)

13 August 1991: Laguna Cartagena, Puerto Rico

Marisol Camacho encountered two strange creatures, with large heads and large black elongated eyes, who were examining a plant at her home during the night. (See pp. 24–5)

19 August 1991: Littlehampton, Sussex, UK
At 3.30 a.m., science teacher Fiona Hamer saw two dimly lit rectangular objects in the sky above a nearby house. 'I was in bed and woke up – I don't know what made me wake up but I couldn't get back to sleep,' she said. 'I looked out of the window and saw two solid rectangles, one under the other, which went over the chimneys and disappeared.' There was no noise and the teacher was convinced the objects were not aircraft. (*Littlehampton Gazette*, 23 August 1991)

20 August 1991: Approx. 200 miles north-north-west of Voronezh, CIS
The crew of Aeroflot Flight 2523 observed a huge, sphere-like object, emerald in colour, from which emitted a beam of light, directed to the ground. (See pp. 181–2)

30 August 1991: Granum, Alberta, Canada
Four children reported observing an oval object hovering over the town at 10.00 p.m. The object was described as 'moving very fast' at some times, then it 'floated' in one position at other times. From its base, blue, red and green lights were flashing intermittently. When the lights were off, the children saw a 'long black thing' streaking across the sky, and then the lights would reappear at another location. At its closest point, the object appeared to hover at the height of a telephone pole. One child described it as a 'big plate with lights on it'. The object made no noise. A circular ground marking was found in front of a garage in the town, and it was thought that the object had 'touched down' there. (Gordon Kijek, Ufology Research of Manitoba associate)

30 August 1991: Blairsville, Pennsylvania, USA
At about 11.15 p.m., two women travelling down Route 22 towards Pittsburgh encountered a large, triangular

object hovering low to the ground on the side of the road. The object was described as having solid white light beams in the outer structure, while the inside had horizontal light beams connecting to the outer structure. There were bright white, non-blinking lights on the beam area. The remaining space of the surface of the object appeared to be transparent, since the witnesses could see the sky behind it. The object made no sound and continued to hover as the women drove by. (Stan Gordon, *PASU Data Exchange*, Issue 18, Pennsylvania Association for the Study of the Unexplained, December/January 1992)

End of August 1991: Cuesta Blanca, Puerto Rico
Ulises Pérez claims to have had a daytime encounter with a creature with a large head and large black eyes. (See pp. 25–6)

8 September 1991: About 40 miles east of Pittsburgh, Pennsylvania, USA
At about 2.00 p.m. an astronomer who was a passenger on board a commercial aircraft reported sighting three disc-shaped objects moving at tremendous speed and flying in a spread-out triangular formation. He is convinced these were not jets. (Stan Gordon, *PASU Data Exchange*, Issue 18, December/January 1992)

11 September 1991: Loudon, New Hampshire, USA
At 7.30 p.m., a mother was driving home with her daughter and son (aged six and ten respectively). As they entered the dead end street where they live, the car radio gave out a lot of static and had to be switched off. The mother parked the car in the driveway and immediately went inside the house to untie the dog. While doing this, her daughter yelled for her to come outside to see something.

Outside, she found her children looking up at two large white discs moving slowly past the house. The discs were identical in shape and light configuration. Surrounding the edge of each disc was a series of pastel multi-coloured lights pulsating in a random sequence. Directly under the discs were three dark circles in a triangular pattern centred on the bottom. Each disc was the size of a small house and they moved side by side. A low-pitched hum was barely audible. The mother estimated the altitude of the discs to be about 100 feet. The brightness of the craft was such that she could see the ground illuminated as they slowly moved out of sight and headed in the direction of Canterbury.

Shortly thereafter, all three witnesses developed strange health symptoms. The daughter started having stomach pain, fever and personality change. The son suffered a major personality change, while the mother began to bruise very easily, and in a short time had multiple bruises on her legs and arms. (New Hampshire MUFON monthly newsletter, January 1992)

15 September 1991: Gulf Breeze, Florida, USA
At 2.00 p.m. a very large UFO and a smaller object were seen in the area of Santa Rosa Shores and Highway 98. Both were described as metallic in colour. The larger object appeared to have appendages which circled it, and what appeared to be layers, or structures, placed one upon the other as plates. Both objects rotated slowly clockwise and moved vertically, with the closest distance to the ground estimated as 500 feet. Finally, the large object shot off and disappeared, while the smaller one slowly disappeared behind the tree line over East Bay. (Joe Barron, *Sentinel*, Gulf Breeze, 21 November 1991)

28 September 1991: Szekesfehervar, Hungary
Truck driver Zoltan Bartus and a companion claim they were followed by a luminous, saucer-shaped UFO, as big as the full moon, while driving near this village in north-east Hungary. On arrival home, the two climbed into Bartus's house through a back window, hoping to shake off the thing, but it shone a green beam into the room. The Bartus family reported that as the neighbourhood

dogs howled, the UFO turned into a cigar-shaped object escorted by two smaller lights, then disappeared. (*Daily Yomiuri*, Tokyo, Japan, 2 October 1991)

Interestingly, some crop circles were spotted in this vicinity in June 1992, and there were numerous UFO sightings reported throughout the summer. A young boy claimed to have seen a yellow dome-shaped object fringed with red light, while his father says he observed a clearly outlined rectangular mass of light over the centre of Szekesfehervar. The object apparently left behind a circle 125 feet in diameter along with several triangles in a nearby cornfield. (*Arkansas Democrat-Gazette*, Little Rock, Arkansas, 12 August 1992)

October 1991: Trowell, nr. Nottingham, UK

This report was prepared by Anthony James of the East Midlands UFO Research Association, who kindly sent me a copy. The witness, who has asked not to be named, signed the following statement about her sighting:

For six days of the week at 04.10 hrs, my alarm wakes me. I get out of my bed and go to dress in the room where my uniform of the Royal Mail hangs. From this room I have an unrestricted view of open countryside, with no lights or buildings of any kind.

One morning in October 1991, I looked out of my window to notice a very bright and unusually situated star. This was in a south-easterly direction and almost directly above Hemlock Wood. I watched the star for several minutes and then went downstairs, where I could still see this star from my kitchen window, and as I had breakfast and prepared for work, I continued to observe it for about fifteen to twenty minutes.

Then I began to notice it was becoming very much brighter and larger, so I immediately thought it was an aircraft en route to East Midlands Airport, about 10 miles away. Several minutes later, I observed a very large bright object heading towards me, very low and close. I rushed outside, only to see a bright haze disappear over the roof of a neighbour's house.

The craft had several lights underneath that shone down vertically. These were different from the lights that were positioned in the centre around the back, which seemed to be

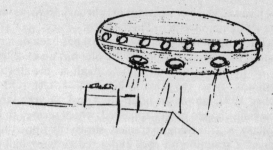

Fig. 14.1   (Based on witness sketch)

coloured and rotating. This craft was no more than 100 feet from the ground, moving very slowly, and there was a faint electrical humming sound that could only have been coming from this object. I had a close view for only a moment, but my recollections of its appearance are still clear in my mind.

Extremely reluctant to report her sighting, the witness only contacted the East Midlands UFO Research Association at the prompting of her husband, and eventually she agreed to an interview with Anthony and Carole James. '[We] believe that this is a genuine sighting by someone who knows nothing about the UFO subject,' they reported. 'It took us a month to coax the information from a very reluctant witness.' (East Midlands UFO Research Association)

2 October 1991: Arkhangelsk, Kazakhstan
At about 6.00 p.m., witnesses observed a UFO which appeared to be pacing the first stage of a rocket booster, following a launch from Plesetsk. (See pp. 165–6)

8 October 1991: Reeves Knob, Boston Mountains, Arkansas, USA
I am grateful to Christine Lippert for sending me details of a wave of sightings (1991–2) which she has investigated in four counties surrounding the Marshall, Arkansas, area in the Ozarks, one of which follows. Note interesting parallels in these cases with the Williamsport,

Pennsylvania, wave of sightings in February 1992, as well as the jet fighter chases in Puerto Rico.

Vickie (surname omitted by request) has been observing these strange craft since 1990. She has an excellent view of the area from her home, high in the Boston Mountains, near the Ozark National Forest. On 8 October 1991, about an hour after dusk, a very large boomerang-shaped object appeared, which seemed to be stationary or travelling extremely slowly. It tipped upwards as if standing on end, and a red glowing ball of light dropped down out of it and headed south. Two jets came from the north as if to chase it or escort it, then it moved off slowly and disappeared.

9 October 1991: Arkalyk, Kazakhstan

A disc-shaped object emitting beams of light crossed the night sky. (See pp. 164–5)

12 October 1991: Chernobyl, Ukraine

Journalist Vladimir Savran photographed a UFO above the nuclear power station. (See pp. 170–2 and photo section)

19 October 1991: Carrasco, Montevideo, Uruguay

Luis Otegui, a control tower operator in Carrasco, Uruguay's main airport, turned on the runway lights when he saw what appeared to be the landing lights of a commercial aircraft. An intense light could be seen at a distance of one mile and at an altitude of 820 feet, but the object did not show up on radar, did not land, and quickly disappeared. Otegui rejected conventional explanations. 'We have been doing this type of work for a long time and know very well what the landing lights of a plane look like, and this one was identical to those,' he reported. (*Diario Popular*, Buenos Aires, Argentina, 21 October 1991)

22 October 1991: Nr. Wigan, Lancashire, UK

The following report by Bill Eatock was passed to me by Tony Dodd of Quest International, who spoke to the witness on the telephone immediately after the incident:

I purchased some walkie-talkie radios today and I decided to test them for range. At about 7.45 p.m., I left one radio with my wife at home and set off in my car, driving progressively further away, speaking to my wife at regular intervals to get some idea of the range of reception. At about 8.00 p.m., I was driving along a country road; it was a dark, clear, dry night, and reception on the radio was very good.

As I drove slowly along the road, I suddenly saw a wall of fog in front of me and was surprised that it started so suddenly. I drove into the fog and immediately heard a very high-pitched whining sound. The sound was gaining in intensity, to the extent that it was hurting my ears. I was unable to see anything due to the fog. By this time, the sound was overpowering and I reached for the car radio to see if it was turned on, but it wasn't. My ears were really hurting by this time and I was fast becoming disorientated. In desperation, I pulled the wires out of the car radio in case it was coming from there, and I made certain the walkie-talkie was turned off, but the sound continued.

At this stage, everything got confused, and the next thing I remember was driving out of the fog to a totally clear road and the sound had stopped. Another strange thing was that this road is usually quite busy with other cars, but I never saw one. I drove home feeling sick, with my left ear and left side of my face burning. On my arrival home, my wife noticed that the left side of my face appeared to have been sunburned. I don't know what caused this, but I feel ill . . .

Additional reports of UFO activity that night were received and published by the *Wigan Reporter* (31 October 1991), although it is evident to me that many of these were caused by a laser display at Blackpool.

2 November 1991: Mar del Plata, Buenos Aires Province, Argentina

A videofilm taken at 11.30 a.m. by Marta Julia Cassiccia revealed the presence of a circular object in the sky, which after hovering moved away swiftly, leaving a long trail. According to experts, the tape showed no signs of fraud or superimposition, nor was there any mechanical defect in the camera. (*La Nacion*, Buenos Aires, 30 November 1991)

5 November 1991: Gulf Breeze, Florida, USA

A UFO was photographed by MUFON representative Patti Weatherford, an auditor for the State of Florida, and Anne Morrison (also MUFON), in the presence of numerous witnesses (see photo section). 'I could see a definite curved structural shape above the blazing red light at its bottom,' reported Bland Pugh, another MUFON member, who observed the object through binoculars. (Gary Watson, *The Islander*, Pensacola, 15 November 1991, plus additional sources)

6 November 1991: Beit She'an, Israel

'It was a shining object, quite large compared to other objects seen in the sky at the time,' said the local police chief, describing the sighting of a UFO over this Israeli town. District Superintendent Yitzhak Mordechai told Army Radio that he was first informed about the sighting by a taxi driver at about 3.30 a.m. The driver, Yossi Ben-Ha'ash, said the object resembled a shining half ellipse. 'We came to the area where the UFO was seen, and we followed it while driving east,' said Mordechai. 'It was some 200 metres off the ground until the morning hours. Then, at about 6.00 a.m., it disappeared.'

Asked to describe the object's flight, he said: 'It moved to some point, stopped, made turns around itself and after several minutes moved in a northerly direction and then back to the spot where it had initially stopped . . . A police force was with us and they saw the same scene.' (*Jerusalem Post*, 7 November 1991)

9 November 1991: Eastern Pennsylvania/Maryland border, USA

At 6.50 p.m. a police officer who is very familiar with aircraft observed a huge object heading in his direction at an altitude of no more than 1,000 feet. Viewed against clouds, the completely silent object was described as a huge triangle or flying wing, larger than a Lockheed Galaxy, with three lights separated across its front. The officer radioed to another patrol car, 5 miles away, in the direction the object was travelling. About two minutes later, the second officer also saw the object. Its speed was estimated to be 150 mph. (Stan Gordon, *PASU Data Exchange*, Issue 18, December/January 1992)

15 November 1991: Nr. Marshall, Arkansas, USA

A group of coon-hunters observed a tremendously large object hovering silently over them in the woods, near the Alred area, south of Marshall. The craft was boomerang-shaped and estimated to be as large as at least three football fields, with very bright, pulsating white lights. At some point, three big red lights evidently separated from the main object and moved away. [Fig. 14.2]

Fig. 14.2   (Christine Lippert)

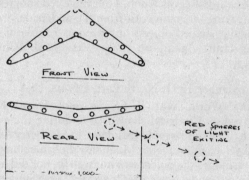

The men were so afraid that they fled. Later, jet aircraft activity was noted in the vicinity, which is unusual in this rural area. (Christine Lippert)

17 November 1991: St Petersburg, CIS

At 3.35 a.m., Anna Gromova observed two triangular-shaped objects hovering motionless above the city. (See p. 184)

21 November 1991: Witts Springs, Arkansas, USA

Here follows investigator Christine Lippert's account of a personal sighting:

. . . at approximately 6.30 p.m. or after dusk, while out tending my cows, I looked up into the sky to see a brilliant red/orange ball of light, stationary directly to the east. It appeared approximately ten times as big as the brightest star. Then I heard jets and turned to focus on them to the north of the object. Suddenly, the jets (which appeared to be military fighters) looked as if they were trying to intercept this object. The object just blinked off and disappeared, then it reappeared farther to the east, with the jets pursuing it. Again, it just blinked off and was gone. This was over several minutes, and was like a game of cat-and-mouse. Afterward, the night sky was full of jet aircraft, which was unusual for this area. Later, I was to find out that this same event was witnessed by many others in the area . . .

On the same day, Vickie (see 8 October 1991) observed a V- or boomerang-shaped craft move from the east towards Reeves Knob. Four huge red spheres were seen leaving the main craft from the underside. Smaller, triangular-shaped objects appeared to be following the larger craft. Again, no noise was heard. (Christine Lippert)

24 November 1991: North Port, Florida, USA
Former World War II fighter pilot David Kersky observed a cylindrical-shaped UFO during the evening which came right over his residence in Mayberry Avenue. Kersky's neighbour, Rita Maul, saw the same thing. Both witnesses said the object was not well lit, nor did it make any sound, and it flew faster than a jet. (Beth Sumner, *Sun Times*, North Port, 27 November 1991)

27 November 1991: Taunton, Somerset, UK
Anne and Fred Hickox claim that a UFO flew over Taunton at 10.00 a.m. 'We clearly saw a round thing going across the sky with two "legs" hanging out,' said Mrs Hickox. 'There was a rectangular bit at the top. It was humming and it moved quickly across the sky.'

Mr Hickox described the object as 'like a huge jellyfish' and dark grey in colour. (*Somerset County Gazette*, 29 November 1991)

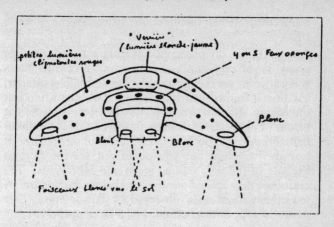

Fig. 14.3 (SOBEPS)

27 November 1991:

Object seen over Saint-Nicholas, Liège, Belgium (see Fig. 14.3)

4 December 1991: Hoveton, Norfolk, UK

Mr Roxham, a former military pilot, reported that at 6.00 p.m., while driving with his daughter, he observed a cigar-shaped object at about 1,500 feet altitude. The object had an intense white light at each end and a row of yellow-coloured ports. As they watched, it suddenly moved instantly to about 300 mph. Mr Roxham stopped his vehicle, opened the window, switched off the engine, and got out in order to have a better view.

The object then passed directly overhead, carrying red, green, blue and white lights on its underside. After a few moments, it returned and again passed overhead, eventually coming to a standstill a short distance away. 'We watched the object for forty-five minutes,' said Mr Roxham. 'It was certainly not a helicopter or aeroplane as we know it. Its size was that of an A310 Airbus.' (Anthony Dodd, *UFO Magazine*, Vol. 11 No. 1, March/April 1992)

6 December 1991: Teynham, nr. Sittingbourne, Kent, UK

A large UFO was observed hovering a few dozen feet above Teynham Church at 5.45 p.m. Mrs Lynne Yates was called to see the object after her children spotted it. 'At first it looked just like a huge star,' she said, 'but something shot off from it and then lots of different beams of light started flashing. It stayed round for about half an hour. It is nothing like I have ever seen before. It was oval on top, but you could not see the bottom because of the red, yellow, green and blue lights.' The craft then flew up and disappeared below the horizon. A few other witnesses also observed the phenomenon. (*East Kent Gazette*, Sittingbourne, 11/18 December 1991)

7 January 1992: Nr. Prague, Oklahoma, USA

A rancher, his wife and daughter and another couple observed an extraordinary phenomenon during the night. First, two large white lights were seen hovering between their home and a microwave telephone tower, just over half a mile to the south. Frightened, the wife retired inside and did not witness the rest of the events.

A small red ball then appeared and moved in on the larger lights and apparently went behind one of them and was not seen again. The remaining four witnesses watched for perhaps forty-five minutes as the two UFOs hovered. Then, from out of the river valley to the west came a large number of helicopters. These broke into two groups, one swinging around below the level of the farmhouse and the other hiding in the valley. One of the groups moved in on the UFOs, which remained stationary. The second group of helicopters then appeared from the east, prompting the UFOs to speed away.

The helicopters remained in the area, moving back and forth over the terrain. Finally they flew away. Shortly afterwards, the two UFOs returned to their original position, remained a short time, then sped away again. The rancher's cats and dogs went berserk during the sighting. (Ken Memoli/Richard Seifried, *Oklahoma*

MUFONews, 1916 Inglewood Drive, Norman, Oklahoma 73071, April 1992)

10 January 1992: Huntsville, Alabama, USA

A health-care professional driving to work at 5.45 a.m. witnessed a circular craft surrounded by multiple lights at the base, with a diameter of a long-bed pickup truck, and joined to a top section with three square windows and dim lights inside them, she claimed. It was hovering over Blake Bottom Road, and the witness tried unsuccessfully to get underneath it. 'The lights went off when I slowed down,' she said. 'I didn't get afraid until I couldn't get under it. I sped up at tremendous speed, and I thought, "This thing is going to fall in front of me." '

Approaching Highway 53, the woman didn't look back, and arrived at work at 6.00 a.m. Air traffic control officials at Huntsville International Airport picked up nothing unusual. 'I don't know if they saw it or not,' the witness commented, 'but they couldn't miss it.' (Paige Oliver, *Times*, Huntsville, 12 January 1992)

24 January 1992: Tetbury, Gloucestershire, UK

A woman who prefers to remain anonymous reported sighting a large, gold, five-pointed 'star' which moved slowly at about 500 feet over her home between Tetbury and Malmesbury, early in the morning. The object appeared to rotate slowly and made a humming sound, then took off at a terrific speed towards Cirencester. The woman said the object was about the size of a small plane and had a row of black dots along its underside. (Tom Flint, *Wilts & Gloucestershire Standard*, 31 January 1992)

25 January 1992: Gulf Breeze, Florida, USA

Together with a group of people, private pilot Glen Bradley spotted a UFO – one of many sightings reported and filmed in this 'hot spot' in 1992. The incident took place at 7.55 p.m.:

. . . I looked to the east and saw something that was not like any airplane I had ever seen. It was a very large red light of great intensity, moving slowly to the south (into the wind). It appeared to be about 8 miles away. As this glowing red unidentified flying object moved to the south, another identical red light appeared below and to its left. This second brilliant red light faded in and out occasionally, while the first light disappeared behind the trees that were almost in front of me . . . I was handed a pair of binoculars. [Through these] the light's intensity was really impressive . . . It was not at all like any light I have seen in over twenty years of flying . . .

(Glen Bradley, *Islander*, Pensacola, Florida, 31 January 1992)

28 January 1992: Nr. Bramfield, Suffolk, UK
Mrs Wood was driving with her six-year-old daughter in the direction of Bramfield. It was very cold and clear. Suddenly, a very bright light moved towards them, low in the sky. A few hundred yards farther on, Mrs Wood decided to stop the car and get out to obtain a better view. She noticed that several other vehicles had pulled in to watch.

The UFO was now visible as a very large, circular object, with a powerful 'searchlight' pointing down to the ground from its underside and smaller lights around the circumference, also shining downward. [Fig. 14.4]

Fig. 14.4   (*Based on witness sketch*)

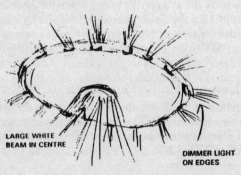

LARGE WHITE
BEAM IN CENTRE

DIMMER LIGHT
ON EDGES

On several occasions, the object, which was moving very slowly, stopped and hovered for a few minutes, then moved over a nearby field and remained stationary again. Mrs Wood was startled to see a large number of white lights 'interweaving with each other' or 'blinking on and off' in the field. During the incident, the main aerial device moved away at high speed, only to return a few minutes later. Although no sound could be heard from the object, Mrs Wood felt a vibrational-like hum, 'as if the sound was out of our hearing range'. For several minutes the witnesses watched the display, then Mrs Wood continued on her journey home. (Anthony Dodd, *UFO Magazine*, Vol. 11 No. 1, March/April 1992)

30 January 1992: Nr. Marshall, Arkansas, USA
At approximately 9.10 p.m., a giant 'flying wing' with numerous bright white lights was observed south of Marshall, flying silently about 1,000 feet above treetops. The size was estimated to be that of an aircraft carrier, or larger. Jets were said to be in the vicinity, either observing or escorting the craft. The aircraft appeared to be very tiny in comparison. (Christine Lippert)

5 February 1992: Williamsport, Pennsylvania, USA
A wave of sightings of very large, boomerang- or triangular-shaped objects was reported by numerous witnesses from 6.00 p.m.–8.30 p.m. (see Chapter 9).

7 February 1992: Carleton Moor, nr. Skipton, Yorkshire, UK
At 10.00 p.m., as Brett Young was driving across Carleton Moor and approaching the National Security Agency/GCHQ microwave aerial, a glowing ball of blue light flew in front of his windscreen. The object maintained this position for a short time, despite the car travelling at about 30 mph. The witness stopped on the road and the object stayed in front of the windscreen. Suddenly, it 'shot off' into the distance at a very fast speed.

Brett Young described the object as 'bone-shaped', surrounded by a blue neon-like glow, which gave the impression that it was circular until it was close enough to see through the glow. At one point the object was no further than 3 feet away from the witness, who estimated its size to be approximately 10 inches across. (Anthony Dodd, *UFO Magazine*, Vol. 11 No. 1, March/April 1992)

8 February 1992: Nr. Hebden Bridge, Yorkshire, UK
At about 9.30 p.m., Frank Skinner and two of his relatives were on their way home by car to Halifax when Mr Skinner, a rear-seat passenger, sighted an object which looked like a single-decker bus with lit-up windows and which seemed to be rotating. On its top and down the sides appeared 'a string of fairy lights' that were flashing and rotating. Mr Skinner alerted the driver, his cousin, who nearly lost control of the car when he saw the object, which seemed to be above a hilltop. After thirty seconds, the object suddenly disappeared. (*Skylink*, No. 2, April 1992, London UFO Studies, 10A Tudor Road, Barking, Essex, IG11 9RX)

9 February 1992: Llangurig/Llanidloes, Powys, Wales, UK
At 5.00 a.m., two security guards on duty at a government establishment reported an object which they described as glowing bright blue, and of the classic saucer shape with a dome on top. 'The witnesses said that at the time of their observation, there had been a total power failure in the area as the object hovered nearby,' reported Tony Dodd, a retired police sergeant who directs investigations for Quest International. 'Whilst they continued to observe the disc, both witnessed the device perform manoeuvres, first flying to their left at great speed, and then turning quickly to their right. The object was within a quarter of a mile and visible for some thirty minutes.

'Some five hours later, the object returned – this happening during our conversation. The gentlemen terminated the call, because they were afraid of being traced by the authorities.' (Anthony Dodd, *UFO Magazine*, Vol. 11 No. 1, March/April 1992)

10 February 1992: Henri-Chapelle, Belgium

During February 1992, Dr Steven Greer and members of his research group, the Center for the Study of Extraterrestrial Intelligence (CSETI), travelled to Belgium from the USA to meet principal witnesses to, as well as investigators of, the extraordinary series of sightings (of mainly triangular- and boomerang-shaped UFOs) reported in that country, which now number over 3,500 since 1989. Dr Greer and his team were themselves successful in witnessing a number of anomalous objects, and here follows Dr Greer's description of one of those sightings:

On the night of February 10, 1992, we proceeded with Dr Brenig [of the Belgian research group, SOBEPS – Ed.] to a high ridge near the town of Henri-Chapelle, about 10 miles from Eupen . . . About 10.00 p.m. we observed a convoy of military/official trucks . . . It was obvious that the cargo in question was a hazardous material of some sort which required a high degree of security . . .

Dr Brenig left around 11.00 p.m. to return to Brussels . . . We continued to remain at this site for several more hours, and at around 12.30–1.00 a.m. observed another, even longer convoy of vehicles . . . under tight security . . . While observing this event, we noticed through a break in the clouds a bright, large yellow-white light appear, which moved slowly and was larger than the full moon. It should be noted that we could see the moon through thin clouds in the opposite direction from this other light. This light was in the clouds over the area of the transport convoy, and was soon obscured by rapidly moving clouds.

A few minutes later, after the convoy had moved out of sight, we heard – and felt – a deep vibratory rumble directly over our car, which lasted ten to thirty seconds. This vibration was coming from the clouds directly overhead . . . It was unlike anything any of us had ever heard; it certainly was not the distant rumble of thunder or jets, nor was it a sonic boom. Each of us felt that this sound was emanating from an immense and powerful object directly overhead in the clouds – like a million transformers humming, almost to a roar or boom . . . this sound did not appear to be coming from a moving object, and a second episode of vibratory rumbling occurred shortly after the first one . . .

(Steven M. Greer, MD, *MUFON UFO Journal*, No. 289, May 1992)

11 February 1992: Calumet, Oklahoma, USA
Following cattle mutilations in the area, Travis Dean and his girlfriend observed a brilliant light, with additional coloured lights, above a field at 8.15 p.m. The object began to follow the witnesses in their car, who in turn tried (unsuccessfully) to follow the object. (See p. 192)

15 February 1992: Warrington, Cheshire, UK
Mr W. was driving along the M62 towards Manchester in the vicinity of Birchwood at 7.15 p.m. when his girlfriend in the passenger seat reported seeing a UFO in front. As they turned off the motorway at Gorse Covert, the object now appeared much closer. Dome-shaped, with a mass of white windows or lights rotating on the base, it hovered over the Risley Nature Reserve before disappearing into a large cloud. (Manchester UFO Research Association, *Northern UFO News*, No. 155, June 1992)

19 February 1992: Hillingdon, Middlesex, UK
At about 10.27 p.m., a female driver (name known to me) encountered a huge disc-shaped object at the junction of Pield Heath Road, Lees Road, and Harlington Road. An investigation of the incident was conducted by Darren Gillett, who sent me the following report:

. . . It appeared to be glowing like a ceiling light tube does, with a pure white light all over its surface. The dome and upper surface were also the same white colour and, according to the witness, the object did not appear to be giving off any haze or glow. The lower surface was ringed by a series of round lights, apparently of the same colour and intensity: these were equally

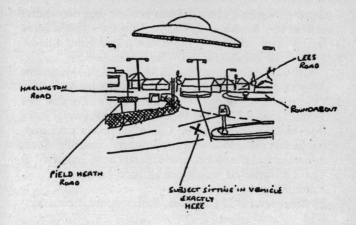

Fig. 14.5 (Darren Gillett)

spaced and contained within a narrow band which was only slightly duller. She noted to me during a follow-up session that the object appeared to be slightly tipped towards her right. She does not remember if the underside was lit up but does not believe it was.

The sky that evening was clear with a little high cloud. The stars were very clear and the moon was visible but not behind or near to the object. Earlier in the evening a blimp had been in the area, but she knows the difference between one of these and the object she saw ... Her car did not appear to be affected. She noted that some other vehicles were in the area but they did not appear to be affected, nor did anyone else seem to notice the object, which I have estimated to be easily 250 metres in diameter. This was driven home by an examination of the site and questioning of the witness ...

'I sat there in total awe at the size of this UFO,' the witness wrote to me (Editor) in November 1992. 'There was no sound coming from it but I was about 100 yards or more away. It was completely motionless and filled the sky ... I think I observed the object for about three minutes – or it seemed like that – then I decided to go and get some witnesses to watch it with me, so I drove to my daughter's friend's house. I was ecstatic, but they didn't believe me. Anyhow, they came with me straight away [after] three minutes or more, but it had gone. I drove around the whole area, [but] there was nothing . . .'

I should point out that RAF Northolt, Heathrow Airport, as well as the Headquarters, Military Air Traffic Operations, Uxbridge (co-located at the London Air Traffic Control Centre at West Drayton) are not far away from the sighting location. Could the object have been tracked on radar? Via a former air traffic controller, I was informed that the object would merely have registered as 'ground clutter' at such a low altitude, however.

25 February 1992: East Fork, Bath County, Kentucky, USA

At 9.30 a.m. Bill Goldy, alerted by James Carpenter, an employee, observed an unusual object, about 100 feet up, at Goldy's 87-acre farm. It appeared to be a small object (Fig. 14.6) which then landed in trees in a hollow, turned on its side, or unfolded, until it looked like a very bright aluminium circle which was flashing extremely bright blue, green and yellow colours.

Fig. 14.6 (Bill Goldy)

Goldy went over the hill to feed his cattle, then returned to look for the object in the hollow. Nothing was found, even after a subsequent three-hour search. 'I don't know what it was, where it came from, or where it went, or anything,' Goldy said. 'I don't want publicity . . . I just saw the object and that's all I can tell you.' (Andy Mead, *Herald-Leader*, Lexington, Kentucky, 13 March 1992)

3 March 1992: Concord, New Hampshire, USA

At about 7.50 p.m., motorist Roger Cross saw a huge, roughly triangular object along Route 3A/South Main Street, in Concord near the Interstate 93 overpass (see photo section). The object had pulsating bluish-white lights and disappeared over the tree line near Broadway. Cross described the object as 'awesome in size', flying just above the tree tops, and making a sound 'like increasing rain on a summer night on a canvas tent'. Starting at about 6.00 p.m., other reports came from observers in Claremont, Newport, Bradford, Salisbury and Penacook, as well as Concord. (*Union-Leader*, Manchester, New Hampshire, 7 March 1992)

3 March 1992: Greensboro, North Carolina, USA

Robert Benson, together with his girlfriend, Cathy Kenny, and another friend, Melvin Ferguson, were in the yard of Kenny's mobile home in Woodlake Mobile Home Park off Randleman Road at around 8.40 p.m. when they spotted an object encircled with strobe-like lights flying low at a slow speed and making a humming noise.

'It looked about the size of a DC-9,' said Benson. 'My first thought was, "That plane is awful low". It was about 250 feet off the ground. I thought it was going to crash.' Kenny's cat seemed mesmerized and was unable to move a muscle. The object disappeared over a nearby hill, then turned around and came back. Kenny and Benson jumped into a car and drove along Creekridge Road.

'It seemed like it was following us down the road,' Benson said. At about the same time, an anonymous witness called the *News & Record* office to report seeing a loud and brightly lighted object hovering near Lees Chapel Road and Church Street in north Greensboro. (Jim Schlosser with Bernie Woodall, *News & Record*, Greensboro, 5 March 1992)

4 March 1992: Disley, Cheshire, UK

At 8.30 p.m., Miss B. was walking her dog near Lyme Park when she observed a brightly lit 'donut', with a bump on the base and lights or windows studded into the sides. The brightly glowing object appeared to be the relative size of two double-decker buses and moved at some speed as it climbed from trees and headed north towards a quarry. (Roy Sandbach, *Northern UFO News*, No. 155, June 1992)

5 March 1992: Perth, Western Australia

A witness was heading north along Wanneroo Road when she noticed a bright white light to her right which seemed to keep pace with her car. Turning left and heading west into Whitfords Avenue she was surprised to see an object almost directly in front of and overhead her vehicle. It was large and triangular-shaped, with a white light at the apex of each triangle. Off-centre – more towards the rear – two white lights shone a green light. No sound was heard and the object seemed just to vanish. (Brian Richards, UFO Data Collection Centre/ UFORUM)

9 March 1992: New Kensington, Pennsylvania, USA

Two boys, eight and ten years of age, were playing near a cemetery located within a mile of the Alcoa Research Center, when at about 6.30 p.m. they noticed an aerial object approaching them from the east. It gave the boys an impression of a 'flying car' with two lights. The object flew with a fluttering motion that allowed them to see both the top and bottom sections of the object as it appeared to be banking back and forth.

The object was disc-shaped and of a grey or silver

colour, with two protrusions on top. When it reached about the centre of the cemetery, the two headlight-type lights went off and a very bright beam of light emitted from the bottom central part. At the same time, a larger number of round white lights came on that followed the perimeter of the object on both the upper and lower surfaces. The light beam was so intense that it hurt the boys to look at it. The object emitted a jet-like sound and was about the size of a truck.

Frightened, the boys hid behind a tombstone, but the object then hovered above, illuminating them with the beam of light. Both boys then ran for cover towards the road, about 100 yards away. When the younger boy reached the road, he ran in a circle and realized that the object was following his movements. Once both boys had reached the road, the object turned and headed back towards the cemetery.

Interestingly, the Alcoa Research Center is said to be involved in research for the Strategic Defense Initiative (SDI – or 'Star Wars'). The primary investigator of this case was Dennis Stadterman, a PASU member who is a police officer and an emergency management supervisor. (*PASU Data Exchange*, Issue 19, April 1992)

10 March 1992: Kings Lynn, Norfolk, UK

This case was investigated at my request by David Dane, the well-known Norfolk artist, after I had read an article about the sighting in the *Lynn News & Advertiser* of 10 April 1992. His report follows:

The evening of Tuesday, March 10, was to be like none other for Marilyn Preston and her daughters Kim and Kerry. The Preston family live at Woodwark Avenue, Kings Lynn. Marilyn works at the Sydney Dye home for the elderly. On this particular Tuesday, Marilyn was working the 2.00 p.m. to 9.00 p.m. shift. She drove home then left again at about 9.30 p.m. to take her daughter Kim's boyfriend home. As they left, they became aware of crackling noises emanating from the car radio speakers. This was unusual, since the radio was not even switched on.

After dropping off the boyfriend at nearby Middleton at around 10.00 p.m., Marilyn and her daughters Kim (17) and Kerry (11) started to make their way home. Driving along, they noticed what appeared to be a very bright star and commented that maybe it was the pole star, but soon realized that the star was moving and seemed to have a red tail. The 'star' seemed to increase in size dramatically, and in a matter of minutes a brightly illuminated object descended above the roadway just ahead of them.

Fig. 14.7   (Kerry Preston)

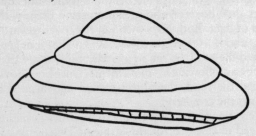

Described and drawn by Kerry [see Fig. 14.7] as a saucer-shaped craft, the object hovered between the factory premises of Campbells and Jaeger, and seemed wider than the four-lane highway near the Hardwick roundabout.

At this point, Kim was sitting in the back of the car, verging on hysteria and shouting, 'Keep where all the lights are!' as she didn't want the object to follow them into a dark street. The now stationary object, which they described as of metallic appearance and shrouded in steam or vapour, seemed so close that the family felt they could reach up and touch it.

According to Kerry, the underneath of the object was lit by bluish fluorescent-type lights on the outer edge and a bright yellow-white light in the centre. The family say that on passing underneath the object, the car felt as if it were floating, and also that they had the distinct feeling that everything around them was dead and of no significance. Although the car windows were open, the object was noiseless. Marilyn wanted to stop and take time to fully appreciate the spectacular object, but the terrified Kim wanted only to reach home as soon as possible. And then Kerry turned around to see the object moving away and then upwards, at tremendous speed.

The family proceeded home. On their return, Kim looked

very pale and shaken, but both Marilyn and Kerry were in a state of excitement. Husband Kevin was amazed at the story, and soon came to realize that they had indeed had an extraordinary experience.

These events were reported to the Kings Lynn police on Saturday, March 14. About a week after the incident, the Preston family was visited by a local taxi driver who said he had had a similar experience a week earlier.

As a further point of interest, Marilyn's parents – Mr and Mrs Eglin, who live opposite the Preston's home – had a strange experience some five years previously. They were awoken in their bed in the early hours one morning by a loud buzzing sound. Furthermore, the bedroom was brightly illuminated, and they found that they were unable to move until the light faded and the noise diminished. According to Marilyn, the Eglins later contacted nearby RAF Marham and were advised to 'keep quiet about it'.

13 March 1992: Bellevue, nr. Green Bay, Wisconsin, USA

At 10.00 a.m., while filming a two-minute weather shot, David Hooker, chief photographer for WFRV-TV, the local CBS affiliate station, inadvertently videofilmed a cigar-shaped UFO. The film (a copy of which was kindly sent to me by Mr Hooker) has been analyzed by MUFON photoanalyst Jeffrey Sainio, who rules out the possibility of the object being an aircraft, bird or lens flare. The UFO is seen to travel from the right to the left of the frame, passing behind a windmill and then reappearing on the same trajectory, at an estimated altitude of 25,000 feet and speed of approximately 7,000 mph.

14 March 1992: Gulf Breeze, Florida, USA

As many as thirty witnesses, including members of the Gulf Breeze Research Team and others conducting a skywatch from Santa Rosa Island, observed a total of five UFOs for about ten minutes, after 8.00 p.m. In a cloudless sky, a white light appeared about 50 degrees off the horizon, then turned bright red. It was followed by a second, third and fourth, then finally a fifth red light, in roughly the 4, 5, 8 and 9 o'clock positions.

'They didn't fly in, they just kind of "blinked in" from nowhere,' said George Crumbley. 'Two started moving directly toward us,' said Art Hufford, a member of the research team. 'As an experiment, using a 500,000 candlepower spot light, we had been directing a repetitive sequence of high-intensity flashes at the uppermost UFO. The movement toward our location began after the object appeared to respond to our signals by repeating our sequence of flashes. The approach lasted about thirty seconds . . .' (Patti Weatherford, *Islander*, Pensacola Beach, Florida, 27 March 1992)

16 March 1992: Perth, Western Australia

At 12.15 p.m., a witness was driving in the Kelvin and Chitterbrook Road area, Kalamunda, when he saw two metallic-grey discs travelling low and fast from west to east. They were so low that he thought they were going to crash, but no sound could be heard. His first impression was that they were jet trainers of the RAAF, but the absence of any protuberances and the disc shapes precluded this. (Brian Richards, UFO Data Collection Centre/UFORUM)

19 March 1992: Nr. Colchester, Essex, UK

A family of five, driving along the A130 by-pass near Colchester, noticed a diamond-shaped object hovering to the left of the road at 9.45 p.m. Pulling in to a lay-by, the witnesses saw that the object was deep green in colour, with three other objects or lights spinning around it, coloured red, blue and yellow.

'It was just sitting there not doing a thing, apart from the lights spinning around it. We did not notice any other cars on the road during the hour-and-a-half we watched it, which was most strange. Also, [everything] seemed very quiet. At 11.15 p.m., the diamond-shaped object just blinked out, leaving a hazy image for about ten minutes. We heard no noise whatsoever.' (Ron West, Essex UFO Research Group)

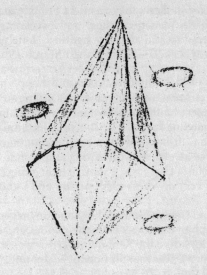

Fig. 14.8   (Witness sketch)

19 March 1992: Haines City, Florida, USA

Police officer Luis Delgado was driving a patrol car north on 30th Street in south-eastern Haines City at 3.52 a.m. when a large, disc-shaped, bright green light came up behind his car. The light hovered around the car at about 10 feet above the ground, for about a minute. Delgado reported that after he pulled in to the side of the road to avoid crashing into the object, his car engine mysteriously shut off and his walkie-talkie stopped working.

'I grabbed the radio to talk, but everything went out. The car lights went out. After that, I just stood there and it was really cold. I could see the breath coming out of my mouth.'

Another police officer found Delgado at the site, shaking and crying in his car. Although he found the experience stressful, Delgado said it was also exciting.

Haines City [police spokesman] Lt Frank Caterino said
that Delgado passed physical and psychological tests
administered to him after the sighting. (Jeff Osterkamp,
The Ledger, Lakeland, Florida, 20 March 1992)

20 March 1992: Islington, London, UK

A witness claims to have observed a fluorescent, disc-
shaped object 'with red all around the edge' above Essex
Road, sometime between 7.30–8.00 p.m. from her home
in Islington. 'It hovered for a couple of minutes then, in
the blink of an eye, shot off through the clouds,' she said.
'It was so fast. There was a shaft of light going on and off
. . . I'm a very down-to-earth person and I know what I
saw.'

Gary and Debbie Hines of Highbury managed to take a
photograph of the object from their home, and the object
does not look like the Renault advertising airship which
was put forward as the solution to the sighting. (*Islington
Gazette*, London, 26 March/9 April 1992)

23 March 1992: The Dalles/Dufur, Oregon, USA

A woman driving along Highway 197 reported being
pursued by a UFO, just before 9.00 p.m. Shortly afterwards, another witness reported that three triangular
objects in the sky followed him from Tygh Valley to The
Dalles. (*Chronicle*, The Dalles, 24 March 1992)

24 March 1992: Havelock, North Carolina, USA

When a Havelock woman went outside at about 7.30
p.m. to take her laundry off the clothesline, she saw
something hovering motionless and silently above some
trees about a half a mile away. Together with her
fourteen-year-old son, she watched as the thing came to
about 75 feet above them, then stopped. In the dark, they
were unable to discern the shape, but it seemed to be
about 90 feet long, with four bright lights on one end and
a red light at the other. Between these lights, the body
appeared to be grey. As they watched, they felt it was
watching them. Suddenly, the object split into three

sections: the central section remained still but the section with the red light zoomed behind them, while the yellow lights slowly descended. The two witnesses fled into their house.

Seconds later, the whole family, including the woman's husband (a former Marine) rushed out in time to observe the yellow lights drifting across the town and the red lights flying faster to the north. 'You would have had to prove to me there are UFOs,' said the woman, 'and now you'll have to prove to me there are not. To tell you the honest truth, if they can discredit me, that's fine. But I want a logical explanation.' (Randall Patterson, *Herald-Sun* Durham, North Carolina, 31 May 1992)

24 March 1992: Gulf Breeze, Florida, USA
Bland Pugh, a MUFON field investigator, reports as follows:

The Gulf Breeze Research Team had gathered at South Shoreline Park for our usual skywatch, when in the north-western sky the 'UFO' appeared, and seemed to be determined to out-do the sighting of March 14. The red light appeared as usual, then another light next to the first [which] proceeded to move completely around the first one. After five minutes, the smaller light faded out and disappeared. Then to everyone's surprise, it or another one blinked in, just to its lower right, both slowly moving to the south-west before fading out, as if turned off by a rheostat . . .

Other witnesses included a CBS Television crew, who filmed the entire sighting. (Bland Pugh, *Islander*, Pensacola Beach, Florida, 10 April 1992)

28 March 1992: Nr. Bury St Edmunds, Suffolk, UK
A family driving at night through open countryside, about 4–5 miles out of Bury St Edmunds, were confronted by an unusual aerial object. 'It was stationary and quite large, with red lights,' said the mother, who asked not to be named. 'At first we thought it was a tower of some kind, but when we got closer we realized there was

nothing underneath. My husband stopped the car and he and the children got out to have a better look.

'Two main beams of light shone down into a field and then started to turn on to us, as if attracted by the [car] lights we had left on. Then very slowly it went off across the fields.' There was no sound or only very faint noise from the object, which was estimated to be some 300–400 feet in the air. No shape was discernible. (*Lynn News & Advertiser*, Norfolk, 3 April 1992)

28 March 1992: Nr. Irwin, Pennsylvania, USA

At about 3.30 a.m., a fourteen-year-old boy was shaken when the bedroom of his rural home suddenly became bathed in a bright yellow-orange light, emanating from outside. The boy noticed a humming sound, and a large mirror in the room made it easy to see what the source of light was. About 150 feet from the house, behind a tree, was an oval-shaped object, the size of a large car, yellow-orange in colour, hovering about 50 feet above the ground. After about twenty seconds, it rose above the trees and passed over the house, heading toward Route 30. The humming stopped and the object departed. About fifteen minutes after the sighting, the boy's parents and other members of the family heard what sounded like the rotor blades of two helicopters which seemed very close, but nothing could be seen. (Stan Gordon, *PASU Data Exchange*, Issue 19, April 1992)

13 April 1992: Washington, DC, USA

At 5.45 p.m., George Wingfield and others observed a total of eleven UFOs which put on a 'display' above the Washington Monument for over twenty minutes. (See Chapter 3)

14 April 1992: Nr. Durant, Oklahoma, USA

Elizabeth (name changed) was in her mother's bedroom trying to put her little boy to sleep at about 10.00 p.m. when she noticed a red light shining through the window. She went outside. Two objects could be seen: one which looked like a fireball about 18 inches across, and the other quite large. Throughout the sighting, faint sounds of different intensities and pitches could be heard. The larger craft moved slowly along the roadway, then over an adjacent field, and stopped.

The craft was silver, with a protuberance with a red light or antenna on top. All around the protuberance Elizabeth could see what appeared to be square or rectangular windows, and there was a line of blue lights in the middle and a line of red lights on the bottom of the object. Several antennae were seen on various parts of the hull. The bottom was flat, except for a long, possibly round protrusion. This area opened up partly and a white light shot down to the ground near where she stood. Elizabeth felt this was aimed at her.

By this time, Elizabeth was frightened and crying, though extremely happy. She took two jumps to the left. The object's sound changed and it seemed to respond by 'jumping' or jerking two 'steps' to her left. Elated, Elizabeth jumped two steps to the right, and the UFO did likewise. This exchange was repeated several times. Just before her brother came outside, the beam seemed to be drawn up into the UFO, gradually becoming shorter, and the bottom part closed. The mother shouted at them to come back inside the house, and the UFO moved away.

Investigator Richard Seifried, who interviewed the witnesses, reports that Elizabeth recalled seeing written 'words' along the whole side of the object. Also, at about 7.00 p.m., her radio began to emit static, so possibly the craft was in the vicinity for as long as three hours. Finally, the family's puppies and chickens appeared to be very agitated throughout the incident. (Richard Seifried, *Oklahoma MUFONews*, June 1992)

18 April 1992: Komsomolsk-na-Amure, CIS
The crew of a military transport plane watched for an hour as a UFO described a series of aerobatics. (See p. 186)

19 April 1992: Kyeemagh, nr. Sydney International Airport, Australia

The four members of the C. family were fishing off the rocky embankment on the west side of the mouth of the Cooks River, just below the Endeavour Bridge, at 7.30 p.m., when Mrs C. noticed a stationary, noiseless object in the north-western sky above the street lights on the bridge.

The object looked like a metallic upturned saucer with a dome on top (Fig. 14.9), and had a flat, circular bottom

Fig. 14.9   (UFO Reporter)

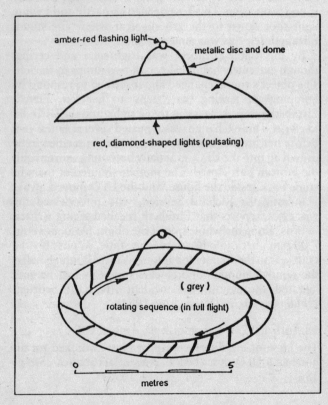

with a ring of red lights inside the rim. The lights within this ring were fluctuating, and a separate, bright amber light could be seen blinking on top of the dome.

After about ten minutes, Mrs C. called her husband, who was standing 5–10 metres from her, and he joined the rest of the family to watch the object. Mr C. estimated the still motionless object to be about 7 metres in diameter, 45–50 metres above the level of the riverbank, some 35 degrees up, and 80 metres away. Shortly after Mr C. had joined the group, the object pitched over about 45 degrees away from them, so that they could clearly see its circular base. The red lights making up the circle around the bottom edge were diamond-shaped, with well-defined edges. As the object flipped, the slowly flashing light on the nearby Kingsford Smith Airport control tower sped up and an alarm (a series of very loud beeps) sounded. All lights on the object then became brighter, and the ring of red lights pulsated faster, as did the amber-red light on the dome.

The UFO then started to move off soundlessly 'at about 40 kph' in a north-northeast direction towards Sydney's Central Business District (CBD), travelling at an angle of about 40 degrees overall, and moving erratically in a series of little jumps. Once the object had moved away, the alarm on the control tower stopped and the blue light slowed down to its original rate. After seven to ten minutes, the object apparently levelled off, but was still visible as a single red blinking light high above the CBD.

The C. family was surprised that, although other people around them saw the object, they seemed stunned and did not take much interest in what had happened. There were no reports in the Sydney newspapers the following day, and when the Sydney Airport control tower was contacted, the family was informed that nothing unusual had been reported. (Frank Sinclair and Paul Sowiak-Rudej, *UFO Reporter*, UFO Research New South Wales, Vol. 1 No. 2, June 1992)

28 April 1992: Rainham, nr. Chatham, Kent, UK

At around midnight, Elsie Bassett-Burr saw a large object hovering above Herbert Road. 'It was round like a wheel and it had spikes. It had at least 100 lights, all white. I was not scared, I was just excited,' she said. (*Chatham Standard*, 5 May 1992)

28 April 1992: Lajas, Puerto Rico

Freddie Cruz, Director of the Civil Defence Agency of Lajas, was one of several witnesses who observed a US jet fighter chasing a 'flying saucer' at 5.00 p.m. (See pp. 131–2)

1 May 1992: Polegate, nr. Eastbourne, Sussex, UK

Justin Lycett, a photographer for the *Eastbourne Gazette*, was shaken by the sighting of what appeared to be an aircraft about to crash, as he was driving into Eastbourne with a friend, Steve Hazelgrove. It was 10.20 p.m. and they had just gone through the traffic lights at Polegate and were approaching Willingdon on the A22 when the incident occurred, reported as follows by Justin Lycett:

I noticed a red flashing light in the sky on the Downs side of the road and as I drove I saw the silhouette of a plane. It was very low and I thought perhaps it was in trouble. I told my friend to look and he saw the flashing light. We pulled into a bus stop near the new garage to have a look.

I could see the outline of a plane – it was a DC-9 or BAC-111 – just above the skyline above the Downs at Butts Brow. It was getting lower and lower but there was no noise. I was convinced it was going to crash. Then the nose pulled up and it turned towards us. I just put my foot down. I thought it was going to hit us. We stopped near Church Street and looked back, but there was nothing. We even drove around searching, but found nothing. There were no aerials or anything with red lights on. My hands were shaking. We were both a bit scared.

Police told the *Gazette* that they had no reports of low-flying aircraft on the night in question. (*Eastbourne Gazette*, 13 May 1992)

Justin Lycett confirmed these details when I spoke to

him, and supplied some additional information. As an aviation enthusiast, he was certain that the 'aircraft' resembled either a DC-9 or a BAe One-Eleven. I should point out that, had it been an actual aircraft of either type, it would have been heard (a BAe One-Eleven is particularly noisy), unless the engines were off – in which case it would have crashed. The aircraft was flying very slowly, and the only lighting was a red flashing light on the top of the tail fin. Justin said that he and his friend were baffled also by the lack of cars and people in the vicinity at the time, which was unusual for this road. Furthermore, there was a strange atmosphere, 'as if something was about to happen'. Even the sky looked strange, he told me. The entire episode lasted for about ten minutes.

5 May 1992: Cooma, nr. Stanhope, Victoria, Australia
At 6.30 p.m., Yvonne Matthews heard a thumping sound outside her Midland Highway farm at Cooma, east of Stanhope, and alerted her husband Chris. 'The banging continued, from the top of the house, running down the side. It shook all the windows,' Chris reported. Noticing

Fig. 14.10   (*Chris Matthews*)

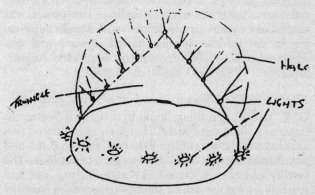

a bright light shining through the curtains, he pulled back the blinds and saw a conical object which he believes was on the ground in a paddock across the highway.

'It had orange lights around the top and along the side,' said Chris. 'There was a glow of light around the top and then lights dimmed from the top and the ones along the side turned a pale blue.' He estimated the object to be 10 metres wide and the same in height. It was shaped like 'a triangle on top, like a tent, with an egg shape on the bottom.' (Fig. 14.10)

Chris phoned his brother Mark, who saw the object from 15 kilometres away then drove to Mark's farm and tried in vain to take a photograph as it hovered about 400 metres away. Another brother, Shane, arrived shortly afterwards with a video camera, and Mark joined him in giving chase to try to film it. The object was noiseless as it moved in a north-south line, and they followed it until it disappeared in the direction of an old quarry at the end of Cooma Road. Three police units converged on the quarry but failed to find anything. (Juanita Greville, *News*, Shepparton, Victoria, 6/7 May 1992)

8 May 1992: Bruce Highway, Sunshine Coast, Queensland, Australia

A woman travelling south down the Bruce Highway, from the Sunshine Coast to Brisbane, observed a bright stationary light above the tree line. The object was shaped like a plate, clearly defined, with a slight hump on top in the middle. It then moved upward and disappeared. (*The UFO Encounter*, No. 148, August-September 1992, UFO Research Queensland)

17 May 1992: Collector, New South Wales, Australia

G, E, and K, returning home by car from Sydney to Canberra along the Federal Highway, encountered two unusual aerial objects from 9.00 p.m. to 9.15 p.m., and pulled in to the side of the road to get a better look. The smaller object was shaped like a child's top and had several stationary white lights, arranged in parallel

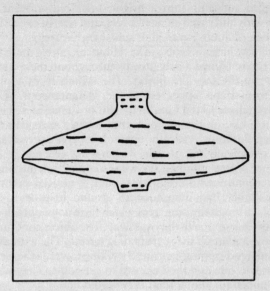

Fig. 14.11   (UFO Reportér)

bands, around the top and bottom surfaces (Fig. 14.11). The small lights flickered irregularly but quite slowly within their bands, and were also irregularly spaced.

There appeared to be smaller cylinders at the top and bottom of the object, with similar rows of small white lights. The object had sharp edges and was 'about one and a half times as wide as a full moon'. (E indicated that the small lights on the upper surface were greenish, and those on the lower surface were reddish – not white.)

The second object was a larger, brighter, but more diffuse yellowish-white light source, with soft edges, and a slightly flattened, 'saggy' appearance (that is, elliptical or oblate). It appeared to be sinking gradually towards the ground, but the witnesses could not be sure. Both objects were completely silent.

After hovering for a minute or two, the top-like object

changed suddenly into a bright, brick-red crescent of light with fairly well-defined edges, and started executing a series of loops, arcs, flips and figures-of-eight, away from the larger 'blob'. The elliptical blob's path of descent remained fairly steady throughout these gyrations by the top-like object. The switch from top to crescent shape appeared to be instantaneous. This 'active' phase lasted for about eight or so minutes. Then the top-like object stopped and hovered momentarily before shooting vertically upwards at great speed, and was completely out of sight within a few seconds.

After several minutes, the witnesses got back into their car to continue home. At this point, E noticed that the large 'blob' had descended to ground level and was visible through the pine trees which form a windbreak on the low hill opposite the causeway. The object continued to glow and lit up the surrounding terrain. The witnesses considered stopping again and walking towards the blob, but it was late and they wanted to get home. They were also uncertain about what they would find.

All three were surprised that although many cars passed them during the incident, none stopped to watch the objects. (E. Mudge, C. Williams, B. Dickeson, M. McGhee, *UFO Reporter*, UFO Research New South Wales, Vol. 1 No. 2, June 1992)

10 June 1992: Coatesville, Pennsylvania, USA
According to Evelyn Walker, spokesperson for the Lukens Steel Company, several workers reported seeing an unidentified object land in the middle of the steelyard at about 4.30 p.m. The source of the report, who is the husband of a Lukens worker and who asked not to be identified, said that the object touched down briefly and then took off towards the old Coatesville Hospital. Walker refused to answer a reporter's questions about how many people saw the object, or precisely what they saw, but added that the company had not yet come up with 'a reasonable explanation' for the report. (Michael

Rellahan/Barbara Mastriana, *Daily Local News*, West Chester, Pennsylvania, 12 June 1992)

14 June 1992: Topanga, California, USA

According to the Lost Hills/Malibu Sheriff's station, a shaken man reported that he and his girlfriend were followed by an unidentified bright light, sometime after midnight, in Topanga Canyon. 'Suddenly it was over us, we lost control of the car and it lifted us up in the sky – lifted us up over the ground ... We don't drink, don't take drugs, and have no history of psychological problems.' What happened next was vague, according to the driver, who reckons they both lost memory for 'maybe a couple of minutes, and then we were put down. Suddenly it wasn't there anymore.'

Shortly afterwards, another call was received by the Sheriff's station from a witness, who together with his girlfriend saw three flying discs high up in the Canyon. 'They were following us above the car, and we stopped and got out ... we watched them and within maybe three seconds, they were gone – straight up into the air.' Several other witnesses reported UFO activity in the area at the time. (Colin Penno, *Messenger*, Topanga, 2–15 July 1992)

18 June 1992: Clavering, Essex, UK

At 6.45 p.m., Mr and Mrs Smith-Hughes were driving in the vicinity of Clavering, 6 miles south-west of Saffron Walden, when their attention was drawn to a brightly shining object which was hovering about 100 feet above a wood, half a mile from their position. Mr Smith-Hughes described the object as about 50 to 60 feet in diameter and shaped like two soup dishes laid one on top of the other.

As the couple observed the object, it suddenly began to descend behind the trees and went out of view. Mr Smith-Hughes followed the road until he came to the other side of the trees, but by the time he arrived, there was no sign of the object. Both witnesses work at an airport, and are adamant that the object was not an aircraft, helicopter, nor a balloon. (Anthony Dodd, *UFO Magazine*, Vol. 11 No. 3, July/August 1992)

27 June 1992: Nr. Tooradin, Victoria, Australia

A woman motorist driving near Tooradin saw a very bright pulsating light in her rear-view mirror – too high to be another car. The light came speedily from the south and overtook her car, at which point she was able to discern that it was egg-shaped. The witness stated that she felt 'as though all the air had been taken out of her' and suffered considerable shock, necessitating a visit to a doctor. (*Australian UFO Bulletin*, Victorian UFO Research Society, September 1992)

27 June 1992: Nr. Raeford, North Carolina, USA

At 12.30 a.m., alerted by something that sounded like a freight train, which rattled their trailer home, Mrs Diane Messing and her mother saw an extraordinary object in a hayfield surrounded by woods about 300 feet away. The object was circular in shape, measuring about 15 by 15 feet.

'It looked like a fire burning in the woods,' said Mrs Messing, 'but the more you looked at it, it was like orange windows around it . . . And it was quiet. That's why I called the police. I didn't know what it was going to do next.' By the time the two returned from making the phone call, however, the object had disappeared, and the six Sheriff's deputies saw nothing when they arrived.

At daybreak, the two women went to the landing site and found a circle of pressed grass. (Larry Bingham, *Observer-Times*, Fayetteville, North Carolina, 2 July 1992)

7 July 1992: Stonehenge, Wiltshire, UK

Steve and Jean Shipton had been sight-seeing in Wiltshire and had parked their camper down a side road close to Stonehenge when, at 12.15 a.m., Steve noticed a ball of very bright white light which had come into view. He described it as moving slowly across the sky at low altitude, with a strange jerky movement. 'It was very strange,' he said, 'it would move then stop, then move then stop continually. It was about the size of a two-pence piece held at arm's length but seemed to occasionally grow to twice its size.' Both witnesses were shaken by the observation. (Anthony Dodd, *UFO Magazine*, Vol. 11 No. 3, July/August 1992)

7 July 1992: Upavon, Wiltshire, UK

'During the early hours of the morning of 7th July,' investigator Maria Ward informed me, 'a young farmhand was awoken from sleep by the frantic cries of the farm livestock. John (pseudonym) left the comfort of his bed to go in search of the cause for this unusual behaviour. When he reached the courtyard below, he found that several of the horses had broken out of the paddock, breaking a fence in the process. The sheep and cattle were making "an awful din", so he then went in search of the horses.' John takes up the story:

. . . As I reached the top of the bluff, behind the farm, I saw a light moving in the cloud. From out of nowhere, a long thin taper of silvery light appeared. I stood where I was, with my hands in my pockets. I was scared stiff . . .

This thing – this narrow beam of light – seemed to be turning. It got faster and faster, and I thought, what the hell is it? You know, I was kind of frightened and curious at the same time. Anyway, this beam – this knitting needle-like thing – suddenly poked into the wheat. The light in the clouds disappeared and so did the beam. Where it had hit the wheat, a circle spread out. It just flattened out – just like that . . . I can't get over the speed of that thing: it all happened so fast.

I didn't know what to do. My boss was away on holiday, and he don't take kindly to all this crop circle stuff. He [had] told me not to let anyone on the land . . .

'Fortunately for the researchers,' Maria continued, 'John contacted a friend of his, who managed to get him to tell his story to one of them. Some crop from within the circle was sent for laboratory analysis, and we are still awaiting the results. Also, aerial photographs of the site were taken. The circle itself was harvested as soon as the landowner returned from his holiday; in fact, before he had even unpacked his luggage! John was reluctant to talk about the sighting, because of fear of losing his job, hence the use of a pseudonym. The sighting affected him greatly.'

If this account is factual – and Maria is confident of the witness's truthfulness – it provides us with a rare instance of a crop circle apparently being produced by an anomalous aerial device of some kind. (Maria Ward, Circles Research)

18 July 1992: Nr. Colchester, Essex, UK

A chartered accountant driving home from Colchester at midnight was alarmed by a very large, triangular-shaped object, which swooped very low over his car, heading north. 'There was no noise as it passed over me, or afterwards,' he reported. 'It was about 150 feet up. It was massive – at least a span of 400 to 500 feet – a blackish colour and had three pointed ends at the rear with rods sticking out. There were no lights or other markings to be seen.' [Fig. 14.12]

Fig. 14.12 (Witness sketch)

'Another car heading towards me swerved towards me, but managed to right itself in time to avoid a crash. I was shaking like a leaf [and] also felt very sick. I had to

stop the car to recover . . .' (Ron West, Essex UFO
Research Group)

24/25 July 1992: Alton Barnes, Wiltshire, UK

At 11.57 p.m., members of Dr Steven Greer's CSETI
team witnessed two fleeting lights encircling their group.
One of the witnesses, Ron Russell, tried to take photographs but his camera refused to work, although it was
perfect the following day. At 12.05 a.m., three separate
balls of light appeared to emerge from behind the
Tawsmead Copse. The orange lights moved rapidly and
soundlessly, although Edward Sherwood experienced a
'metallic ringing noise' as he approached the edge of the
copse. Later, he suffered from severe irritation of his right
eye and a swollen eyelid.

   Returning at 2.00 a.m. from the CSETI skywatch,
Maria Ward, Edward Sherwood and Simon Cooper were
driving on the road to Devizes when their vehicle was
followed by a ball of bluish-white light. Smaller than a
football, this appeared by the driver's window and at
times lit up the interior of the car. The light darted
through hedgerows and trees alongside the road, and at
one point moved behind the car and lit up the rear-view
mirror. It continued to pace the witnesses until the car
emerged on to the A361. During the incident, Maria and
Edward experienced severe 'pressure' in their heads and
chests, eye irritation and disorientation. (Maria Ward,
Circles Research)

26/27 July 1992: Alton Barnes, Wiltshire, UK

Several members of the CSETI team observed an extraordinary series of lights, apparently attached to an object
of at least 75 feet in width, which seemed to respond to
signals from the group. (See pp. 63–4)

28 July 1992: Alton Barnes, Wiltshire, UK

At about 1.00 a.m., eleven members of the CSETI team
observed four large brilliant balls of orange light, which
seemed to emerge from Tawsmead Copse. 'They moved

one after the other in a jerky fashion and were absolutely silent,' reported Maria Ward. (Maria Ward, Circles Research)

28 July 1992: Alton Priors, Wiltshire, UK

John and Julie Wakefield, plus several other witnesses, observed a large ball of orange light, estimated to be 35 feet across, as well as a smaller ball of light which came from it, from 10.15 p.m. to 10.35 p.m. (See pp. 64–6)

29 July 1992: Purcell, Oklahoma, USA

At about 10.00 p.m., a family of four observed a large object moving in the sky, which they said was approximately as wide as a football field and two to three football fields in length. The estimated altitude was from 3,000 to 5,000 feet. It appeared to be oval in shape, with white lights on the front and back area. The father and son stated that they also saw blue and green lights flanking the space between the white lights. The object moved overhead silently, steadily and slowly, in a westerly direction. As it did so, the father and son noticed, through binoculars, that the underside of the craft appeared to be made of a grey, dull silver metal.

Suddenly, the object 'split in two', and a small disc-shaped object allegedly ejected from the larger craft and headed directly north and out of sight. The larger craft headed south-westerly into a turn, and then south-easterly out of sight. The father, however, was able to follow it through a telescope. The son ran into the street in his socked feet, trying to follow it. Coming to the edge of a field, he was able to see the object in the distance as it zigzagged around for about fifteen or twenty seconds. Then it stopped and hovered, shot straight up an additional 2,000 to 3,000 feet, and disappeared in a northerly direction. (Ginny Meyer/Jean Waller, *Oklahoma MUFONews*, September 1992)

29 July 1992: Mount Rainier National Park, Washington, USA

Mr and Mrs Phinney, together with their friends Marlene and Robert Hansen, were hiking up a small peak called Dege (or Dega) Peak in the early morning. When Mrs Phinney reached the top, she noticed a shining object towards the north-west, and called her husband. Mr Phinney, who holds an MA degree in mathematics and was employed by the Bell Aircraft company, observed the object through binoculars, and said that it appeared to be rectangular then, as it turned, trapezoidal in shape. After about ten minutes, as the witnesses looked in a different direction to admire the scenery, the object disappeared. (Richard Seifried, *Oklahoma MUFONews*, September 1992)

30 July 1992: Goldhanger, nr. Maldon, Essex, UK

'. . . between 2.00 a.m. and 3.00 a.m. I was in bed but unable to sleep because of the humid weather,' a witness reported. 'I looked out of the window and saw an object which I would describe as oblong and very big. The whole thing was an orange square with what I would describe as white pinpricks of light. We looked at it through binoculars but they didn't help . . . The object reflected light into my bedroom window [and] was at least 500 yards [away]. The light remained in one place and I watched it for at least ten minutes. It was still there when I went back to bed and the light was still shining on the wall. I was just about to go to sleep [then] I got up to have another look and it had gone.' (Ron West, Essex UFO Research Group)

4 August 1992: Mansfield, Nottinghamshire, UK

Just before midnight, four teenagers observed a large black object with triangular lights around its edges and a red dome in the middle, which 'hummed and whirred' its way from a westerly direction. The witnesses said the object flew too low and was too large and multi-coloured to be an aircraft. (*Chad*, Mansfield, 12 August 1992)

8 August 1992: Broome, Western Australia

Up to forty witnesses are believed to have seen an unusual UFO in the vicinity of this coastal town in the north of Western Australia, and a few of those reports follow:

6.45 p.m. – Robert M. and his wife, his brother Peter, and Peter's wife Sandy, were preparing camp 10 kilometres south of Tom Price on the Paraburdoo Road, when they suddenly noticed an object the colour of dull aluminium in the sky, travelling in a SSW-NNE direction. Robert described the spherical-shaped object as having a sort of darker spot in the centre, and it appeared to be creating a disturbance or shock waves, because of a fuzzy effect around it. The sighting lasted thirty to forty seconds. (Brian Richards, UFO Data Collection Centre/ UFORUM)

8.00 p.m. – Two prospectors were camped out in the bush 47 kilometres ENE of Nullagine when they saw a light blue, half-moon-shaped object at a height of about 30 metres and at a distance of about 150 metres. It hovered motionless for a while then shot straight up and vanished. (Brian Richards, UFORUM)

8.10 p.m. – Norm Archer, together with four other adults and about four children, was camped in a valley on Sunday Island when a large yellow light the shape of a crescent moon standing upright cruised above the hill in front of them. The object was yellow, with a mist or cloud around it. It seemed to be at low altitude, and Archer said that it appeared to be relatively about five times the size of the moon. The object moved from east to west, following the contours of the hill on the island. When it came to the end of the hill, it turned (at this point appearing like a yellow pencil) then shot straight up in the air and vanished. (Report by John Kernott, 24 August 1992, sent to UFORUM)

8.20 p.m. – Chris Davis and Lella Bailey, co-managers of the Willie Creek pearl farm, 37 kilometres north of Broome, observed a crescent, quarter-moon-shaped object flying overhead vertically at about 2,000 feet, with the crescent points trailing. It seemed to be enveloped in a sort of mist, giving it an overall fuzzy appearance. Both witnesses said it was accompanied by a faint droning sound. (Brian Richards, UFORUM)

14 August 1992: Nr. Blairsville, Pennsylvania, USA

Several motorists claim to have seen a UFO while driving along Route 22 in Indiana County during the night. According to investigator Stan Gordon, the witnesses saw the object when they came within view of the Homer City power plant. 'These people were really shook up,' said Gordon, who said that 'a large triangular shape about 150 feet off the ground' flew over their vehicles, with 'structural beams and white lights glowing'. (Jeff Himler, *Dispatch*, Blairsville, 3 September 1992)

29 August 1992: Seymour Mountain, British Columbia, Canada

At 2.30 a.m., Frank Riley (pseudonym), a police officer with a military background, observed what appeared at first to be a shooting star over the Blue Ridge area of Seymour Mountain. Through the bathroom window he observed three red and white pulsating cylindrical lights. The sensor alarm in the patio was activated and the light which illuminated the lane went out. One of his dogs, outside the house, started to whine. Panic-stricken, Frank tried to wake up his wife, but it took all his effort to awaken her for just a brief moment before she fell back to sleep 'like a rag doll'. This had never happened before. Their nine-month-old child was 'giggling' in the other room – another unusual occurrence. By 3.00 a.m., the lights had disappeared. Frank remarked that he had never been so frightened in his life. (Lorne Goldfader, UFO Research Institute of Canada)

30 August 1992: Colchester-Chelmsford, Essex, UK

Three independent witnesses watched an oblong-shaped object, with one white light at each end and red lights moving around it, at 7.15 p.m.

'Driving along the A12 from Colchester towards Chelmsford, I noticed this oblong-shaped object in the sky,' said one witness. 'It had very bright white lights at each end and numerous smaller red lights moving around it. It seemed to be travelling level with my car. I had slowed down to 30 mph to watch, and it seemed to pace me. I pulled into a lay-by to get a better view. The object then stopped and allowed me to watch it. Two other vehicles pulled into the lay-by and their occupants got out and we discussed what we were seeing. After about twenty minutes, the object just seemed to disappear in front of us.' (Ron West, Essex UFO Research Group)

31 August 1992: Midland, Western Australia
Mrs June R. was travelling along the Great Northern Highway, 7 kilometres from Midland at Herne Hill. She noticed a flashing red light ahead, to the west of the highway, and thought it was some kind of beacon illuminated by a red warning light. Stopping shortly afterwards to investigate, J.R. saw that the red light had no tower or beacon beneath it. It was hovering at an undetermined height about half a kilometre away over some vineyards. Below the light, but not attached to it, was a dark rectangular shape larger than a jumbo jet. The sides of the rectangle looked like a rubber inflatable boat or the rounded skirted sides of a hovercraft. The object remained stationary for about three minutes, then there was a flash of blue light and it started to move away towards Perth in the south. (Brian Richards, UFO Data Collection Centre/UFORUM)

31 August 1992: Bacup, Lancashire, UK
Three fifteen-year-old Rossendale girls claim to have observed a green and red flashing object late in the evening. 'We watched it for at least five minutes from about a half-mile away,' said Joanne Ellidge. 'It was hovering silently about a metre above the ground. It had lights all round, like a circle. There was no way we could guess the size because of the distance. We were too

frightened to get closer because it was getting dark. It suddenly sped up to about 40 mph and disappeared into the woods . . .' (Neil Graham, *Rossendale Free Press*, 4 September 1992)

APPENDIX

Australia

UFO Research & Investigation Canberra, PO Box 382, Woden, ACT 2606.

Australian Centre for UFO Studies, PO Box 728, Lane Cove, NSW 2066.

UFO Data Collection Centre/UFORUM, 36 Loris Way, Kardinya, W. Australia 6163.

UFO Research Australia, PO Box 229, Prospect, S. Australia 5082.

UFO Research Queensland, PO Box 222, 50 Albert Street, Brisbane, Queensland 4002.

Victorian UFO Research Society, PO Box 43, Moorabbin, Victoria 3189.

UFO Research New South Wales, PO Box Q95, Queen Victoria Building, Sydney, NSW 2000.

Canada

Canadian UFO Research Network, PO Box 77547, 592 Sheppard Avenue W., Downsview, Ontario, M3H 6A7.

Centrale de Compilation Ufologique de Quebec, CP 103, Drummondville, Quebec, J2B 2V6.

UFO Research Institute of Canada, Dept. 25, 1665 Robson Street, Vancouver, British Columbia, V6G 3C2.

Ufology Research of Manitoba, PO Box 1918, Winnipeg, Manitoba, R3C 3R2.

United Kingdom

British UFO Research Association, Suite 1, The Leys, 2c Leyton Road, Harpenden, Hertfordshire, AL25 2TL.

Contact International (UK), 11 Ouseley Close, New Marston, Oxford, OX3 0JS.

East Midlands UFO Research Association, 8 Roosa Close, Hempshill Vale, Bulwell, Nottingham, NG6 7BL.

Essex UFO Research Group, 95 Chilburn Road, Great Clacton, Essex, CO15 4PE.

Plymouth UFO Research Group, 40 Albert Road, Stoke, Plymouth, Devon, PL2 1AE.

Quest International, PO Box 2, Grassington, Skipton, N. Yorkshire, BD23 5UY.

Scottish UFO Report Line, (0426) 983401.

Surrey Investigation Group on Aerial Phenomena, 126 Grange Road, Guildford, Surrey, GU2 6QP.

United States of America

Citizens Against UFO Secrecy, PO Box 218, Coventry, Connecticut 06238.

J. Allen Hynek Center for UFO Studies, 2457 W. Peterson Avenue, Chicago, Illinois 60659.

Fund for UFO Research, PO Box 277, Mount Rainier, Maryland 20712.

The International UFO Museum & Research Center, 400 North Main, Roswell, New Mexico 88202.

Mutual UFO Network, 103 Oldtowne Road, Seguin, Texas 78155–4099.

Operation Right to Know, PO Box 2911, Hyattsville, MD 20784.

Pennsylvania Association for the Study of the Unexplained, 6 Oak Hill Avenue, Greensburg, Pennsylvania 15601.

UFO Reporting & Information Service, PO Box 832, Mercer Island, Washington 98040.

THE CROP CIRCLES

Centre for Crop Circle Studies, SKS, 20 Paul Street, Frome, Somerset, BA11 1DX, UK.

Circles Phenomenon Research, PO Box 3378, Branford, Connecticut 06405, USA.

Circles Research, 1 Louvain Road, Greenhithe, Kent, DA9 9DY, UK.

Phenomenon Research Association, 12 Tilton Grove, Kirk Hallam, Ilkeston, Derbyshire, DE7 4GR, UK.

SOME UFO JOURNALS
(Australia, UK and USA)

Communique, PO Box 382, Woden, ACT 2606, Australia.

Flying Saucer Review, FSR Publications Ltd., PO Box 162, High Wycombe, Buckinghamshire, HP13 5DZ, UK.

International UFO Reporter, 2457 W. Peterson Avenue, Chicago, Illinois 60659, USA.

MUFON UFO Journal, 103 Oldtowne Road, Seguin, Texas 78155–4099, USA.

Northern UFO News, 37 Heathbank Road, Cheadle Heath, Stockport, Cheshire, SK3 0UP, UK.

UFO, PO Box 1053, Sunland, California 91041–1053, USA.

UFO Magazine, PO Box 2, Grassington, Skipton, N. Yorkshire, BD23 5UY, UK.

UFO Reporter, PO Box Q95, Queen Victoria Building, Sydney, NSW 2000, Australia.

UFO Times, Suite 1, The Leys, 2c Leyton Road, Harpenden, Hertfordshire, AL5 2TL, UK.

SERVICES

Books on UFOs

Those requiring books which are not available in bookshops should write, enclosing a stamp, to: Susanne Stebbing, 41 Terminus Drive, Herne Bay, Kent, CT6 6PR, UK, or Arcturus Books, 1443 SE Port St Lucie Blvd., Port St Lucie, Florida 34952, USA.

UFO newsclippings

Those interested in receiving regular newsclippings on UFO reports (many of which appear only in local newspapers) should write for subscription details, enclosing a stamp, to the UFO Newsclipping Service, Route 1, Box 220, Plumerville, Arkansas 72127, USA, or the British UFO Newsclipping Service, CETI, 247 High Street, Beckenham, Kent, BR3 1AB, UK.

Video/audio tapes and official UFO documents

Write for details, enclosing a stamp, to Quest Publications International Ltd., PO Box 2, Grassington, Skipton, N. Yorkshire, BD23 5UY

UFO Call

The British UFO Research Association and British Telecom run a 24-hour news update service on (0898) 121886.

UFO hotlines

Quest International has a 24-hour UFO hotline for reporting sightings in the UK. Telephone (0756) 752216. In the USA, a similar service is provided by the 24-hour Pennsylvania UFO Hotline, (412) 838 7768, and the UFO Reporting & Information Service, (206) 721 5035. In Australia, contact the UFO Research New South Wales Hotline on Sydney (02) 588 6058.

Computer UFO networks (USA)

Computer UFO Network: connect at 300/1200/2400 bps, eight data bits, no parity, one stop bit: USA (206) 776 0382. Address: Box 832, Mercer Island, Washington 98040. ParaNet Information Service can be accessed by computer and modem up to 9600 bps by calling (303) 431 8797. Address: PO Box 928, Wheatridge, Colorado 80034.

MUFON *amateur radio net (USA)*

80 metres – 3.930 MHz – Saturdays 9.00 p.m.
40 metres – 7.237 MHz – Saturdays 8.00 a.m.
20 metres – 14.264 MHz – Thursdays 9.00 p.m.
10 metres – 28.470 MHz – Sundays 3.00 p.m.

Alternative if 10 metres is dead:
20 metres – 14.264 MHz – Sundays 3.15 p.m.

All times are Eastern Standard or Daylight (USA)

REPORTING SIGHTINGS

The majority of UFO sightings turn out to have a conventional explanation, such as aircraft, aircraft landing lights, balloons, airships used for advertising purposes (Richard Branson has one shaped like a flying saucer!), meteors (shooting stars), computer-controlled laser displays (which often look like illuminated discs flying in a circle), planets and stars (Venus and Sirius being commonly mistaken for a UFO), re-entry of terrestrial space hardware, and satellites, etc., but if you *really* think you have seen something exotic, do contact one or more of the organizations listed above. In addition, the police will investigate a sighting if it is considered sufficiently important, and they are required to submit a report to the Ministry of Defence (MoD), as are military bases and air traffic control officers (in the UK), but in most cases the report is simply filed away and neglected. The MoD takes UFO sighting reports seriously and will be glad to note down all the details if you approach them directly but, unless specifically requested, seldom notify witnesses of their findings. The main point of contact for the MoD is (071) 218 9000 (office hours). Ask for the Secretariat (Air Staff) 2a.

If your sighting is particularly impressive (*not* just an odd light in the sky), I recommend that you contact the newsdesk of a national newspaper office, radio or television station, in order that we may all learn about it with the minimum delay. Also, local newspapers will be glad to publish your report, together with an appeal for any additional witnesses. Local radio or TV stations should be contacted too, ideally during the sighting (if the object has been visible for some time). Finally, try to get some evidence on film.

INDEX

Index

Index